Internationalizing Business Education

Meeting the Challenge

Internationalizing Business Education

Meeting the Challenge

Edited by S. Tamer Cavusgil

Michigan State University
East Lansing
1993

All Michigan State University Press books are produced on pape
which meets the requirements of American National Standard o
Information Sciences—Permanence of paper for printec
materials ANSI Z23.48-1984.

Michigan State University Press
East Lansing, Michigan 48823-5202

Printed in the United States of America

01 00 99 98 97 96 95 94 93 1 2 3 4 5 6 7 8 9 10

Library of Congress Cataloging in Publication Data

ISBN 0-87013-332-2

Internationalizing business education : meeting the challenge /
   edited by S. Tamer Cavusgil.
         p.   cm. — (International business series ; #1)
   Includes bibliographical references and index.
   ISBN 0-87013-332-2
   1. Business education—United States—Curricula. 2.
International education—United States—Case Studies. 3.
Business schools—United States—Case Studies. 4. Business
education—International cooperation. I. Cavusgil, S. Tamer II.
Series: International business series (East Lansing, Mich.) ; #1.
HF1131.I584 1993
650'.071'073—dc20
                                                93-27983
                                                CIP

Acknowledgments

Numerous individuals contributed to the success of the Roundtable on Internationalizing Business Schools and Faculty and the resulting publications. Professors Michael Schechter of Michigan State University and Attila Yaprak of Wayne State University were involved actively from the planning stages to actual implementation. Both have also read each manuscript and provided comments for the authors. We are grateful to them for their input, guidance and enthusiasm throughout the project. Our gratitude also goes to Ms. Doris Scarlett, Associate Director of Michigan State CIBER, for her exceptional organizational and administrative skills. She assumed full responsibility for the planning and implementation of the Roundtable, and contributed tremendously to its success. She was also responsible for the production of the accompanying publication, *Internationalizing Business Education: Issues and Recommendations by Leading Educators.*

We must also acknowledge the valuable assistance of Ms. Hilla Mody Motiani, a graduate student at Michigan State University, in bringing this project to fruition. Hilla assumed the primary task of editing each manuscript, providing feedback to authors for several rounds of revisions, and preparing the manuscript for publication. Her editorial skills are largely responsible for a manuscript that is well integrated, insightful, and readable. Hilla also prepared the subject index and other parts of the book.

Ms. Tamie Phetteplace of Michigan State CIBER provided skillful, cheerful and enthusiastic secretarial services. Tamie corresponded numerous times with each author throughout the project period and was instrumental in completing the project.

It is also appropriate to acknowledge the cooperation of Michigan State University Press with this publication aimed at serving the business education community. We also appreciate their willingness to initiate an International Business Book series, of which the present book represents the inaugural volume. In particular, we applaud Dr. Fred Bohm, Director of MSU Press, for having the wisdom to launch the International Business Books series. Our thanks go to Ms. Laura Luptowski of the MSU Press for very competent copyediting and preparation of the book for publication.

Last, but not least, we are grateful to each of the authors for their willingness to share their experiences and insights with the business education community. Their cooperation and patience during the review and editing process were exemplary, for which we are thankful.

Contents

PART I: CONCEPTS AND CONCERNS

PART II: HISTORICAL PERSPECTIVES

PART III: RESOURCE CENTERS

PART VI: NON-U.S. PERSPECTIVES

Foreword

Clearly, the internationalization of business education is one of the key challenges facing U.S. institutions of higher education. Just as the business community is grappling with the challenge of global competitiveness, business faculty, administrators and students are having to design creative responses to a changing global marketplace by incorporating international and comparative dimensions into business education.

Such efforts must be undertaken by business schools in an environment of critical financial limitations and by a relatively few "change agents." Each institution is going to have to discover what this challenge—the internationalization—means to them. Relevant in this soul-searching will be the mission, history, structure, culture, clients, and resources of the particular institution. It is essential that any response to the internationalization challenge be proactive and programmatic. Specific objectives must be formulated in advance, and performance must be monitored.

This resource book, *Internationalizing Business Education: Meeting the Challenge*, could not have come at a better time. As concerned educators are searching for ideas and direction, the contributions in this collection begin to provide some answers. Each author addresses one or more dimensions of the internationalization challenge, such as faculty development or curriculum, and shares experiences and recommendations for others. Recognizing the multidimensional nature of the process—ranging from student life and activities to business outreach—many aspects are discussed by an impressive group of colleagues, who are truly "pioneers" in the cause to internationalize business education. Perspectives are rich and varied—from small to large schools, from private to public schools, and so on. I believe the illustrations highlighting specific institutional models and experiences will be especially valuable to readers.

The Center for International Business Education and Research (CIBER) at Michigan State University is extremely pleased to offer this contribution to the business education community. Thanks are in order to each of the authors for sharing their insights. Congratulations to Michigan State CIBER for hosting the 1991 Roundtable on Internationalizing Business Schools and carefully producing this book. We gratefully acknowledge the guidance and encouragement of Ms. Susanna B. Easton of the U.S. Department of Education in the completion of this project.

Richard J. Lewis, Dean
The Eli Broad Graduate School of Management
Michigan State University
Immediate Past President-AACSB

Foreword

Most elementarily, we should internationalize business schools because business is a worldwide, universal activity, whether private or public, profit or nonprofit. As we teach the disciplines of domestic marketing, accounting, finance, business law, etc., each is merely one species of a family of varied practices comprising (after the creation of the Commonwealth of Independent States) some 180 nations and several hundred major cultures. The path to the distant global village is still an unbeaten one. To the extent that what we teach is U.S.-oriented, it is literally specious, lacking in external validity.

Thirty years ago I headed a faculty task force proposing the introduction of an international business (IB) program at the University of Chicago. The proposal was killed, due to the pervasive local influence of George Stigler, who stated that "economics is economics, whether in chicago or Buenos Aires," and that "all you need if sent to Argentina is your (Chicago) MBA and some Spanish." Intercultural differences were dismissed as merely matters of degree. Nobel Prize not yet in hand, the distinguished economist overlooked that a difference in body temperature between 37°C (98.6°F) and 40°C (104°F) is also a mere matter of degree, though the prognosis may be dramatically different. Analogously, teaching jungle medicine and teaching medicine in the jungle are two different things.

Insightful observers in other countries have pointed out that much of U.S. management writing, from Philip Kotler's well-known marketing text to most Harvard-type cases, has limited applicability in these nations. Even worse, this also applies to much of our so-called "basic" research findings.

By our benign neglect of the environment beyond our borders, we have been short-changing management as a universal discipline. But we have also been short-changing our future *managers*, as literally every company is now either directly engaged in IB or dealing with foreign competitors or overseas cultural influences in our own market. Why, even the village barber must be attuned to changing styles of coiffure, or face the hair-raising prospect of extinction! What is more: by going cross-cultural we gain a deeper understanding of our own culture—and this applies even to FASB accounting standards.

A major stimulant in efforts to internationalize our B-schools is that academia still has a chance to be *proactive* relative to a business community that is becoming increasingly short of managerial personnel with either training, in or personal experience of, IB. This is in stark contrast to, say, the area of Total Quality Management, where academia is seriously lagging behind developments in the world of practice.

We should also be aware of the fact that others are already in the running. In many areas, such as in the formidable International Marketing and Purchasing project, European research is already setting the pace. And it is, of course, symptomatic that IMD (the former IMEDE and CEI) in Lausanne, and INSEAD at Fontainebleau, were world pioneers as all international B-schools. In the United States, as of 1960, only Harvard and Stanford had significant international programs. IMEDE was co-founded by Harvard and Nestle, and Harvard ran its own summer programs for international executives and business faculty. Stanford's ICAME (International Center for Advanced Management Education) was a Ford Foundation sponsored institute for the training of management teachers in developing countries and was rather independent of the B-school. Symptomatically, the program was discontinued as the Ford money ran out. Much has happened in the last few decades in this country (as detailed in several contributions to this book), but it would be a vast overstatement to say that our B-schools are internationalized. No wonder we are caught relatively empty-handed when called upon to assist in the transformation of Eastern European management systems!

It is against this background that the initiative of the CIBER at Michigan State University is particularly praiseworthy. As demonstrated by this book, the discussions at the Roundtable were as thorough and multifaceted as required by the overarching topic of internationalization of the business schools. It is also timely. One can only hope that this pioneering work will be as widely recognized—and impact as much on our schools—as the Gordon-Howells and Pierson reports were 30 years ago. Encouraging in this regard is the federal sponsorship of the numerous CIBERs around the country, which, if properly orchestrated, could have a dramatic effect.

In the light of the many excellent contributions to this book it would be presumptuous to attempt to develop an overall philosophy of B-school internationalization by way of a foreword. A few personal observations will have to do.

1. The fact that one can *still take a Ph.D. (DBA)* in many, or perhaps most, B-schools offering the degree *without taking a single internationally oriented course* is an outrage. An internationalized faculty is clearly a *sine qua non* for the future.

2. Re the perennial discussion whether the curriculum needs *a special IB program or internationalization of "all" courses*: large schools *need both*. IB programs are needed now, internationalization of the curriculum at large is a question of a decade or a generation, requiring a basic change of mindset of both faculty and textbook writers.

3. Increasing the enrollment of *foreign students per se does nothing for B-school internationalization*. It will contribute only if they are systematically used as resource persons. There are no cross-cultural gains when Japanese students congregate on one dormitory floor, Germans on another, and Latin Americans on a third. The International House ideas may have been a good one before 1950; it is now an idea whose time has gone.

4. The linkages between geography, economic development, and business activity are many and exciting. Especially in view of the weakness of U.S. high schools in geography teaching, we need more attention to *economic geography*. Some of the outstanding Scandinavian B-schools have an obligatory course in this area.

5. U.S. multinationals are *missing out on the Viking spirit* of many freshly graduated American MBAs (international recruiting is generally confined to natives of countries where subsidiaries are located). Instead, an American MBA is typically offered an overseas assignment several years later, when that special spirit has gone out of the individual and s/he is a spouse in a dual-career marriage. As part of their outreach programs B-schools need to educate the U.S. business community on this important point.

6. As long as business generally does not hire fresh graduates for international assignments, there is clearly *a major market for postgraduate international executive programs.*

7. As emphasized by several contributors, there is no single road to internationalization; in general, experimentation is to be preferred. But diversity can also lead to fragmentation, or even dissipation, of effort. To this observer *internecine competition among American universities in developing countries* and, of late, in Central and Eastern Europe, *has reached dysfunctional proportions.* We would do host countries as well as ourselves a major service by exploring much more seriously consortia (such as the Midwest Universities Consortium for International Affairs, MUCIA) and joint ventures. There is also a crying need for a central database concerning the overseas engagements of U.S. B-schools.

8. Again, to *overseas engagements*: Everyone has such linkages, but, as pointed out in the summary report of the Roundtable, "as the number of faculty and students with interest in a particular linkage is exhausted through exchange participation, interest begins to lag." In an article on strategic networking a few years ago I pointed out that *network maintenance* is an indispensable antidote to entropy. Rotating liaison personnel, with a trip to the overseas institution, should be seen as a key part of sustaining activity. Another powerful tool is for one institution to help arrange for contacts and open doors for researchers visiting from the other. Personal experience suggests this is especially important in developing countries.

9. Salute should be extended to institutions such as Michigan State University, University of Texas at Austin, and Columbia University (as well as IMEDE) for their effective involvement of *overseas alumni* in various aspects of their internationalization programs. While other schools no doubt are making similar forays it appears that in many cases, foreign alumni constitute a semi-dormant major natural resource.

10. Finally, a modest promotional plug: experience indicates that *strategy simulations in the executive game form* are a particularly powerful tool in teaching multinational business operations. This book is likely to appear about the time when we will release the *International Operations Simulation Mark 2000* (INTOPIA), which as far as we know is a state of the art educational instrument.

The world of IB is fraught with rapid and often unpredictable change. At times one might wish that the pace would calm down for a few years, so that our B-schools could hone their IB research, teaching, and outreach activities. On the other hand, that very turbulence makes life exciting—as every international business manager knows.

Hans B. Thorelli
Indiana University

Preface

BACKGROUND

In the 1990s, business enterprises will continue to address the challenge of staying competitive in an increasingly global market environment. Accordingly, business schools need to internationalize their curriculum, faculty, and student experiences if they are to remain competitive and relevant. Observers note that the response of U.S. business schools to the globalization of markets has been slow and inadequate. Others emphasize that there is a lack of knowledge about effective ways business educators can meet this challenge. Information about alternative strategies and models of internationalizing business education is not widely available, and the experiences of successful schools have yet to be disseminated among concerned business faculty and administrators.

As a response to these challenges, the Center for International Business Education and Research (CIBER) in the Eli Broad Graduate School of Management at Michigan State University hosted a two-day conference of leading international business educators from North America, Europe, and Australia. This Roundtable on Internationalizing Business Schools and Faculty was held June 6 and 7, 1991. Twenty-three business faculty and administrators gathered in East Lansing to share their perspectives and experiences and to brainstorm about approaches to internationalizing business education. These educators are eminently qualified to serve as resource people: each brought a unique perspective on internationalization from their leadership positions at a diverse set of business schools, the Academy of International Business (AIB), the American Assembly of Collegiate Schools of Business (AACSB), and the U.S. national resource centers in international business education (CIBERs).

This book is one of two publications that resulted from the Roundtable on Internationalizing Business Schools and Faculty. The earlier one, which became available March 1992, contains the recommendations of the experts on ten dimensions of business school internationalization. These dimensions ranged from curriculum and

xix

faculty development, formulating strategies and action agendas, to outreach to business community and overseas linkages. The first publication, *Internationalizing Business Education: Issues and Recommendations by Leading Educators*, was edited by S. Tamer Cavusgil, Michael G. Schechter, and Attila Yaprak and published by Michigan State CIBER. This 28-page booklet has already proven useful to faculty and administrators who are searching for specific ideas, action plans, and examples that can be helpful in meeting the challenge of internationalization.

The present book, *Internationalizing Business Education: Meeting the Challenge*, represents an in-depth treatment of the issues, perspectives, and strategies. Each Roundtable expert has shared his or her insights on a broad range of issues through the essays featured in this book. The contributions have been revised several times by the authors in light of the discussions and comments before, during, and after the Roundtable. The essays have been edited carefully in order to minimize redundancy and to produce a coherent and well integrated book.

THE RATIONALE

There were a number of explicit premises underlying the convening of the June 6-7, 1991 *Roundtable on Internationalizing Business Schools and Faculty* and particularly behind the commissioned papers contained in this book. These propositions included:

- The time for discussing "why internationalize" our schools of business is past; it is now time to enunciate strategies, tactics, and structural alternatives and constraints.
- Internationalization of business schools is a multi-faceted process involving curricular reform; faculty development; administrator reorientation; research; linkages with the business community, including training, executive programs and consulting; and student life (e.g., campus activities, internships, overseas study).
- While strategies for internationalization must be institution-specific, there are important lessons to be learned from other schools' prior positive and negative experiences, including from schools of different character from one's own and at a different phase in the internationalization process.
- Heretofore, too much of the inter-institutional sharing of experiences has been verbal and anecdotal; a publication was desperately needed, authored by leading international change

agents who could elaborate, compare, and draw lessons from a variety of institutional experiences.

- The internationalization of business schools is too often pursued in the absence of a comprehensive, strategic plan: a publication recounting other institutions' experiences with internationalization should facilitate the future development of such plans.
- There is much to be learned about resources related to internationalization efforts, including innovative funding sources, and methods for resource conservation and sharing through exchange and consortium arrangements.
- The internationalization dialogue has been too enthnocentric; there were lessons for U.S. institutions to be learned from non-U.S. institutions and lessons to be learned from non-business faculty.
- Insufficient attention has been given heretofore to methods for evaluating the success of various internationalization undertakings.
- The CIBERs' impact on the internationalization process can be magnified through: (a) sharing of information as to their experiences on their own campuses and with other institutions with which they have worked; (b) discussions resulting in division-of-labor among themselves to take advantage of particular institutional strengths, to avoid duplicative efforts, and to conserve vital human and financial resources; and (c) agreeing on mechanisms to insure wide dissemination of information about the resources that they have available for other institutions wishing to work with them.

As the following contributions eloquently demonstrate, these presumptions were validated: there is much that each of the authors has learned from others. We also believe that much can be learned from the historical and theoretical papers; the case studies, comparative and individual, of programs more advanced on the international track and those less so, that focus on the undergraduate, MBA and Ph.D.; those based on U.S. experiences and those from outside; and that have succeeded and those that have been less successful.

THE ORGANIZATION

The book is organized into six major parts and a concluding chapter. Part I establishes the scope of the book and introduces key concepts and concerns. In the first chapter S. Tamer Cavusgil proposes an integrative framework for the internationalization *process*. In Chapter Two, Jeffrey Arpan elaborates on the curricular and administrative dimensions of internationalization in the business schools.

Part II offers historical perspectives on internationalization. Lee Nehrt, who has been a strong proponent of internationalization perhaps longer than anyone else, discusses the evolution of the challenge and efforts by the Academy of International Business, the American Assembly of Collegiate Schools of Business (AACSB), and by individual institutions. Brian Toyne presents a thoughtful essay on the complexity of the issues faced.

The four chapters in Part III address the role of centers/institutes in internationalization efforts. Both Ben Kedia and Susanna Easton discuss the role of CIBERs. Robert Grosse emphasizes the business community links, Michael Czinkota reports on the experience of one resource center, and Rob Scott on the CIBER Maryland experience.

Part IV offers perspectives on appropriate institutional strategies. Michael Schechter pleads for building bridges between business and other disciplines, while Jack Lewis and Paul Beamish illustrate two models of institutional initiative.

Part V features illustrations of seven schools. Each author elaborates on his or her institutional experience with some aspect of internationalization. These chapters are of interest to those readers who are interested in case studies. While experiences of other schools cannot be simply adopted, common patterns and lessons are instructive.

Part VI presents some non-U.S. perspectives on internationalization. Claude Cellich offers experiences of the International Trade Centre (UNCTAD/GATT) in developing country institutions; Nigel Barrett describes a program from Australia; Tevfik Dalgic elaborates on European approaches; and Daniel Van Den Bulcke focuses on doctoral programs in Europe.

Finally, the Conclusion presents integrative thoughts and comments on the challenge of internationalizing business education.

S. Tamer Cavusgil
East Lansing, Michigan

Internationalization of Business Education: Defining the Challenge[1]

S. TAMER CAVUSGIL

INTRODUCTION

The past decade has seen the emergence of a global economy. Virtually all of the free world's economies are linked together directly. East Bloc economies are anxiously looking forward to participation in free trade and competition by free enterprise.

The scale of manufacturing, and especially technology, has grown to the point where national markets are too small to support efficient operations. Environmental problems do not respect borders and cannot be solved on a country-by-country basis. Finding solutions to economic, technical, and environmental problems requires transnational cooperation. As a result, an increasing number of firms face immense pressures to compete on a global basis. This is reflected both in the increase in the importance of international operations for many large firms and the emergence of strategic alliances among often competing firms from the Triad region.

Internationalization of business has taken on many facets. Competitive activity has assumed an international dimension in trade, investment and ownership, manufacturing and sourcing, markets and customers, finance, and technology and R&D. It is safe to expect then, that before the end of the 1990s, the ongoing globalization of all businesses in the industrialized world will be completed. Businesses will be either "globetrotters" or "globewatchers." You become a globetrotter by engaging in a form of international business such as foreign manufacturing, exporting, or outsourcing. You become a globewatcher by engaging either in competition or cooperation with foreign companies in your domestic market or by

1

at least scanning the international scene for relevant developments.

Among the globetrotters, internationalization is evidenced increasingly in the selling rather than the buying end of marketing. Large-scale players like Ford and General Motors have long notified their thousands of suppliers that, in the interest of the sustained viability of their industries, they are pursuing a policy of global rather than national sourcing. Internationalization is gradually forcing itself upon even the most parochial enterprises.

THE CHALLENGE FOR BUSINESS EDUCATION

How should the education community respond to these changes? What are the implications of this new global environment for business education? What kinds of expertise do college graduates need to help prepare companies to compete globally?

There is universal agreement that there is an increased need for global knowledge on the part of firms and their managers. Indeed there is almost a national outcry for us to take some dramatic steps to cope with at least the widely acknowledged of our failings, including our students' ignorance of geography and lack of a sense of even recent history.

Globalization has indubitably established that:

- all business graduates will be affected by international aspects of business;
- many business graduates will become involved in international business later in their careers;
- managers need a depth of knowledge in history, politics, literature, arts, culture, religion, and language— in addition to functional business disciplines;
- we need to move away from parochial thinking.

It is imperative therefore that graduates, through the educational process:

- gain broad training in the humanities and social sciences;
- develop cosmopolitan orientations, sensitivity, adaptability to cultures other than their own (cultural empathy);
- acquire foreign language skills; and
- are exposed to international dimensions of business.

The role played by education is even more important today than before. This is because company policies increasingly confine the traditional source of international expertise—the overseas expatriate assignment—to fewer and fewer managers.

At a recent conference on business education, concern was raised that large, multinational companies were shifting to local nationals for management of overseas operations. Lee Morgan, a retired CEO and chairman of Caterpillar Inc., noted that from the early 1950s through the late 1970s, his company placed thousands of employees abroad and as a result, five out of six top managers have had international experience and are well equipped to deal with global competition. However, he noted that there has been a marked fall in these figures, and wondered how future generations of Caterpillar managers will gain the expertise that is, and will continue to be, a key factor in the company's competitive success.

Richard Huber of the Chase Manhattan Bank expressed a similar concern and believes that the United States is failing to build a pool of middle-level managers with international experience. All of the corporate people present agreed that it is critical that a substitute be developed to replace expatriate experience as a means of gaining international competence for corporate managers.

Similarly, Rex Adams from Mobil Oil, whose international career has proved valuable as he has risen through the managerial ranks, wondered how Mobil would supply international expertise to its managers when economic constraints now prevent expatriate careers for all but a very small proportion of managers.

All this suggests that the contribution of the education process assumes an even greater significance in creating international expertise. It implies that we need to use the educational process in lieu of direct international exposure through expatriate assignment abroad. And this requires the internationalization of business education.

Internationalization becomes a redundant, superfluous concept when we stop making a distinction between domestic and international markets. To the so-called global companies that view the entire world market as an integrated marketplace, the domestic-international distinction is trivial. Interestingly, many European business schools draw a similar parallel as they do not offer "international" courses, apart from very specialized topics. Rather, the practice is to treat both "domestic" and "international" dimensions in all core courses.

Beyond this distinction, it is important to recognize the multidimensional nature of internationalization. For true internationalization to take place, progress must be made simultaneously on several fronts:

- courses and curriculum;
- study of foreign language and international studies;
- instructional and resource materials;
- student life (through campus activities, internships, overseas study, etc.);
- faculty and administrators; and
- linkages with the business community.

A certain degree of synergy or complementarity exists among the components. Efforts on any one front tend to reinforce progress on others. In addition to proactive planning, encouragement and guidance from leaders of the organization can go a long way.

In sum, internationalization requires a shift in our mindsets, a change in the organizational culture, and a sincere commitment to the cause.

WAYS AND MEANS

There are a wide variety of means to achieve the goal of internationalization. The choice depends, in part at least, on the structure, mission, finances, past history, knowledge and experience of the faculty, and the politics of the institution. What is apt for one institution at a particular point in its history may be far from the ideal strategy for that same institution to pursue at another time, much less for another institution of a very different kind. Therefore, each institution will need to formulate its own unique approach to internationalization.

Exhibit 1 presents a conceptual framework that identifies the constituent elements of the internationalization process as "inputs" to a "value adding" process. The latter amounts to what business programs ought to be involved in. The output of this process results in graduates, knowledge, and a comprehensive program. The inputs include faculty, students, resources, and so on.

The following discussion elaborates on the eight classes of inputs or components that aid in internationalization efforts. The nature of these components are summarized in Exhibit 2.

EXHIBIT 1

A Conceptualization of the International Process

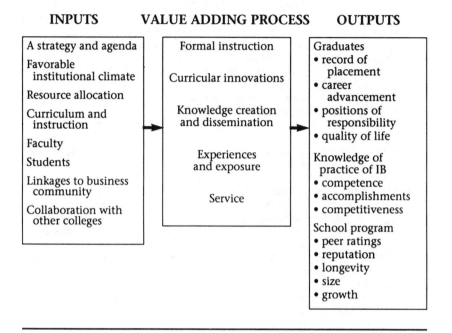

INPUTS   VALUE ADDING PROCESS   OUTPUTS

INPUTS	VALUE ADDING PROCESS	OUTPUTS
A strategy and agenda Favorable institutional climate Resource allocation Curriculum and instruction Faculty Students Linkages to business community Collaboration with other colleges	Formal instruction Curricular innovations Knowledge creation and dissemination Experiences and exposure Service	Graduates • record of placement • career advancement • positions of responsibility • quality of life Knowledge of practice of IB • competence • accomplishments • competitiveness School program • peer ratings • reputation • longevity • size • growth

1. COMPREHENSIVE STRATEGY AND AGENDA

The starting point in a proactive effort to internationalize a business program is the formulation of an overall strategy and an action agenda to guide the internationalization drive. As mentioned above, this strategy will need to be customized to each institution. Its purpose is to serve as a blueprint or roadmap to achieving the goals of internationalization.

In addition to a carefully crafted strategy and action agenda, it is essential that one or more "change agents" emerge in the institution, providing support and encouragement to the effort.

Change agents could fuel an internationalization fervor by motivating, facilitating, and providing vision and leadership. Ideally, they serve as principal resource persons for critical choices to be made along the internationalization path. In the marketing terminology, their contribution amounts to one of serving a "product champion." When they are not available within the institution, they must be identified and brought in from outside.

EXHIBIT 2

Internationalization Checklist

1. Comprehensive Strategy And Agenda
   - Is there a comprehensive strategy for internationalization?
   - What are the principal thrusts of this strategy?
   - Is the strategy translatable into an action agenda?
   - Are there individuals who can serve as change agents?
   - If not available internally, can they be secured from outside the institution?
2. Favorable Institutional Climate
   - Is internationalization adopted as a legitimate institutional goal and reflected in its mission?
   - Is there senior administrative commitment?
   - Is there suitable support infrastructure?
   - Does the internationalization effort permeate the entire organization?
3. Resource Allocation
   - Are there adequate monetary resources for various initiatives?
   - Have sources of external support been tapped?
   - Have competitive grant applications been made for government support?
4. Curriculum And Instructional Materials
   - Have adequate instructional materials been prepared and/or acquired?
   - Is the library properly equipped?
   - Have foreign language and international studies been integrated into business programs?
   - Which of the curricular strategies is the most appropriate? Infusion? Addition? Specialized majors?
5. Faculty
   - Are there adequate professional development opportunities for faculty?
   - Are there opportunities for international experiences?
   - Can faculty incorporate international dimensions into their research, teaching, and consulting activities?
   - Does the reward system accommodate internationalization efforts?
6. Students
   - Are there enriching overseas study opportunities?
   - Do interested students have access to international internships and jobs?
   - Does student life on campus offer sufficient international experiences? (e.g., residence hall activities, films, visitors, etc.).
7. Linkages With The Business Community
   - Are there meaningful vehicles for cooperation with the business community?
   - Can internships for students and faculty be created?
   - Can business sponsorship be gained for specific curricular initiatives, study abroad programs, lecture series, etc?
   - Can meaningful outreach and business assistance services be offered?
   - Is there any potential for lifelong education programs?
   - Would a business advisory board contribute to the internationalization drive?
8. Collaboration With Other Educational Institutions
   - Which external partners add synergy to the efforts?
   - How can a coordinated agenda be developed?
   - In what areas does collaboration make sense?

2. A FAVORABLE INSTITUTIONAL CLIMATE

A supportive institutional environment is most critical to successful internationalization. Such a climate requires that internationalization is adopted as a legitimate institutional goal and is reflected in its mission statement. It also means that there is senior administrative commitment to the objectives. An infrastructure, often in the form of a central support office (center or program office), is also essential. The internationalization efforts should be undertaken in a cross-cutting manner within a college or the entire institution, rather than be identified with a particular unit or group of people. In other words, it is best if the institution as a whole can rally behind the endeavor.

3. ALLOCATION OF RESOURCES

Financial resources are essential for implementing a variety of initiatives, including professional development of faculty, travel, release time, internships, visiting lecturers, and so on. Without a minimum level of monetary support, the effort will be crippled. In addition to looking internally to generate the necessary resources, an institution can seek external support. External support for internationalization can be secured from the business community, alumni and friends, industry/trade associations, and state and federal agencies. Businesses can sponsor curricular initiatives, individual students or faculty, a lecture series, and so on. Title VI-B of the U.S. Department of Education also makes annual grants to educational institutions to internationalize programs. These competitive grant programs include "Undergraduate International Studies and Foreign Language," and "Business and International Education." Another federal body, the U.S. Information Agency, also provides financial support for facilitating linkages with overseas educational institutions.

4. CURRICULUM AND INSTRUCTIONAL MATERIALS

A comprehensive plan for internationalization must also consider the curriculum aspects. Principal issues here include preparation and acquisition of instructional materials, equipping the library, integration of foreign language training into business programs, and the choice of curriculum strategy. When it comes to internationalizing the curriculum, three alternative strategies emerge—infusion, addition, and majors. Each alternative carries with it the implication of breadth at the expense of depth or vice versa. Mission goals and resource constraints will also play their role in influencing which strategy should be adopted and could work.

5. INTERNATIONALIZATION OF FACULTY

It is clear that faculty development is the key to the internationalization of business schools. In particular, there is a need to stimulate international teaching, research and outreach on the part of faculty in the mainline functional areas such as marketing, management, economics, and finance.

However, the problem does differ substantially across functional areas. For example, business faculty recognizes at this point that marketing, strategy, and macroeconomics are inherently international. Yet, technical fields, such as logistics, management science, the management of information systems, and microeconomics, are areas where internationalization is accorded a low priority.

Key areas to target for internationalization include marketing, economics, organization studies, and to some extent, production. Courses such as the environment of business, business ethics, and business strategy also lend themselves to internationalization. Nonetheless, the prime focus should be mainstream faculty in the primary functional areas. There is a need to identify key people in each functional area and get them involved in international business instruction and research.

What then are some workable approaches to internationalizing faculty? Perhaps the first priority should be to legitimize internationalization by having respected people in the functional fields work on international problems. One solution might be a rotating chair for a visiting professor who does international teaching and research.

Second, it would be worthwhile to appeal to the intellectual integrity of faculty by demonstrating that current models have been developed in a limited context—that of the United States or North American business environment. There is no reason to assume that these have general validity unless they are developed and tested in the context of global or worldwide business.

Third, the need to provide faculty with some international experience cannot be overemphasized. Even a limited international experience can broaden an individual's horizons and develop an interest and commitment to internationalization and international business. Also, by providing overseas internships, sabbatical opportunities to undertake research abroad, or even relatively short-term travel, one can begin to develop the sort of expertise and knowledge the faculty needs to be effective if they are going to internationalize their teaching and research.

Fourth is the role of the dean. Even though many deans are committed to internationalization, the dean's support, beyond mere commitment, is critical.

Commitment at the top however, is necessary though not sufficient. For many schools, an international umbrella "structure" is appropriate, rather than a separate international business department. A center, institute, or program office that can plan programs and channel resources to encourage internationalization of faculty, teaching, service, and research could provide the necessary organizational framework.

Fifth, a "change agent," or a "product champion," can be a remarkable catalyst. Having a senior and respected member of the faculty who is willing to make a strong commitment to internationalization of his or her business school is very helpful.

To that end, it is critical that resources within business schools be diverted to classroom and research activities that are internationally oriented. The business community may be able to help in this area by providing funding specifically aimed at internationalization of research or course development. One of the best ways of stimulating faculty to acquire international expertise is to award professional development grants on a competitive basis for special projects involving curricular development, resource material development, and travel

Each of the strategies discussed above calls for faculty and staff effort beyond what they have traditionally expended. Accordingly, successful internationalization strategies may require a modification of an institution's *reward system* to underscore the importance of participation in the institution's internationalization efforts. Achievement of such a bold, yet almost cost-free step, requires that the institution insure that its major decision-makers have a commitment to internationalization efforts. Current emphasis in U.S. business schools on research productivity and publications, while not incongruent with the objectives of internationalization, may have to change.

6. INTERNATIONALIZING THE STUDENT BODY

In today's global environment, students often serve as the catalyst for change. Growing up in an era of global communication and travel, young people are quite anxious for an internationally enriching educational experience. Often, they demand and initiate international experiences. These could include overseas study programs, international internships, and cultural activities that enhance student life.

7. LINKAGES WITH THE BUSINESS COMMUNITY

The business community has been quicker to acknowledge the globalization of the marketplace than business schools. And, traditionally, business educators have not fully exploited the fruits of meaningful cooperation with the business community. (The term "business community" is used broadly to include groups/associations of firms, world trade clubs, district export councils, and –individual enterprises.) Here are some suggestions for business-education cooperation:

- Business schools and firms can cooperate to provide internships for both students and faculty to aid in internationalization.
- Businesses can sponsor curricular initiatives, study abroad programs, lecture series, individual students or faculty (e.g., in the form of fellowships), or any other international project.
- Business firms can help to stimulate international applied research through funding and, more importantly, by facilitating access to international data and research sites.
- Business schools can be more active in responding to the applied research and counseling needs of particularly small and medium-sized companies. Often an outreach office becomes a center for this activity.
- Executive development/management education is an area that inherently requires company-school cooperation. Internationalization of this area is critical if managers are to obtain the international expertise they need to compete in the global environment. However, management education can also be used as a lever to help internationalize the curriculum.
- And, of course, business schools and companies can work together to insure that international education is valued in the recruiting process. Demand for internationally educated students will do much to stimulate internationalization of curriculum and faculty.

One of the best ways of achieving a healthy and productive business-education partnership is to create a Business Advisory Board.

In fact, more and more colleges are establishing these advisory groups to seek input and counsel on even sacred academic artifacts like the curriculum.

In establishing a business advisory board, the question that has to be addressed at the outset is: "What do we really want from this board? Do we need a 'prestige' board to provide visibility for the institution or the specific academic program?" Of course, there is nothing wrong with lining up some business leaders to meet every once in a while and hear a provocative speaker after a nice meal. It makes for good public relations and many executives are more than willing to help out in that way.

However, a "working" board may be what is really needed. Although they may represent lower managerial levels than CEOs, working boards can and should be invited to join in active academic problem solving and program development.

8. COLLABORATION WITH OTHER EDUCATIONAL INSTITUTIONS

While the agenda for internationalization is demanding, the reality of funding and the current modest levels of experience and expertise often dictate a collaborative approach. Schools are better off engaging in cooperative ventures in this area for simple economic reasons as well as for maximizing the impact each one can make in their respective institutions. Cooperation, and especially a coordinated agenda for internationalization, are essential for institutions in a region receiving their funding from the same government agency.

Universities with a strong public service thrust are especially open to serve as resources. For example, at Michigan State University, various units and programs welcome opportunities to lend expertise to other institutions. These MSU units include the International Business Centers in the Eli Broad College of Business, the Office of the Vice Provost for Lifelong Education, the African Studies Center, the Center for Advanced Study of International Development, the Japan Center, and many others.

The newly established national resource centers—the CIBERs—should also play a major role in terms of pioneering innovative approaches to international business education. A special mission of these exemplary programs is to disseminate new approaches to teaching and researching international business. Thus the larger business school community should benefit from the academic outreach activities of these centers through shared experience and resource materials. The universities where the national resource centers had been established as of late 1992 are the following: Michigan State, Michigan, Illinois, Indiana, Chicago, Purdue, Pittsburgh, Bentley College with Fletcher School, Columbia, Georgetown, Maryland, South Carolina, Duke, Miami, Texas, Texas A & M, Memphis State with Southern Illinois, Brigham Young with Utah, Washington, Southern California, UCLA with San Diego State, and Hawaii.

CONCLUSION

Internationalization of a business program is an exciting, multifaceted enterprise, which can be achieved in a variety of ways. Tailoring strategies to an institution's unique needs and resources, rewarding faculty, staff and student participation, and coordinating activities across the institution are essential to achieve the greatest impact. This effort also provides an opportunity to take a fresh look at curriculum. (Periodic re-examinations of the curriculum are far more appropriate today than ever.) Internationalization can also be tied to ongoing efforts to sensitize the campus community to cultural/ethnic diversity. In fact, internationalization is just one dimension of diversity.

Certainly, there are many barriers to overcome in the quest to internationalize our schools. Some are created by the slow nature of the institutional change process in academic institutions. College administrators tend to be more bound by tradition, often at the expense of something else.

Problems on the corporate side, too, serve to inhibit the internationalization of business school faculty, students and curriculum. Perhaps most hindersome are perceptions of corporate hiring and career development programs. Corporations come to campus to hire specialists: accountants, financial analysts, salespeople, or marketing researchers. Not only is there scarce attention paid by corporate recruiters to hiring people with international expertise, but many students perceive that corporations do not value their international experience or knowledge. In fact, corporate recruiters may even give the impression that international knowledge, foreign language proficiency, or international business expertise are sometimes seen as a negative in that they may take the place of additional functional knowledge and expertise. Also, actual hiring is done by human resource people who tend to look for competent and narrow functional specialists.

One of the most important steps, therefore, that could be taken by corporations to aid in the internationalization of business school faculty, students, and curriculum is for top management to pay more attention to the hiring process and to the career development of junior employees. It is difficult to promote internationalization of business schools when one cannot assure students that the time spent on acquisition of international knowledge and expertise will be valued when they enter the job market or in the early years of their careers.

A final point remains to be made. Today we have come to recognize that acquiring international expertise is a lifelong task and cannot be accomplished within the limited time span of a business program. Ideally, the process should start in public schools and be reinforced through college education. The early formative years of the individual represent a critical period of acquiring both cultural empathy and language skills. (It is ironic to hear the Japanese argue that our educational system is partly to blame for poor U.S. competitiveness.) Thus, internationalization of managers requires that individuals develop the capability and motivation to continue to learn on their own beyond what a formal program teaches, and to make effective use of any international experiences they encounter.

As a logical extension, executive or management education will also become increasingly important given the market decline in the availability of expatriate experience.

It is appropriate, in conclusion, to repeat and reacknowledge the long-term nature of the internationalization process. Whether one is talking about an individual or an institution, the process is best viewed as a gradual one that can be an enriching experience for everyone involved. Such a special mission always provides a deep sense of satisfaction and gratification to the individuals concerned.

NOTE

1. This chapter is based on the article by S. Tamer Cavusgil, "Internationalization of Business and Economics Programs: Issues and Perspectives," *Business Horizons* 34, no. 6 (November-December 1991): 92–100.

Curricular and Administrative Considerations—
The Cheshire Cat Parable

JEFFREY ARPAN

The time has passed to debate the *merits* of curriculum internationalization. Nation states are inexorably enmeshed in the fabric of the global economy. International business impacts virtually every industry, firm, and person, either directly or indirectly, whether they know it or not. Hence the relevant questions for business schools are HOW to accomplish internationalization—questions of methods, not merit.

The intertwined issues of internationalization strategy and structure brings quickly to mind the infamous "structure-strategy" paradigm, or in its more modern form, the "structure-strategy-context" paradigm. In other words, there is an important relationship between the *strategy* selected for internationalization, the organizational/administrative *structure* selected for it, and the context in which "internationalization" is to take place. However, because management scholars have yet to resolve whether structure follows strategy or strategy follows structure, it would be ill-advised for me to attempt to do so in the more specific case of internationalization. This said, I believe it *is* worthwhile to discuss some strategic aspects of structure and strategy for internationalization and how they influence each other. The remainder of this paper is devoted largely to this task. But first, as a point of departure, a few paragraphs are in order concerning *goals* and strategy.

THE CRITICAL IMPORTANCE OF GOALS

Far too often, educators neglect the paramount points of departure and future reference: *goals*. Recall Alice's encounter with the

Cheshire cat in Lewis Carroll's *Through the Looking Glass*. Alice gets lost in the woods and arrives at a junction where several paths branch out from the one she has been traveling. The infamous Cheshire cat appears with his resplendent, luminescent smile, and Alice asks him, "Which path should I take?" In turn, the Cheshire cat asks Alice, "Where do you want to go?" to which Alice replies, "I don't know." The Cheshire cat then sagely responds, "Then it doesn't matter which path you take. . ."

In internationalizing the business school, the goal(s) of internationalization must be clearly determined before proceeding with discussions of methods, structure, or anything else related to internationalization. Otherwise, much time, effort, blood, sweat, and tears will be spent unnecessarily arguing about advantages and disadvantages of different approaches and structures—all without regard to the basic truth that any method or structure is just as good as another until you decide what you want to accomplish.

During nearly two decades of work related to internationalizing business schools throughout the US and abroad, I have frequently encountered a lack of clear goals for internationalization. (In truth, this situation of goal ambiguity has general application to all aspects of business schools, not merely to the issue of internationalization.) To ameliorate this problem, I offer below what I have expounded for these many years as three primary goals for curriculum and faculty internationalization: awareness, understanding, and competency. The three are not mutually exclusive, but are generally hierarchical in terms of their degrees of complexity and cost.

CURRICULUM

Awareness is where it all begins. If students don't know there's a wider world "out there," they can hardly be expected to understand it or learn how to deal with it. In my opinion, and as an absolute minimum, no student should be able to take courses in the business school without developing an "international awareness"—an awareness of how the national economy and its people are connected to the rest of the world.

From a curriculum standpoint, the "awareness" goal can be achieved generally and relatively easily by the *infusion* method: i.e., placing/infusing some international content in existing courses throughout the curriculum.

Understanding begins where awareness is established, and represents a significantly higher order of learning for the student, and of educational commitment and complexity for the institution. It's one thing for a student to be aware that a country has a balance of trade deficit; it's another thing for the student to understand why the deficit exists or how a trade deficit influences economic conditions, government policies, etc. Because international business increasingly affects everyone's lives and livelihoods, I argue that business school students should not be allowed to graduate without having developed an understanding of the vital links between their economy and people and the rest of the world, what causes international business, and how it affects domestic business, economic growth and standards of living. If this is considered too grandiose a goal, a lesser, more widely adopted one is for all students to understand the international aspects of their major/specialization.

From a curriculum standpoint, achieving the "understanding" goal generally requires more than infusion. It requires *specific international courses* and international course *requirements*.

Competency permits the transformation of understanding into action. For example, awareness provides information that there are markets outside the United States. Understanding then provides information about how those markets *could* be tapped. Competency provides the specific skills needed to tap those markets, to transform knowledge into action. Similarly, competency permits taking the necessary action to strategically position a firm in a global context once a manager has developed an awareness and understanding of global competition and strategic positioning.

From a curriculum standpoint, true international business competency is facilitated by a *specialized degree* of an international and multidisciplinary nature. It requires the development of business skills, foreign language and cross-cultural interaction skills, a global mindset, and, probably most importantly, the completion of a significant "overseas experiential component" during the students' program (preferably working abroad). In other words, true competency can only be developed by first-hand, on-site experiences. This latter point currently precludes most business schools from developing international business competency in their students because the institutions are either unwilling or unable to arrange and require overseas experiences for their students. But even short of requiring an "overseas experience," most business schools make it difficult and/or costly for their students to take courses in other parts of the world, or even in other parts of the same university (e.g., history, foreign languages, political science, international studies, geography, etc.).

FACULTY

The hierarchical goals for faculty internationalization are essentially the same as those for students: awareness, understanding and competency. From an administration viewpoint, at most schools the dominant importance of faculty internationalization is curriculum driven; if the faculty are not sufficiently internationalized, they cannot or will not teach courses that are either international or internationalized. Nor are they likely to be as supportive (if at all) of new international degree programs or international components within existing programs. There is also the research perspective. Because most companies face international competition or are involved in some form of international business, research that is designed to be useful to them should address the international aspects or implications of the topic being studied. Like curriculum internationalization, there are several ways to achieve faculty internationalization, and different structural implications as well. Some of them are addressed later in this paper.

CURRICULUM ISSUES/APPROACHES

As we are often reminded, there are many ways to skin a cat—even a Cheshire one. So also with internationalizing the curriculum. One may typically consider four major methods: infusion, international courses, concentrations, and specialized degree programs. Each has certain advantages and disadvantages and facilitates the achievement of different goals. In my opinion, no method is "optimal" or "better" than the others. Each method must be considered in the light of goals and context (characteristics and constraints) of each institution.

Infusion is a very appropriate method and the one most often used for developing international awareness. Its major comparative advantage is that it does NOT require new courses, new faculty, structural changes, changes in class size, or "deep" faculty internationalization. At a relatively low cost, core and other courses can be altered to include international aspects of existing topics and related readings, cases, or other assignments, and faculty can be trained in how to minimally cover the international material. For example, several professional organizations such as the American Accounting Association and universities such as the University of South Carolina annually offer seminars to help faculty internation-

alize themselves and their courses. Courses can also be internationalized via the infusion of international anecdotes, films/videos,
simulations, and guest speakers. For largely these reasons, infusion
has been the method of internationalization adopted by the largest
number of business schools in the United States.

The comparative weaknesses of the infusion approach are that:

- it is often done as minimally/superficially as possible (therefore, it develops nothing more than minimal awareness),
- more faculty need to be internationalized (albeit minimally),
- many international business topics do not fall logically or easily into existing courses,
- more coordination of the internationalization process is necessary, and
- as a method, it does not develop international skills or much
understanding.

However, at most institutions, infusion clearly constitutes a starting point for internationalization. I would also argue that infusion
should be implemented even when other internationalization
methods are employed because it increases all students' exposure to
the international aspects of business and typically heightens their
interest in taking more in-depth, specialized courses in international business.

International courses are more appropriate for the goal of developing "understanding" because they permit the in-depth coverage
that is necessary. For example, gaining an adequate understanding
of international finance requires at least a full course on international finance (rather than an internationalized finance course) in
order to treat all the major international finance topics, their interrelationships, and their nuances. Even a general "survey" study of
an international business course is useful, and in my judgment
needed, to provide an understanding of the various aspects of international business, how they relate to each other, their impact on
what's happening today, and their implications for the future.

If "*minimal* understanding" is the internationalization goal for
all students, then all students should take at least one international
course. If the goal is "*more than minimal*" understanding, two or
more international courses are needed, etc. And if "broad understanding" is the goal, then a concentration (major) in international
business is in order.

International courses have several advantages, the most significant being the time and material available to explore the interna-

tional aspects, complexities, and nuances of a particular functional subject, such as marketing. In addition, an international course reveals the interactions and interrelationships between activities within a functional area and among functional areas—something difficult, if not impossible, to achieve under the infusion method. An East-West Business course, for example, teaches how the international aspects of marketing, finance, management, and accounting must be combined effectively in order to conduct business successfully in an East-West context.

The major cited drawbacks of the international course approach are that:

- new courses must be designed and added to the curriculum if they don't already exist,
- there is a shortage of faculty with sufficient expertise to teach complete international courses,
- from a pedagogical standpoint, at least for functional areas, it's better to introduce the international aspects of an activity immediately after its discussion in a theoretical or domestic context (as in the infusion method).
- another potential drawback is the size of classes if an international course is "required," and particularly if only a specific course is required at the undergraduate level. At some institutions in the US, such a decision has resulted in class sizes of over 300 students, given the large number of students who are required to take the course and the shortage of faculty at the institutions available to teach the course. A solution to this class size problem taken by many schools has been to require an international course from an array of several designated courses.

There are also a different variety of international courses often neglected or rejected by business schools: the numerous "international" courses offered *outside* the business school. Many of them can and should be considered as being suitable for business school students, such as world geography or world history, comparative sociology or religion, and anthropology, to name just a few. One advantage of such courses is that they don't add to the teaching load or class sizes of business school faculty.

Concentrations (majors), if nothing else, are symbolic indications of a student's interest and area of specialization. Similarly, an institution's offering of an IB concentration (either as a major, co-major, or minor) is a symbolic indication of its belief and interest in international business education. In a sense, it legitimizes international business as a field of study and specialization.

From a curricular standpoint, IB concentrations require a certain designated number of courses (credit hours) in international business. The major curriculum questions center on how many hours/courses, which courses, and what sequencing and/or prerequisites. Few schools consider offering IB concentrations of any variety until they already offer at least three international courses. Majors typically require four or five courses, some of which may be offered by departments outside the business school. However, the biggest, most complicated and hotly debated issue usually concerns offshore programs: should they be utilized, required, etc. To date, most business schools have not utilized or required offshore programs, for a variety of reasons, although the trend seems to be turning upward toward greater utilization.

The most frequently cited disadvantages of concentrations are:

- There is a strong obligation to offer the requisite courses on a regular basis (compared to intermittently offering them as electives).
- There is a need to offer counseling/advisement to students in any concentration, and some schools may not have the expertise or resources to provide such "services" to students concentrating in international business.
- It may be more difficult (require more or at least distinct effort) to place students with international business concentrations.
- Somewhere in the organization of the business school there needs to be a person or persons with oversight/administrative responsibility for the concentration. Hence for the first time, there is a formal organizational-structural implication of internationalizing the curriculum.

Special Degree Programs represent the biggest commitment and the most radical and comprehensive approach to curriculum internationalization. The main reason is because they are multidisciplinary (or if you prefer, interdisciplinary): combining courses in business, foreign language, and area studies. And in their most complete and complex form, they are also truly international in the sense that they involve offshore course work or internships. They thus combine the two most feared, dreaded, complicated, and hence usually avoided characteristics of programs from an administrative perspective: interdisciplinary curricula and international operations. Other administrative dimensions include having faculty and/or staff responsible for admitting, advising, and placing students; promoting the program to potential students and employers; arranging for and evaluating instruction in the program; and a host of other administrative activities normally associated with a degree program. For such reasons, special international business degree programs are usually avoided, and clearly constitute the minority in terms of internationalization approaches adopted in the United States.

To accommodate the multidisciplinary nature of the curriculum, time must be provided for course work taken outside the business school. Because most business schools don't want to disrupt their normal scheduling of classes, this often means utilizing the period before the students enter the business school for such course work. For example, at the undergraduate level, this typically means the first two years of a bachelor degree program before the students gain official admittance to the business school program. For graduate programs, this typically means the summer before students begin the program, and/or the summer between the first and second year of the program. The percentage of non-business school courses in specialized IB degree program varies considerably by institution, depending on each program's goals, objectives, resources, and constraints. For example, several existing programs require a general foreign language proficiency as a prerequisite to entry, shortening considerably the portion of the program needed to be devoted to language instruction.

Similarly, the offshore component of a specialized degree program typically disrupts normal program scheduling unless it occurs in the summer—hence the dominance of summer abroad programs, either study abroad or overseas internships. Further, the complicated and often expensive nature of offshore program development and operation often results in consortia being formed for such purposes or the utilization of other institutions' existent programs.

In sum, special degree programs carry significant curricular and organizational/ administrative considerations. These should not be taken lightly or underestimated in terms of cost, complexity, time and effort required. Further, existing approaches taken to date do not necessarily constitute ideal ones. There remain many yet-to-be-truly-tested curricular and structural configurations for such programs, and many of the "best ones" currently in existence continue to undergo experimentation and modification.

STRUCTURAL ISSUES/APPROACHES

I use the word "structural" to encompass a variety of administrative and organizational issues. In this sense, for example, "structural" would not pertain to the way a curriculum looks (what others might call the curriculum structure), but would pertain to how decisions were made to configure the curriculum in a certain way, how internationalization was implemented, and how it is administered.

Internationalization does not take place automatically. Someone or some group(s) must decide to internationalize. They must then decide how and how much to internationalize, and how to monitor, evaluate, and in some instances, administer the results. Hence some of the major structural issues of internationalization include the following:

- Should there be an internationalization committee established, and if so, should it be temporary or permanent, intra-college or inter-college (single disciplinary or multidisciplinary), advisory or operative (administrative)?
- Should there be a "department" of international business commensurate with other functional departments of the college, an "institute," or some other type of formal organizational unit?
- Is a matrix the most suitable and/or desirable form of organization for internationalization?

The answers to the above, in no particular/corresponding order, are "no," "yes," "maybe," and, like in the old fortunetelling eight ball, "ask again later". In other words, it again depends on goals and contexts. However, in addition to the curriculum-related issues of structure mentioned earlier in this paper, there are other issues that also need to be considered, most of which relate to faculty concerns and predispositions. And as a final point of departure, deciding whether strategy follows structure or structure follows strategy is less important than recognizing that each affects the other, especially over time.

ADMINISTRATIVE AND STRUCTURAL EVOLUTION

Just as the administration and organizational structure of a company change over time as the firm moves from domestic to global operations, so do those of a college of business. Initially, a little internationalization will take place on a serendipity basis: some faculty will internationalize their courses and research because of their own international backgrounds or their perceptions of needs and benefits. Some internationalization will also occur as a result of having "foreigners" as students, research assistants, or colleagues. However, internationalization via serendipity is erratic, at best, and seldom leads to any major degree of faculty or curriculum internationalization.

More directed steps forward result from senior administrator involvement, be it cajoling/threatening, encouraging, or actually supporting! For example, I know one dean who asks all faculty members during their annual performance reviews, "What have you done during the last year to internationalize your courses and research?" Because faculty generally don't like to report zero activity in an area of interest to the dean, internationalization gets more attention than it would otherwise. Better yet are deans or department chairs who provide incentives to faculty to internationalize. I know of several deans who have paid for their faculty to attend curriculum internationalization workshops, seminars and conferences, such as those organized by the American Assembly of Collegiate Schools of Business (AACSB), the American Accounting Association (AAA), the American Marketing Association (AMA), the University of South Carolina, American Graduate School of Management (Thunderbird), and the University of Hawaii. A dean at a midwestern school of business allocates $10,000 per year for up to ten of his faculty to take an international trip. Others provide teaching load reductions for faculty to internationalize themselves, their courses, and in some cases, their school's curriculum. However, while such administrative direction is laudable and in virtually all cases necessary, it is rare. Perhaps more importantly, it is not likely to achieve as much internationalization as fast, or with as long-lasting effect, as efforts brought about via structural change. Therefore, some structural change is typically both desirable and needed.

Initially what seems to work well at most institutions is the creation of an "international" committee—often a rather ad hoc group of faculty with international backgrounds and interest—charged by a senior administrator to develop a strategy for internationalizing the curriculum. This advisory committee serves essentially as a think tank or brainstorming group, typically comprised exclusively of business faculty. It can even be comprised initially of faculty from a single department, especially when the goal is internationalization of a single department's curriculum or faculty. Such a committee can clearly facilitate internationalization by focusing attention on it, identifying opportunities and constraints, generating alternatives, and recommending specific courses of action. If and when they are combined with strong administrative support, such committees can exercise the wherewithal to actually implement internationalization recommendations or take other substantive action.

Beyond the internal committee is the broader, multidisciplinary committee that adds faculty from non-business disciplines. The inclusion of non-business faculty usually adds a considerable amount of international experience, expertise, information, and contacts—individual and institutional. While more likely to be established for undergraduate curriculum internationalization or for specialized degree programs (because both are more likely to involve course work outside the business school), this type of committee can be useful for any internationalization effort. However, most multidisciplinary committees tend to be "advisory" only. Therefore, someone or some other organizational unit with "authority" will most likely be needed to push further and implement the internationalization effort.

Another structural change is to establish an international "institute" or "center," indicating a stronger commitment to international business education and research. Members of such institutes are typically appointed by deans or higher level university administrators, and hold such positions in addition to their normal tenure track positions in departmental faculties. I am aware of only a few cases where members' promotion and tenure are truly affected by their being a member of an international business institute or center. Nevertheless, having an international institute/center can help obtain funds and create more ongoing activities and synergy than committees usually can. They also can administer international programs of both an educational and research variety. Further, if they belong to an international business center or department faculty with international expertise are more identifiable to students and others groups, and are more likely to provide advisement and career counseling concerning international business education, research, and careers.

Beyond an international institute or center is an international department, similar to those of finance, marketing, accounting, etc. Here the key distinction involves tenure and promotion decisions. If operated as a true department, the department's faculty are promoted and tenured in terms of their *international* education, research, and service activities. Such faculty see themselves *first* as international business faculty, and *second* as faculty with a specialized interest in a functional area such as marketing or finance. Until recently, less than a half dozen international business departments existed in the United States. Now there are more than twice as many, but these numbers still cover only a very small number of business schools. The major advantage of an international business department is it establishes a group of faculty with a clear mandate and responsibility for internationalization. It also lends itself to synergistic activities that typically don't occur when international expertise is dispersed throughout several different departments. The main arguments usually put forth against establishing international business departments are that:

- international business is not a distinct discipline, and
- there may be less internationalization of other curricula and faculty because the other faculty perceive internationalization to be the responsibility of only the international business faculty. It is also possible that international business faculty will not work as much with non-international business faculty in internationalizing courses and research projects if they are departmentally separated.

Theoretically, to solve the potential disadvantages of a freestanding international business department, a few business schools have adopted a matrix (or grid) structure in which internationally oriented faculty belong to both an international department and a functional area department. Tenure and promotion decisions are based on assessments by each of the two faculty groups, and one usually needs support from a majority of the combined faculties (and in some cases, a majority of each faculty) to be promoted and tenured. The ambitious goal of the matrix structure is to capture the benefits of having international specialists in their own department (as listed above) and in functional area departments (e.g., serving as international catalysts for other "less internationally oriented" faculty in their departments). The potential downsides of matrix structures are the schizophrenic behaviors they often induce and the fact that pleasing one faculty group can and often does antagonize the other group. Promotion, and particularly tenure, get more difficult to achieve under such circumstances.

Somewhere, and sometimes amidst these administrative and structural changes, a specific *international administrative position* can appear, such as an associate dean for international business educa-tion and research—or in shorter parlance, international activities. These persons are usually charged with encouraging, overseeing, and/or coordinating international activities in the college of busi-ness, and also perhaps interfacing formally with counterparts in other colleges or administrative units of the university. Fund rais-ing and serving as the focal point or major point of contact for international activities typically comes with their territory. They also can and do serve as chief administrators of international busi-ness degree programs.

A final administrative and/or structural issue worth mentioning, concerns *international experiential components* of curricula, such as study abroad or international internships. Key decisions include who and which unit(s) of the business school will have responsibil-ity to investigate, evaluate, promote, arrange, administer, and monitor them. These are not unimportant or simple decisions. The administrative complexities of offshore activities are a major reason why international experiential components are either absent or not required in virtually all business schools.

In sum, and as in business, there is no optimal administrative approach or organizational structure for internationalizing curricu-lum and or faculty. Each institution must make and implement such decisions with reference to their internationalization goals, resources, and constraints. However, based on what I have seen and experienced, I conclude that the most comprehensive internation-alization of the curriculum and faculty occur when there is a group of faculty whose tenure and promotion depend almost exclusively on international activities and criteria. I am equally convinced that this structure is also optimal for specialized international business degree programs.

PUTTING IT ALL TOGETHER: THE UNIVERSITY OF SOUTH CAROLINA EXPERIENCE

Beginning in the early 1970s, the College of Business Adminis-tration (CBA) at the University of South Carolina (USC) pursued several different methods of internationalizing its curricula. Curi-ously, USC's initial approach was and remains its most ambitious and noteworthy: the establishment in 1974 of its Master of Inter-national Business Studies (MIBS) program—arguably the nation's most comprehensive and best graduate program in international business. Equally surprising to many people is the fact that the radically innovative concept and curriculum of the MIBS program was the product of a committee!

THE MIBS PROGRAM

Very early in the 1970s, USC CBA Dean James F. Kane observed two separate but related phenomena. Foreign investment in South Carolina was growing exponentially, and many South Carolina firms were either being adversely affected by imports or were not doing well in their international ventures. As a result, in 1972 he formed a CBA committee to investigate if and how internationalization could strengthen the college's educational activities, image, etc. The committee was comprised of one faculty member with international project administration experience (Agency for International Development projects in Latin America), one who taught international economics, one who had training in international studies, and one who had recently completed an international finance dissertation. At that time there was only one CBA course in international business (a combined grad/undergrad course in international finance), no faculty with degrees in international business, and virtually no international content in other CBA courses.

During the committee's year-long investigation, numerous executives of regional, national, and international business communities were contacted for their opinions and advice—most of which supported a strong international thrust. What evolved was the design of a comprehensive, multidisciplinary, specialized degree program in international business: the Master of International Business Studies program (MIBS). MIBS would add to the traditional MBA core a half dozen specific international business courses, foreign language training—Spanish and German, area studies courses, and most uniquely and importantly, a six-month corporate internship in a foreign country. This raised the key questions of how to implement and operate such a program with virtually no faculty with international expertise, and in such a non-international environment as South Carolina.

Members of the existing business advisory board to the CBA pledged their financial and other support to get the program started, as did several other previously contacted companies who believed in what the program was trying to accomplish. A senior faculty member at Syracuse with substantial international experience was hired to set up the overseas internships and handle program administration duties.

In order to administer and further develop the MIBS program, and to attract tenure track faculty with strong international expertise and commitment, an international business department was created. Several international scholars were brought in to lend their teaching and development expertise, and several tenure track faculty who had significant international business training or degrees were hired. Faculty in USC's Department of Foreign Languages and Literatures designed a new, integrated language program that included an intensive summer course, courses dealing with the commercial aspects of the languages, and advanced language training overseas. Faculty in USC's Department of Geology and Department of Government and International Studies developed a series of area studies courses that they would team teach.

Several years after the MIBS program began, French and Portuguese specializations were added, along with further language training and internships in Belgium, France, and Brazil, and the faculty in the international business department increased to six. During the 1980s, the program added five other language specializations, became larger than the full time MBA program, and assumed flagship program status in the College of Business. The international business department faculty grew to a dozen members, and at least that many faculty with some international training or interest joined other departments of the CBA. Today there are more than 300 students in the MIBS program from more than thirty states and a dozen countries, nearly 1500 MIBS alumni worldwide, several dozen USC faculty members teaching in the MIBS each year, and a MIBS full-time support staff of six, assisted by about a dozen graduate assistants.

NON-MIBS CURRICULA

The expansion of international business faculty permitted the addition of more than a half dozen new international business courses in the non-MIBS curricula. However, these courses were taken as electives only by a small percentage of graduate or undergraduate students. Hence most students in the CBA were not exposed to the international aspects of business. As a result, the international business faculty obtained several grants from the US Department of Education to internationalize additional faculty and core courses at the undergraduate and graduate levels. To further internationalize students, several exchange agreements were initiated by international business faculty with foreign universities, substantially increasing the number of foreign students in the MBA and undergraduate programs, as well as permitting more of USC's American students to study abroad. In addition, a major in international business was added at the Ph.D. level in the early 1980s, and with it, several new international business courses were added strictly for Ph.D. students. Like students in the MIBS program, USC Ph.D. students majoring in international business had to develop a foreign language proficiency and complete a three month overseas experience. In 1986, an *international* business advisory board was established formally to provide continuous input and assistance concerning existing and future activities. In 1989, USC's CBA was selected and designated by the U.S. Department of Education as one of the first national Centers for International Business Education and Research. Through a series of federal and other grants to the Center, the CBA has been able to support an increased level of international business research and educational activities by an ever widening number of faculty—including some in other colleges at USC. And in 1991, the CBA faculty approved curriculum changes in the MBA and professional MBA programs to require all students to take at least one international business course.

So today at USC, undergraduate and graduate business students gain an awareness and some understanding of international business. At the master's and Ph.D. levels, some students can also develop international business competency through the specialized international business degree programs. Most of the CBA faculty have some understanding of the international dimensions of their specialties, and many have high levels of competency. Strong working relationships have been established between the CBA and the College of Humanities and the international business community. Financially, the international business programs and faculty have resulted in millions of dollars coming into USC and the CBA that would not have otherwise been forthcoming.

To be sure, USC's internationalization process was not easy, fast, inexpensive, or painless. In addition, even after more than fifteen years of internationalization, there still remain some operational problems to be addressed and solved. Nevertheless, in the future, USC plans to increase the international awareness, understanding, and competency of *all* business students and faculty. It is safe to predict that numerous paths will be traveled to get there!

Business School Curriculum and Faculty: Historical Perspectives and Future Imperatives

LEE C. NEHRT

INTRODUCTION

The Gordon and Howell report and the Pearson report, both published in 1959, were largely responsible for convincing the AACSB of the need for graduates to be able to utilize the business applications of mathematical techniques, and to understand the business applications of developments in the fields of psychology and sociology. Over a period of years after the publication of these reports, the AACSB accordingly changed its standards and developed interpretations of these standards to provide guidelines for the expected changes in the curriculum. These fields of study were developed in business schools; courses in these fields were gradually introduced into the required "core," and attempts were made to recognize, integrate, and utilize the knowledge and techniques across other courses in the curriculum. Given the need for business professors in most fields to understand and utilize the quantitative and behavioral aspects of their specializations, the doctoral programs in business administration gradually came to require that all doctoral students have a grounding in the quantitative area and the behavioral sciences.

HISTORICAL PERSPECTIVE

The developments in the field of international business and the internationalization of the curriculum have followed a somewhat different path. The first courses in international business per se, as contrasted to foreign trade or export marketing, were offered in the mid-1950s. The Academy of International Business (AIB), the professional organization of the field, was founded in 1959, and within four or five years a fair number of schools were offering courses in international business, with several offering a major in the field at the MBA level. In 1963, a survey[1] showed that 49 business schools were offering one or more courses in the field. A 1969 survey[2] showed that this number had increased to 95 schools, with 69 schools offering international courses at the undergraduate level, 72 at the masters level, and 21 at the doctoral level. A 1974 survey by John Daniels and Lee Radebaugh showed that 213 U.S. schools (this was 64 percent of the schools responding to the survey) were offering at least one international business course. A 1980 survey[3] marked an increase to 262 schools offering one or more international business courses. This was 81 percent of those responding to the survey. Of these 262 schools, 68 schools offered a major in international business at the undergraduate level, 50 did so at the MBA level, and 20 at the doctoral level.

A 1986 curriculum survey[4] used somewhat different methodology and had a lower response rate; the results are therefore not easily comparable, but it appears that by 1986, 382 schools offered one or more international business courses, 84 undergraduate programs had a major in international business, 119 had one at the MBA level, and 49 at the doctoral level. We see, therefore, that international business courses are taught in most of the country's business schools, and a major in the field is available in many of them.

Meanwhile, several meetings were organized and studies published regarding the teaching of international business and the need to internationalize the curriculum. The first such meeting[5] was organized at Indiana University in late 1963 and was attended by deans or their representatives from more than 80 business schools. A number of papers were presented. The main topics discussed were:

- Why should business schools teach international business and what subject matter should be taught?
- How should the international dimension of business operations be integrated into business school curricula?
- How should this international dimension be related to international studies in the rest of the university?
- What are the needs for research and instructional material in the field?

In 1967, the Education & World Affairs organization appointed a study committee to review what business schools were doing to respond to the needs of business. They issued a report, *The Professional School & World Affairs: Business Administration*. After discussing the growing internationalization of business and the consequent need to educate future and present managers in the international aspects of business, the report reviewed the extent to which some business schools had already responded. Various levels and strategies of internationalization of business schools were discussed. The central theme of the report was that most schools had not addressed the international aspects of their professional responsibilities adequately. It then indicated that, in various ways, foundations and the government had an obligation to help business schools to respond to the challenge.

Tulane University organized a meeting in 1968, similar to the one which had been held five years earlier at Indiana University. The Tulane meeting[6] was attended by the deans or their representatives from ninety-eight U.S. business schools. The subject matter and topics discussed were similar to the earlier meeting. In the same year, utilizing a portion of a major Ford Foundation grant for international business development, Indiana University sponsored a study,[7] conducted by eight faculty members from eight different schools, that examined the need for and the methods of internationalizing the curriculum.

NEEDS AND MEANS

Two major efforts were subsequently undertaken by the U.S. National Commission for UNESCO which, in 1970, appointed a task force composed of ten members, including John Fayerweather and Richard D. Robinson. The task force organized a conference that included representatives of business, academe, and government. They discussed business needs for management personnel who possess a perspective that transcends national economies, a sensitivity to foreign cultures and alien environments, and a knowledge of international affairs. The report[8] recommended that:

1. University and continuing education urgently needed to be re-examined to determine to what extent and in what ways the international dimension should be strengthened;
2. Corporations might do well to evaluate their recruitment and promotional policies and their executive development

programs to determine if, in fact, they are utilizing people
who have a knowledge and understanding of world affairs;
3. The business community might consider increasing its support to educational and other organizations that have
   demonstrated an interest and capacity to develop and sustain relevant international programs and to engage in significant research;
4. Schools of management, with the cooperation of the business community, should seek:

- to strengthen the international dimension of faculty and
  curriculum development,
- to initiate new research programs,
- to improve programs of faculty and student exchange,
- to strengthen and increase technical assistance to management education programs abroad and
- to improve programs of continuing education and post-
  experience training for international executives and overseas personnel.

The fall of 1972 saw the U.S. National Commission's second
major effort—the organization of four regional conferences at Indiana University, Georgia State University, Tufts University, and University of Washington. At each of these conferences, forty to fifty
academics and businessmen, plus several government officials,
gathered to hear and discuss a series of papers on the needs and
means of internationalizing management education. Each university produced a "proceedings" of the conference. These were summarized in a report,[9] the thrust of which was similar to that of the
UNESCO task force report described above. An offshoot of the latter
was the inauguration by the AACSB of a quarterly newsletter, *International Dimensions*, containing various ideas on internationalizing
business education.

THE ROLE OF PROFESSIONAL ASSOCIATIONS

Meanwhile, the early 1980s saw several of the leaders of the
Academy of International Business initiate the process of urging
the internationalization of the curriculum—for *all students*—rather
than simply having courses offered for majors and others who
elected to take them. It was felt that institutional pressure needed
to be brought to bear on the AACSB to change its standards. In

1971 the Executive Board of the Academy under the president, Vern Terpstra, prepared a position paper which proposed that the AACSB accreditation standards be modified so that the "common body of knowledge" required for all students would include the international environment and the international influences on business.

The AIB Executive Committee then corresponded with the standards Committee of the AACSB and finally, in April 1973, this author, then AIB President, attended the annual meeting of the AACSB Standards Committee where agreement was reached to add the three key words to the "purpose" of the curriculum: "The purpose of the curriculum shall be to provide for a broad education preparing the student for imaginative and responsible citizenship and leadership roles in business and society —*domestic and worldwide.*" This was adopted the next day at the plenary meeting of the AACSB.

Despite this modification, it became apparent over the following several years that faculty members (who control the curriculum) and deans lacked both knowledge and motivation to incorporate the international dimensions into the core of the curriculum.

Around the same time, the U.S. Office of Education sponsored a conference in Philadelphia to discuss ways in which the government and academe might better communicate their needs to each other in the field of international education. This was followed, in 1973, by a Smithsonian Conference, sponsored by the Bureau of Educational and Cultural Affairs of the Department of State. This latter conference led to the initiation of a series of studies by the American Council on Education (ACE) in August 1973, to re-examine the roles that the academic sector might play to better respond to the needs of government and society. This resulted in their publication of *Education for Global Interdependence* in 1975. The series of studies contained in this publication addressed the needs of liberal arts but ignored business education and the needs of the business community and was, therefore, incomplete. Consequently, the ACE submitted a proposal to the Exxon Foundation for funding to establish a task force on business and international education. Exxon agreed to provide the funding and a task force was organized in November 1975 under the chairmanship of this author. It carried out a series of studies over the following twelve months and ACE published the results in *Business and International Education.*[10]

The studies found that (a) relatively few schools had found a way to internationalize the curriculum, (b) a very high percentage of students were completing their BBA's to MBA's without having taken an "international" course, and (c) 75 percent of graduating DBA's (and Ph.D's in business) had *no* international business courses during their graduate studies and another 10 percent had had only one such course.

WORKSHOPS TO INTERNATIONALIZE FACULTY

One of the studies undertaken by the task force surveyed all AACSB deans. Responses were received from 76 percent of the 178 accredited schools and 65 percent of the non-accredited schools. When asked their opinions as to the desirability of instituting summer workshops in international business for their faculty, 86 percent of the responding deans of accredited schools and 87 percent from the nonaccredited indicated that they felt it was either desirable or highly desirable (see Chapter 5 by Ben Kedlow).

The International Affairs Committee of the AACSB was aware of the results of the ACE survey before the ACE task force had completed all of its work. Consequently, the AACSB, in cooperation with the task force, organized a one-week workshop, in August 1976 in Washington, D.C., for business school deans, to discuss the various ways in which international business might be integrated into the curriculum. It was very well attended and termed "definitely successful" by the participants. This was the AACSB's first effort to assist member schools to meet the needs of business' international environment and comply with the accreditation standard on internationalization.

One of the recommendations of the ACE task force was that a joint AACSB-AIB committee be appointed to develop and direct a three-year program of summer workshops to prepare business school faculty to teach various special international business courses and to internationalize various specific functional courses. It was suggested that this joint committee should seek funding from both government and private sources to subsidize such workshops.

The AACSB's International Affairs Committee subsequently obtained financial assistance from the U.S. State Department to fund a two-week workshop organized by the Graduate Business School of New York University (NYU) in June 1977. This was on the initiative of Professor John Fayerweather who chaired NYU's International Business Department. Its purpose was to provide participants with a background both for teaching international business courses and for internationalizing existing core courses.

The August 1976 seminar in Washington D.C. and the June 1977 workshop at NYU provided the experience needed by the AACSB-AIB joint committee to plan subsequent programs. It created the joint AACSB-AIB committee, chaired by Donald Carroll, dean of the Wharton School. The committee planned seven regional five-day workshops to be attended by thirty-five faculty members from each region, preceded by a three-day plenary session in Washington D.C. that brought the participants into contact with the various parts of government that impinge on international business.

Deans were asked to nominate faculty members for these programs. A total of 450 people were nominated, from which the committee selected 245. The Washington plenary session was held in May 1978. The seven regional five-day workshops were held during June and July of 1978. This was all funded by a grant of $150,000 from the General Electric Company as part of its 100th anniversary celebration. The proceedings[11] were published by the AACSB in 1979. In subsequent years, grants were received from various other sources to continue to subsidize similar summer workshops. There were seven more in 1979, four each in 1980 and 1981, and two each year in 1982-1984. Thus, the AACSB organized about thirty workshops in various parts of the country. Over 1,000 faculty members plus thirty to forty deans participated in them.

In 1981 the AACSB sponsored a study, by this author, to determine the effects of the seven workshops that had been organized in 1978. Published by the AACSB[12] the report contained nine case studies and attempted to provide role models to exemplify how schools had used various approaches to the problem of internationalizing the curriculum.

RECENT PERSPECTIVES

As a further follow-up, during 1984, this author conducted a survey of all of the 564 AACSB member schools in the United States. The initial letter/questionnaire had a 63 percent response rate. A follow-up questionnaire raised the response rate to 80 percent and follow-up telephone calls brought the response rate up to 99 percent. The results of this study were published in JIBS.[13]

Exhibits 1 and 2 summarize the main results of the survey. Exhibit 2 reveals that, at the MBA level, 94 schools required that a student take an international business course. There were 102 schools that had made no attempt at internationalization. My greater concern, however, was for the 286 schools whose faculty simply agreed to include an international dimension in some or all of the core courses; there is no guarantee this is going to be implemented. There are about 28,000 faculty members in the 669 member business schools. Only about 1,000 have attended the AACSB seminars. Perhaps 1,500 other faculty have studied and are teaching international business. Few of the remainder are sufficiently familiar with the international dimensions of their own disciplines to feel comfortable with introducing them into the courses that they teach.

EXHIBIT 1

Internationalization at the Undergraduate Level

112 Schools	Have done nothing
39 Schools	Have a required course for all students
39 Schools	Have all students take an international course of their choice
318 Schools	The faculty have agreed to include an international dimension in some or all of the core courses
13 Schools	Have both a required course, *PLUS* the faculty have agreed to internationalize the core courses
27 Schools	Have all students taking an international course of their choice, *PLUS* the faculty have agreed to internationalize the course courses
548 Schools	

EXHIBIT 2

Internationalization at the MBA Level

102 Schools	Have done nothing
41 Schools	Have a required course for all students
26 Schools	Have all students take an international course of their choice
286 Schools	The faculty have agreed to include an international dimension in some or all of the core courses
17 Schools	Have both a required course, *PLUS* the faculty have agreed to internationalize the core courses
10 Schools	Have all students taking an international course of their choice, *PLUS* the faculty have agreed to internationalize the core courses
482 Schools	

So, we were headed in the right direction and we had good intentions, but were the schools capable of delivering?

If the AACSB had continued to organize seven seminars every summer, perhaps by now a sufficient number of existing faculty members would have provided the critical mass in many schools to accomplish the task. But, what about our future faculty members? What about those who are going through our doctoral programs? Are they being prepared to add an international dimension to the courses they will teach during their future careers?

THE DOCTORAL PERSPECTIVE

As noted earlier, a 1976 survey conducted during the ACE study showed that 75 percent of the Ph.D./DBA graduates of the 25 largest doctoral programs in the country had not studied even one international business course during their graduate studies.

At the time of this author's 1984 study, there were 100 doctoral programs in business in the United States. Of these the largest 53 produced 92 percent of all doctoral graduates. A letter/questionnaire to the directors of those 53 doctoral programs won 48 responses; those 48 schools produced 82 percent of all the doctoral graduates in business. Perhaps the most significant result of that 1984 survey was that, of the 1690 doctoral students who had completed all of their coursework and who would be graduating during the following one to three years, only 287 (17 percent) had studied one or more international courses. This compares to 25 percent in the 1976 study. Thus, the situation was deteriorating while the need was increasing.

I don't know of a more recent study of this type, but I suspect that the early 1990s situation has not improved over 1984, and may be continuing to deteriorate.

Unfortunately, the AACSB accredits only undergraduate and MBA programs—not Ph.D. programs. The AACSB has not concerned itself, to date, with this major problem. Somebody must. *The disease of provincialism will not go away by itself. The disease is genetic—it is inherited from one generation of faculty members to the next.* Provincialism is the weak gene in the double helix of the DNA of our reproductive process.

What can be done to break into the DNA chain and supply the missing link of internationalism?

There are two solutions to the problem of internationalizing the doctoral programs: (a) The doctoral committee of each school/college must change the prerequisite coursework requirements for *all* doctoral students so as to include an International Business course. This can be done at the school/college level, or (b) Each department that offers a major would require that the core courses required for the major include an international course in that discipline (e.g., international marketing for marketing majors). This requires a separate decision by each department, which is more desirable, but more difficult to achieve.

Either of these solutions is simple. The implementation process, however, is not necessarily simple. Each requires pressure from both the dean of the school and the director of the doctoral program to effect this change. The first solution depends upon a vote of the faculty members of the school's doctoral coordinating committee. The second depends upon the chairmen of each department in the school to push the department's doctoral program committee into voting for the change.

FUTURE IMPERATIVES

In summary, there are many strategies that might be selected to internationalize the curriculum. To develop these strategies however, one must understand the dimensions of the problem.

At the national level, we have seen that there are about 28,000 faculty members in the AACSB member schools. If we assume that the rapid growth in the number of business students over the past 30 years has plateaued, and if we assume that the average career of a faculty member is 28 years, then there will be a flow-through (retirees leaving and new faculty entering) averaging about 1,000 per year. If, as it appears, about 800 per year are coming from the doctoral programs of business schools, many of the remainder are coming from the fields of psychology, economics and computer science, none of whom will have had any background in international business. Of the 800 from business schools, we have seen that perhaps 15 percent to 20 percent have studied some international business. So, we have an influx, each year, of 800 to 900 new faculty members who have had no formal training in the international dimensions of their field.

During the late 1970s, when AACSB was struggling to run seven workshops per year to internationalize business school faculty, there was a flow-through of only about 250 faculty members per year. While this strategy does not solve the problem wholly, and would need to be continued ad infinitum, ceterus paribus, it is a strategy that the AACSB should follow and which could be financed by contributions from the business community.

The U.S. Department of Education could clearly assist in this effort by requiring that each CIBER similarly organize several such workshops each year.

This national effort will not solve the problem but would assure an increasing number of faculty members to support the internal efforts of individual business school deans and department heads.

Can the AACSB do more via its accreditation standards? Yes, it must be more specific and require that each graduate, particularly at the MBA level, have at least *one course* in international business and have a *thorough* understanding of (rather than merely an exposure to) the international dimensions of his/her field of specialization. If this were restricted to the MBA level, it would not require the addition of large numbers of faculty with the ability to teach international marketing, international finance, international management, and international accounting. Also, the need for such people could be satisfied largely through the AACSB- and CIBER-sponsored workshops, rather than solely through hiring new international business specialists.

This new type of AACSB standard applying only to the MBA level, while maintaining the current standard for the undergraduate programs, is at least partially defensible in that MBA graduates tend to be hired by firms that are more deeply involved internationally. It would, of course, eventually need to be extended to the undergraduate level.

Also, as most doctoral students have an MBA, or need to satisfy MBA requirements, this will largely solve the current problem of most doctoral graduates not understanding the international dimensions of their own fields. It will have taken place at the MBA level, where the AACSB has standards, rather than at the doctoral level where the AACSB is not involved. This is the *only* solution that I see to the problem of provincialism in the coming generations of new faculty members. It also is the only way I see of avoiding having the large majority of MBA finance majors not understanding international finance, and MBA marketing majors not understanding the international dimensions of marketing and marketing competition, etc.

The AACSB standard will need to have an interpretation which states that a *thorough understanding* means a specific course; otherwise the AACSB accreditation teams will be as lax in their review in the future as they have been in the past.

From the perspective of individual schools, which strategies should be followed?

It is imperative that the dean understand today's business world and that the dean be *committed* to the internationalization of the faculty and the curriculum. With that as a given, what strategic plan should the dean develop?

Most schools have student exchange programs. However, except for a few small private schools, such programs rarely involve more than a very small percentage of undergraduates. Also, whereas students may be able to develop some language and cultural skills of the foreign country, they do not learn about international business in an operational sense. This could be overcome by an internship program.

Student internships with foreign companies, either in the United States or abroad, is a powerful learning experience, but is very costly, and will never affect more than a very small percentage of students.

Both exchanges and internships are useful programs to expand the opportunities for students, but they do not qualify as part of a strategic plan for internationalizing the curriculum and faculty in a way that must affect all students.

Should business schools attempt to emulate the MIBS program at South Carolina or the MIM program at Thunderbird, whereby all students achieve a foreign language skill, an understanding of a foreign culture, and an in-depth knowledge of international business? No; I believe that there is a market niche for such students, but it is a relatively small niche and would become quickly saturated.

Recent articles have described INSEAD, at Fountainebleu, France, and IMD at Lausanne, Switzerland, as the model for business education in today's world, a model for U.S. business schools. However, it is a model which requires students to master three languages—French, German and English—for faculty members to be fluent in two of those languages, and for both faculty and students to come from a wide range of countries with no one country accounting for more than one-third of the total. It depends upon the use of case studies as the primary tool of pedagogy. Finally, it depends upon the fact that the students tend to have five to ten years of business experience and bring that experience from their home countries to benefit the group preparation for case presentations. It is not a model that is transferrable to other countries.

CONCLUSION

So, what is the U.S. dean to do? The primary goal of the dean is to end up with a faculty that sees business from an international perspective. If that can be accomplished, all sub-goals of changes in curriculum design and the ability to implement those changes will follow naturally. To accomplish the primary goal, the dean must:

1. advise faculty search committees that candidates they select will not be approved unless they demonstrate a competence in the international dimensions of their field;
2. advise tenure and promotion committees that their proposals for tenure and promotion will not be approved unless the faculty members have, in teaching and research, shown competence in the international dimensions of their fields;
3. advise all faculty members that salary increases will be linked to demonstration of competence in the international dimension;
4. use the annual budget for faculty research to push faculty into doing research on international problems. Advise the faculty that in year one, 40 percent of such research funds will be allocated to research on international problems; in year two, 60 percent, in year three and thereafter, 80 percent.
5. implement (4) above for two years before beginning (2) and (3).

With the above strategy in place, faculty exchange programs with foreign business schools will be a positive experience with an abundance of volunteers to go abroad, rather than the usual current experience of an inability to find sufficient faculty willing to go abroad.

Without a toughening of the AACSB standard on internationalism, few deans will have the guts to follow through on the above strategy, although a few have already adopted such a strategy. On the other hand, if a dean were to follow such a strategy, the faculty members would, after three or four years, comprehend the need for international understanding by their graduates and make the necessary changes in the curriculum irrespective of AACSB standards. In this case I believe that the chicken comes before the egg. The AACSB must first stiffen the standards, their interpretation, and their implementation, thereby giving the deans the leverage needed to overcome faculty resistance to change.

NOTES

1. This survey was carried out by Professor John Fayerweather, New York University, and published by the AIB.

2. This survey was carried out by Professor Vern Terpstra, University of Michigan, and published by the AIB.

3. This survey was carried out by Professor Robert Gross of the University of Miami, and Professor Gerald Perritt of Ball State University, and published by the AIB.

4. This survey was carried out by Professor John Thanopoulos of the University of Akron, and Professor Joseph W. Leonard of Miami University, and published by the AIB.

5. Nehrt, L.C. and S.H. Robock, eds., *Education in International Business*, Bloomington, IN: Graduate School of Business, Indiana University, 1964.

6. Zeff, Stephen A., ed., *Business Schools & the Challenge of International Business*, New Orleans: Graduate School of Business, Tulane University, 1968.

7. Otteson, Schuyler, ed., *Internationalizing the Traditional Business Curriculum*, Bloomington, IN: Bureau of Business Research, Indiana University, 1968.

8. U.S. National Commission for UNESCO, *Business and Education for World Affairs*, Washington, D.C., 1971

9. U.S. National Commission for UNESCO, *Internationalizing Management Education*, Washington, D.C., 1973

10. Nehrt, Lee C., ed., *Business and International Education*, Washington, DC: American Council on Education, 1977.

11. Nehrt, Lee C., ed., *The Internationalization of the Business School Curriculum*, vols. 1 & 2, St. Louis: AACSB, 1979.

12. Nehrt, Lee C., ed., *Case Studies of Internationalization of the Business School Curriculum*, St. Louis: AACSB, 1981.

13. Nehrt, Lee C., "The Internationalization of the Curriculum," *Journal of International Business Studies* 18, no. 1 (Spring 1987): 83-90.

Internationalizing The Business Administration Faculty Is No Easy Task

BRIAN TOYNE

INTRODUCTION

After nearly three decades of urging by the American Assembly of Collegiate Schools of Business (AACSB), the Academy of International Business, the business community and various government agencies, schools of business are finally responding to the nation's growing need for managerial personnel trained in the peculiarities of international business and worldwide competition. Specifically, they are attempting to (1) internationalize their undergraduate and graduate business programs, (2) provide their faculties with international business skills and knowledge, (3) develop relationships with foreign educational institutions, (4) develop foreign study and international exchange programs, and (5) attract foreign students and scholars to their campuses.

THE FORD-CARNEGIE PARADIGM

While these responses are admirable and constructive, they may be addressing the deficiencies of an education-research system that is increasingly viewed as flawed.[1] For example, Bedeian (1989), Daft and Lewin (1990), Porter and McKibbin (1988), and the Graduate Management Admission Council (GMAC) (1990) have raised serious questions concerning the efficacy of the Ford-Carnegie paradigm upon which much of modern U.S. business education and research is based. Collectively, these critics question the ability of the present education-research system to deliver on the kind of education required in the years ahead. In particular, Porter and McKibbin and the GMAC report argue that the massive and interconnected changes transforming the global environment of business, such as globalization, rapid technological change, and increasing demographic and cultural diversity of the work force, require different approaches.

The GMAC report, which capsulates much of this criticism, came to three conclusions that have important implications for the internationalization efforts of U.S. business schools. First, fundamental changes are required in the content of business educational programs and the way this content is to be taught. Second, schools of business must develop a new synthesis between academic rigor and managerial relevance that will require new collaborations across institutional and disciplinary boundaries. Third, the academic leaders of individual schools need to face the important challenge of developing more appropriate approaches for the recruitment and development of faculty members, including new models of doctoral education in order to meet the knowledge, skills, attitudes, and values required of faculty members in the future.

The purpose of this paper is to examine the adequacy of the internationalization responses in light of these conclusions. This examination assumes that a central issue, if not *the* central issue, is the need to upgrade and reorient existing BA faculties inculcated in a paradigm that is increasingly viewed as antiquated, and the development of a "new class" of faculty who are more responsive to the emerging needs of practitioners.

Most internationalization efforts are predicated on the assumption that past successes can be the foundation for future successes. For example, it is assumed that the governance structures of schools of business, the emphasis placed on systematic research, and the core content of business education programs that have evolved as a result of the Ford-Carnegie paradigm need not be changed, much less examined. It is also assumed that the "received" training and socialization of students in Ph.D. programs need not be altered except, perhaps, in an incremental or ad hoc fashion.

There is, of course, much to be said for past successes. As the GMAC report succinctly summarized:

> In the three decades since the "revolution" codified in the Gordon-Howell and Pierson reports [for the Ford and Carnegie Foundations], business schools have reached ever-higher

levels of consumer popularity and academic respectability. More than 70,000 MBA graduates leave the nation's campuses annually, and the number of individuals taking the GMAT has steadily increased to annual levels of more than a quarter of a million.

The academic disciplines of management have also matured, with rigorously refereed scholarship in hundreds of journals and increasingly sophisticated doctoral education programs. No longer characterized by the mundane descriptive analysis of the 1950s, the disciplines of the management school are now side by side with those of the arts and sciences. Ground-breaking work that uses academic theory to change management practice has been done in such fields as investment theory, consumer behavior, competitive strategy, and organization behavior.

These institutional and intellectual accomplishments have made graduate schools of management especially important components of their universities. Business schools provide a portal for interactions between the campus and the private- and public-sector organizations of the outside world. The development of practice-based theory during the years since the Gordon-Howell and Pierson reports has enabled business schools to provide students with the organizational and analytical tools that will be vital to leadership in the world of the 1990s and beyond (1990, 15).

THE INADEQUACY OF THE FORD-CARNEGIE PARADIGM

The questions that immediately arise on reading of these successes are: Why fix something that has served business schools so well? Why not accommodate new external demands arising from environmental changes, such as the need for internationalization, within the mission established by the Ford and Carnegie reports and the configuration and characteristics of the resources that have emerged as a consequence of these reports? That is, why not just add features, such as an international concentration, or a number of electives, to degree programs that have been shown to have market appeal? The answer, of course, is that the conditions that resulted in the recommendations contained in these reports no longer exist. It is no longer adequate, even proper, to define the missions of individual schools of business in terms of outputs. During periods of rapid and fundamental change, such as we are now experiencing, outputs change. Thus, it becomes more important to define a school's mission in terms of the educational process and the objectives it seeks to satisfy (Miles 1990, 30).

Unfortunately, as Porter and McKibbin (1988) have noted, the success that schools of business and their faculties have enjoyed in the last thirty years, has bred a misplaced sense of complacency and self-satisfaction. The success that schools of business now enjoy has created a governance structure, programs of business education, and a class of faculty that hinder their ability to be responsive to the educational challenges of the 1990s and beyond. Basically, the Ford and Carnegie reports were inward-looking, and resulted in "a shift toward systematic research and away from common sense, prescriptive approaches to teaching" (Daft and Lewin, 4). By focusing on the lack of quality—in faculty, research, curricula, and students—that plagued the field at that time, the reports recommended a mission for business schools that over the years has resulted in an emphasis on departmentalism, research, and academic rigor to the eventual detriment, even neglect, of the ultimate constituencies served. In effect, they de-emphasized the vocational aspects of business education in order to gain academic respectability and credibility within a university setting. As Ouchi (1990, 27) put it, "Professors have sought to establish their legitimacy by defining the business school as a school of applied science." Knowledge accumulation gained ascendancy over knowledge dissemination through education.

More importantly, perhaps, success has resulted in the reinforcement and entrenchment of academic practices that can no longer adequately meet the challenges facing the U.S. business community. For example, Mintzberg (1989) asserts that society has become unmanageable because of a management increasingly trained with a view toward analytical rigor. Dunning (1989) and Daniels (1991) acknowledge the growing complexity of business dominated by rapid technological change and increasing environmental turbulence, and see a need for cross-institutional and cross-disciplinary approaches to research. Unfortunately, such proposals are somewhat unrealistic since the U.S. education-research system is increasingly fragmented and inflexible as a result of its past successes. In particular, the recommendations set forth in the Ford and Carnegie reports have resulted in the following:

1. Business programs (undergraduate and graduate) are artificially constrained by a faculty insistent on building on

models that emphasize disciplinary fragmentation and analytical rigor at the expense of managerial relevance (AACSB and other accreditation organizations are partly responsible). Thus, when changes are recognized as meaningful, they tend to be accommodated in the form of concentrations or electives rather than made an integral part of the entire educational process (e.g., MIB, MIBM, and MIM, to name a few).

2. Educational activity is receiving decreased attention as a result of the inordinate emphasis laid on empirical research by schools of business. Teaching loads have been reduced, and teaching innovation and the development of teaching materials de-emphasized, even penalized in some schools.

3. Ph.D. business programs increasingly contribute to an emphasis on specialization and the entrenchment of departmentalized schools of business through the training and socialization that they provide future faculty members.

4. The specialization and socialization of faculty members and the emergence of strong, narrowly focused functional departments have resulted in an internationally illiterate faculty in most schools.

5. The emergence of functional departments with increasing political sway over the content of undergraduate and graduate programs and the credentials of entering faculty (marketing plus psychology, finance plus econometrics) has resulted in an education-research system that has very little to offer the ultimate constituencies served, or the people to be educated. Essentially, the system has become insulated from external influence.

These internal trends and pressures contribute to a mounting resistance within the ranks of the faculty toward change and innovation—a resistance that needs to be recognized when developing plans to internationalize a school's faculty.

DIRECTIONS FOR THE FUTURE

Essentially, a school of business interested in responding to the dramatic environmental changes of the day must simultaneously come to grips with three basic problems.

1. *The environmental changes affecting the specific missions and capacities of individual schools of business have changed to such an extent that new approaches and new programs of business*

education are needed that simultaneously cater to the need for academic rigor and managerial relevance.

By defining business programs in terms of outputs that consist of inflexible sets of courses predicated on a paradigm that emerged in the 1960s, schools of business are probably catering to the wrong constituencies—students and faculty members. They may be neglecting the long-term needs of the nation and the business community to whom they are ultimately responsible.

Although students are still keen, thus giving credence and support to the current strategies and policies of business schools, firms are beginning to worry. They are beginning to wonder whether business schools are producing the sorts of managers they want. *The Economist* (1991, 4), for example, quoting from Hayes and Abernathy's 1980 paper on western management education, states that there is growing concern that business schools encourage "a preference for analytical detachment rather than the insights that come from hands-on experience, and for short-term cost reduction rather than long-term development of technological competitiveness." The magazine also reports Leavitt of Stanford as saying that business schools "transform well-proportioned young men and women....into critters with lopsided brains, icy hearts and shrunken souls."

The GMAC study supports this view by stating that:

> The curricula of business schools have recently concentrated far more on the building of elegant, abstract models that seek to unify the world economic system than on the development of frameworks to help students understand the messy, concrete reality of international business. Yet this reality seems certain to prevail in a world in which tomorrow's problems are much more difficult to predict, with the only certainty being that they will be different from today's problems (7).

The report goes on to state that long-run success will not belong to graduates who are trained as specialists. Rather, the future will belong to those who have been trained to work with colleagues of different cultural backgrounds or gender, and who can:

> . . .combine the skills of both the generalist and the specialist. They must be well versed in concepts and theory that can be used in coping with a wide range of general management

problems, and they must be equally skilled in identifying and solving specific, functional problems (13).

The bottom line of recent critical reports is that schools of business are in danger of losing touch with the shifting sands of business. To get back in touch with reality, and with the future needs of their customers (whether students or companies), schools will have to aim for a new synthesis of academic rigor and management relevance. Basically, business programs must be radically redesigned to provide students with the skills, knowledge, and intellectual training required for a future that is undergoing fundamental and rapid change.

This, of course, does not mean that managerial relevance must replace academic rigor. Rather, it means that a new balance which recognizes the importance of both in the years ahead needs to be struck. Such a balance cannot be achieved, however, without recognizing that external environmental changes are fundamentally changing the knowledge, skills, attitudes, and values required of tomorrow's successful managers. Nor can it be achieved without recognizing that the governance structures of schools of business and the specialized training and socialization of faculty that have emerged as a consequence of the Ford-Carnegie reports, work against such a balance. Finally, it needs to be recognized that the changes transforming the practice of business can no longer be accommodated in the form of concentrations, electives, and outside experiences. The implications that globalization, technology, and demographic diversity have for the way business is practiced, need to be made integral, inextricable parts of the entire business education process. The artificial departmentalization of business within schools of business hinders a complete and synthesized understanding of the influence that these changes are having on the way business is conducted.

2. *Although of central importance, the "internationalization" of faculty is not enough. It is vital that faculty members demonstrate awareness of the changes that are occurring in the environment and the responses being made by companies. They must also be made aware of the significant and important roles that geography, history, languages, and the other social sciences play in the formulation of these responses. In addition to being researchers, they must be educators in the classical sense, at home with practitioners and the environment in which they function, as well as with peers from their disciplines.*

The faculty challenge facing schools of business interested in internationalizing their offerings is both immediate and long-term. The immediate problem has two dimensions: (1) to find ways of insuring that their present faculties gain the skills, experience and motivation needed to redesign and internationalize their current program offerings and research activities, and (2) to provide an environment that is supportive of such undertakings. The long-term problem is the need to overcome the anticipated shortage of faculty members trained in international business education and research.

For most business schools, the solutions to both problems are not entirely under their control. They are, in part, political problems, both internal and external—internal since departmental and faculty support is needed if the internationalization efforts of the school are to be successful; and external since the institutions responsible for the training and socialization of future faculty members need to be persuaded to focus some of their efforts on the development of teaching skills and the future needs of the business community, including the international dimension.

Most schools of business preparing persons for future faculty positions ignore the international business dimension. For example, in his 1990 report on the Center for International Business Education and Research, University of South Carolina, Lee Nehrt noted that a 1976 survey of the largest 25 doctoral programs found that 75 percent of the students were graduating without having had a course in the international dimension of their fields. A subsequent survey in 1984 found that this percentage had increased to 83 percent. He attributed this trend to the fact that the AACSB does not accredit doctoral programs and has not taken official notice of this deficiency.

It may, however, be wrong to blame the AACSB. A more basic reason for the lack of interest in international business is the paradigm upon which modern business education is based, and the governance structures in place at most schools. That is, the lack of international business awareness and expertise among graduates of doctoral programs may be the result of the increased emphasis on specialized, increasingly narrow fields of research rather than education. Since most schools offering doctoral programs tend to emphasize research, they naturally stress the development of skills associated with the accumulation of knowledge rather than the dissemination of knowledge as education. Reflecting their faculty-controlled standards and the "passive" support given by the receiving institutions, they are graduating increasingly specialized, methodology- and data-bound researchers, rather than business educators capable of discerning and addressing the issues that will be of central importance to U.S. business in the years ahead.

Collectively, these trends suggest that the pool of current and future business educators will continue to consist of persons who are highly skilled, functionally parochial, narrowly focused, and internationally illiterate. They increasingly lack corporate experience, and are discouraged from seeking this experience by the escalating emphasis placed on research (both during their training and subsequently by the faculties of the schools that employ them).

3. *Schools of business need to take seriously the possibility that they may have to change their governance structures in order to be more responsive to the needs of their ultimate, external constituencies. They also need to take seriously the possibility that comprehensive faculty training and development programs may be needed.*

The lack of managerial relevance, and thus international business awareness and expertise among business faculties, may also be traced to the co-joining of the incentives provided business faculty by institutions of higher education on the one hand, and the growing importance and influence of the various departments that make up schools of business and the associations and academies they have spawned, on the other hand. The incentives—in terms of tenure, salary and supplemental income decisions, and budget decisions—are increasingly keyed to research and publication criteria, external recognition, and an ability to generate research funding. Simultaneously, the detailed knowledge required to conduct "meaningful," empirical research for publication in highly academic, scholarly journals is forcing faculty members to become highly specialized and dependent on large data bases. They are also increasingly disinclined to spend too much time, thought, or effort on teaching, teaching innovation, and the development of teaching materials. Although teaching and curricula development/innovation are still encouraged and rewarded at some schools, they are no longer the *raison d'être* for most schools. The problem is made even more acute by the fact that the research undertaken in many schools is increasingly of little value to U.S. companies facing international and global challenges (Daft and Lewin 1990; Byrne 1990).

Regardless of the individual merits of the reasons given for the lack of interest in international business in general, and the international dimensions of the sub-fields of business in particular, serious reservations exist concerning the abilities of schools of business to deliver on the kinds of international business education and research made necessary by a rapidly changing environment. If current and future business faculties are ill-equipped and ill-prepared to develop or provide "internationalized" undergraduate and graduate programs of education, and lack institutional and peer motivations to conduct international business research, the ability of business schools to meet the international needs of the U.S. business community must be questioned. Indeed, the "bottleneck" may not be an inability to develop "internationalized" business education programs per se. Rather, the "bottleneck" may prove to be the inability of business schools to take the bold steps needed to (1) overcome the entrenched, institutionalized biases of their faculties, (2) recruit and develop an internationalized and managerially relevant faculty capable of meeting tomorrow's needs, and (3) provide an environment supportive of cross-disciplinary and internationally focused business research and education.

BUILDING A NEW INTERNATIONALIZED FACULTY VISION

The changing demands of the marketplace for business education can no longer be ignored, or treated in a departmentalized, insular way. Globalization, the rapid—even radical—changes in technology and its use by business, and the growing demographic and cultural diversity of the work force, all point to a need for fundamental change in the way we educate future managers and retrain and upgrade existing ones. Importantly, this requires business schools to inculcate their faculties with a new vision, a new paradigm, that energizes them as individuals and as groups to creatively meet the challenges posed by these environmental changes.

Increasingly, business schools will have to emulate the actions taken by successful companies when faced with new environmental threats and opportunities. They will have to be more creative, more flexible, and certainly more sensitive to the implications and demands that environmental change may have for the qualifications, interests, and educational and research activities of their faculties. As a minimum, they need to be open to the possibility that their mission statements, strategies, and governance structures may have to be modified, perhaps frequently, and their faculties retrained and their educational and research activities refocused. Basically, they need to recognize that the present structuring of their schools, the training, socialization, and career goals of faculty members, and the tenure, peer review, and reward systems, are inextricably bound together and tend to work collectively toward the maintenance of the status quo.

As the other papers included in the Roundtable on Internationalizing Business Schools and Faculty clearly attest, business schools are responding in increasing numbers to the mandate to internationalize their missions, programs, and faculties. And many of these responses are laudable, original, and daring. Of particular interest here, however, are the various approaches being used to (1) raise the international awareness of their faculties, (2) encourage them to conduct internationalized research, and (3) provide them with the skills and knowledge needed to internationalize their courses. Examples of these approaches follow:

INTERNATIONALIZING BA FACULTY THROUGH TEACHING

There are basically three approaches used to internationalize BA faculty through teaching. The first is to have them teach at least one course that exposes them to the peculiarities of international business on a regular basis. The second is to have them teach at foreign institutions. The third is to offer them competitive course development grants to either internationalize existing courses or develop specialized international courses.

There are several benefits associated with each approach, if used with a clear set of objectives in mind. The first approach can be used to expose all members of the business school's faculty to the international peculiarities and ways of thinking that will trickle down into their other courses (see Chapter 15 by Charles Mayers). The experience can be made more managerially relevant if the courses are part of an executive development program, such as the University of Southern California's International Business Education and Research program. The second approach has been used by the University of South Carolina. Individual BA faculty members have taught at several foreign institutions, including the Helsinki School of Economics and Business Administration in Finland and the Universidad de Catolica in the Dominican Republic. Arrangements are also being made to have faculty members teach at the Instituto Catalan de Formacion Empresarial in Barcelona on a voluntary basis. The immediate benefit of this approach is to expose them to at least different social and cultural milieus. The third approach is to encourage non-international faculty to become involved in the internationalization process by providing them with opportunities to gain expertise, and allows those faculty members already knowledgeable in international business issues and problems to deepen and broaden their expertise.

FOSTERING AN INTEREST IN INTERNATIONAL RESEARCH

The opportunity to conduct research can be used to foster an interest in the international dimensions of business. For example, the College of Business Administration at the University of South Carolina has been funding international research and travel since 1986. Between 1986 and 1989, nine faculty members were competitively selected as international fellows for a variety of research projects that involved travel to Western Europe and the Caribbean. These projects were supported by grants from the U.S. Department of Education under Part B, Title VI of the Higher Education Act of 1965, as amended by the Higher Education Amendments of 1986. Since 1989, under the sponsorship of CIBER, a program of Research Fellows has been offered to BA faculty. Elements of the support package provided to these Fellows include a reduced teaching load, a doctoral graduate research assistant, and funds for such research expenses as foreign travel, domestic travel, and data acquisition. During the 1990–1991 academic year, seven faculty members were competitively selected to be Fellows, representing the areas of accounting, management, management science, marketing, and international business. Several other schools, including Michigan State University, offer similar research inducements.

A potential weakness of the individual grant approach is to ignore the call for cross-disciplinary and cross-institutional research that has an international dimension. To overcome this inherent weakness, South Carolina, for example, is encouraging international research projects that cross disciplinary and/or institutional boundaries.

FACULTY DEVELOPMENT

At least two business schools offer faculty development programs: the University of Hawaii and the University of South Carolina. Both programs are designed to develop the teaching skills and professional knowledge of business school faculty interested in adding international concepts to their courses or in teaching courses in international business. The University of Hawaii's International Faculty Development Program is designed to assist faculty of business and other disciplines to enrich the content of existing courses or to develop new international courses in their home institutions. The program consists of a three-week session involving some seventy hours of instruction on major dimensions of international business, area studies and curriculum development. The University of South Carolina's Faculty Development in International Business (FDIB) program is composed of eight concurrent two-week seminars of twenty-seven classroom hours each. Registrants can select one or two seminars for the internationalization of such functional areas as accounting, economics, financial management, information systems, management, theory and research, or a general introduction to international business. As of 1991, this program was supplemented by an FDIB Seminar on the Role of Central Europe in International Business.

Another approach is to hire international business scholars to work closely with one or two designated faculty in the internationalization of their courses. The designated faculty can then pass on their experiences to other interested faculty and doctoral students. The benefits of this admittedly more expensive approach is the individualized attention given the designated faculty as they work through the process of internationalizing their courses.

HIRING NEW FACULTY WITH INTERNATIONAL SKILLS AND EXPERTISE

One approach receiving wide acceptance is to hire new faculty members with international business expertise. To reduce some of the inherent problems associated with hiring individuals with interests that are outside a particular department's central interests (isolation, unaccommodating peer review and reward processes), a few schools have created departments of international business. The benefits are similar to those sought by companies when creating international divisions. The structure concentrates a school's international business expertise in one sub-unit, and is a way of insuring that the international dimension of business is treated in a comprehensive way. Importantly, it also provides for the development of a social structure and peer review and reward system that encourage internationalized educational innovation and international business research. The University of South Carolina adopted this approach in 1976 in order to support its Master of International Business Studies (MIBS) program launched in 1974.

VISITING SCHOLARS

An awareness of the international dimension can be encouraged by drawing on the expertise of visiting foreign scholars or international business scholars. Through collaborative research projects, seminars, and teaching assignments, these scholars can be used to introduce members of the faculty to the peculiarities of international business education and research.

The following four recommendations address the fundamental issues raised in this paper. They will be used to illustrate the institutional problems that may be encountered when attempting to internationalize the BA faculty in an ad hoc, individualized way that the approaches described above implicitly advocate.

1. *The BA faculty should be encouraged to add to their traditional disciplinary knowledge a broader understanding of the economic, social, political, and technological context of firms involved in international business.*

2. *The BA faculty should be encouraged to add the competencies of the educator to the methodological skills required for effective research: skills in curriculum design, pedagogy, and student advising.*

3. *The BA faculty should be encouraged to acquire a capacity for cross-disciplinary, cross-institutional teamwork and the ability to manage internal as well as external change and diversity as collaborative efforts expand, new programs are introduced, and the needs of the marketplace change.*

4. *The BA faculty should be encouraged to develop an outward-looking vision that seeks closer ties between traditional research methodology and business practice. This will require a deeper understanding of the managerial workplace, possibly through work experience prior to doctoral training, faculty internships, and a greater emphasis on and appreciation for consultancy and case writing.*

While some of the approaches described earlier will certainly contribute to an increased understanding of the broader educational and research issues and problems associated with the conduct of international business, they do not explicitly take into account the internal structuring of business schools and the peer review and reward systems that work against their eventual success. Nor do they explicitly recognize that the internationalization effort requires the active and committed involvement of the school's entire faculty. Basically, all of the approaches are designed to accommodate the increasingly individualized and specialized approaches that have been adopted by faculty members toward research and education. They also seem to be predicated on the trickle down effect assumption made famous by the Reagan Administration. Essentially, they are incremental approaches which assume that individual faculty members, with no apparent ties other than a general interest in international business, will become a collective, internal force for educational and research reform.

These comments should not be construed as advocating the removal of the core components of a school's governance structure (e.g., tenure and peer review). What they do suggest, however, is that the activities measured, and the measurements used, may need to be changed. The tenure system, for example, need not be an obstacle to the acquisition of new knowledge. It can, as in the case of the Japanese lifetime employment approach, be viewed as providing faculty members the security needed to explore new grounds and new bodies of knowledge for a better, deeper, and broader appreciation of business. Unfortunately, the peer review and reward processes, and the senior faculty to whom junior faculty must be responsive, can inhibit such activities.

For example, the first recommendation suggests that the faculty, even those late into their careers, be encouraged to take "time out" from their current research and educational activities to explore new academic areas. Increasingly, the requirement is for widely read faculty members, not narrowly read ones. However, most peer review and reward systems systematically work against such forays. Also, professors, especially those who have built successful careers in fairly narrow areas, and who now identify themselves and their careers with those areas, may see no reason for rethinking what they are doing. And yet, given the present environment and structuring of most schools, it will probably be these faculty members who will ultimately decide whether new approaches and new perspectives are adopted and supported. One possible way of inducing faculty members to enlarge on their areas of interest and to explore new areas is to provide incentives for doing so. For example, the granting of sabbaticals and research grants could be tied to these objectives.

The second recommendation would require a reorientation of doctoral programs. While most doctoral programs provide future faculty members with an opportunity to gain classroom experience, the experience is generally of limited value since it indoctrinates them to an educational process that emphasizes disciplinary fragmentation and analytical rigor at the expense of managerial relevance. Nor does this approach encourage teaching innovation.

To overcome these problems, all incoming doctoral students at the University of South Carolina are now required to attend a two-day workshop designed to introduce them to the various pedagogical techniques employed in the classroom, and to the issues and problems associated with teaching both large and small classes.

Also, Ph.D. students concentrating in international business are required to teach at least one course in their minor (cognate) area in addition to teaching an international business course. Moreover, the dean of the college of business administration has asked his faculty to modify the college's Ph.D. programs to ensure that each Ph.D. graduate has a basic understanding of the international dimensions of his or her academic area of concentration.

In addition, most faculty members, particularly those late into their careers, have received no formal instruction in teaching. This would suggest that the teaching recommendation can be met only in a systematic and comprehensive fashion. All faculty members need to be introduced to the skills and concepts required for effective teaching. This, of course, cannot be done on a voluntary basis if the goal is to enhance the teaching effectiveness of the entire faculty, and to systematically introduce managerial relevance into a school's program offerings. Such an idea, of course, is counter to current trends and individual academic freedom. However, there is movement in this direction at the University of South Carolina. Each year, those faculty members recognized for their outstanding teaching are asked to share their experiences with the other faculty at breakfast seminars sponsored by the University's president. Faculty members are also encouraged to participate in the doctoral teaching workshops.

The third recommendation may also be resisted. Today, faculty members are taught and socialized to be concerned with individual scholarly accomplishments, external peer review, and academic freedom. However, these deeply ingrained tendencies must be supplemented by a commitment to educating future managers, an appreciation for teamwork, and a respect for individual and cultural differences. Unfortunately, the training received in doctoral programs, and the subsequent socialization of faculty members work against teamwork. These tendencies can be overcome, but it will probably require changes in the procedures used to evaluate and reward faculty members. For example, faculty members can be encouraged to participate in large, multimember international research projects by rewarding them for doing so.

The fourth recommendation is probably the most difficult to achieve. To be successful, it too implies fundamental changes in the peer review process and reward systems of most schools, particularly those systems that now stress research and publications in the scholarly journals. A central question that needs to be addressed by a school's administration is whether the selected approaches will result in fundamental changes in the research and teaching interests of the targeted faculty. Although it is probably assumed that this will occur, it need not. For example, it can be argued that the sponsored research approach will be viewed opportunistically and not result in any permanent, long-term change in the research interests of most faculty members receiving support. This approach will be effective only if institutional encouragement is provided. It will be ineffective, for example, if the faculty responsible for making retention decisions are lukewarm or opposed to the emphasis being placed on the internationalization effort, and if they consider these journals willing to publish the research to be lacking in recognition and prestige. Thus, these key faculty members must be persuaded to make a recognizable commitment to the internationalization effort. Again, it is suggested that this can be done only by modifying the procedures used to evaluate and reward faculty members. Not only must the insecurities of junior faculty be addressed, the proclivities of the more senior faculty need to be recognized and dealt with. In other words, it requires a change in the school's culture and the resocialization of the faculty that goes unattended in the approaches described above.

Together, the four recommendations and their dependency for success on a comprehensive understanding of the internal and peer pressures that faculty members are currently experiencing, underscore the need for administrative direction and support. Unfortunately, none of the approaches directly address the three internationalization challenges identified earlier, which are central to the four recommendations listed above. First, while individual courses in a school's traditional programs may ultimately be internationalized, they will tend to be approached in an ad hoc, sporadic fashion that does not address the output-process question raised earlier. Second, most of the faculty can remain apart from the issues of central importance—academic rigor *and* managerial relevance. Third, the indoctrination of the junior faculty to a more internationalized way of thinking about their responsibilities as educators and researchers will be successful only to the extent that they are allowed to pursue activities that might break with internal traditions (norms, values, attitudes). Fourth, the hiring of faculty with international business or functional expertise also has inherent weaknesses. These faculty members are often viewed as peripheral members of the departments in which they are to be tenured and promoted. The same is true of the departmental approach, except that the demarcation occurs at the group level instead of the individual level. Moreover, the other faculty members have an excuse not to become involved, either through teaching or research, in the internationalization process. Finally, the benefits derived from these approaches may be slow in materializing. They will also tend to be faculty-member specific. Thus, if the faculty member leaves or is not tenured, the school will lose the benefits it has been seeking.

None of the recommendations can be obtained/met without the active and committed support of the school's administration, particularly its dean. Nor can they be successfully achieved without fundamental changes to the governance structure of the school and the development of a more flexible and creative structuring of the functional areas involved. This, again, requires a dean who is committed to the internationalization process—who is aware of the strongly entrenched norms, values, and attitudes of his/her faculty.

CONCLUSION

In summary, the internationalization of BA faculty is no easy task when viewed within the context of the 1959 Ford-Carnegie paradigm and the governance and social structures that subsequently emerged and are now influencing the educational and research interests of faculty. Unfortunately, the task will not be any easier in the foreseeable future, since most doctoral programs are not addressing the educational and research implications stemming from such fundamental forces as globalization, rapid technological change, and the growing diversity of the work force. These forces necessitate substantial changes in the way future managers are to be educated, and the way faculty members view their responsibilities as educators and researchers. Individual schools of business, like many companies today, will have to assume the responsibility for the retraining and resocialization of their faculties on a more or less ongoing basis.

More specifically, it has been argued here that schools of business must recognize that the training, socialization, and teaching/research proclivities of faculty members as individuals and as functional departments will tend to work against their internationalization efforts. It cannot be assumed that the internationalization of BA faculty will proceed without administrative and institutional support. Nor can it be assumed that the effort simply involves targeting certain faculty members for specialized training and development and the provision of "one-shot" inducements. Long-standing commitments must be gained from all of the parties involved in the business education process. That is, the internationalization effort requires the implementation of a comprehensive plan with a clearly articulated set of objectives.

Any attempt to internationalize the BA faculty must be tailored to the situation facing the administration of a particular school of business. It must take into account the governance structure in place and the characteristics, proclivities, and history of the faculty, particularly the school's entrenched, tenured faculty. It must also take into account the fundamental and far-reaching changes that are required in the structuring and content of business programs. The international business skills and knowledge deficiencies of the total faculty are actually secondary and would be quite manageable within a properly structured environment.

NOTE

1. See, for example, "Survey Management Education," *The Economist*, 2 March 1991, 18–26; *Leadership for a Changing World: The Future Role of Graduate Management Education* (Los Angeles: Graduate Management Admission Council, 1990); Lyman W. Porter and Lawrence E. McKibbin, *Management Education and Development: Drift or Thrust into the 21st Century* (New York: McGraw-Hill, 1988); *American Excellence in a World Economy* (New York: Business Roundtable, 1987); U.S. Congress, *Omnibus Trade and Competitiveness Act of 1988* (Washington, D.C.: U.S. Government Printing Office); National Commission on Excellence in Education, *A Nation at Risk* (Washington, D.C., 1988); Arthur G. Bedeian, Totems and Taboos: Undercurrents in the Management Discipline, Presidential Address, Academy of Management Meeting, August 1986; and Richard L. Daft and Arie Y. Lewin, Can organization studies begin to break out of the normal science straitjacket? An editorial essay, *Organization Science* 1, no. 1 (1990): 1–9 .

REFERENCES

American Excellence in a World Economy. 1987. New York: Business Roundtable.

Bedeian, Arthur G. 1989. Totems and Taboos: Undercurrents in the Management Discipline, Presidential Address, Academy of Management Meeting, August.

Byrne, John. 1990. "The Best B-Schools: Is Research in the Ivory Tower 'Fuzzy, Irrelevant, Pretentious'?" *Business Week*, 29 October, 62–66.

Daft, Richard L., and Lewin, Arie Y. 1990. "Can Organization Studies Begin to Break Out of The Normal Science Straitjacket?" An Editorial

Essay. *Organization Science* 1, no. 1: 1–9.

Daniels, John D. 1989. "Relevance in International Business Research: A Need for More Linkages." *Journal of International Business Studies* 22, no. 2: 177-86

Dunning, John H. 1989. "The Study of International Business: A Plea for a More Interdisciplinary Approach." *Journal of International Business Studies* 20, no. 3: 411–36.

The Economist. 1991. "Survey Management Education," 2 March, 1826.

Hayes, R. H., and Abernathy, W. J. 1980. "Managing Our Way to Economic Decline." *Harvard Business Review* 58 (July/August): 67–77.

Graduate Management Admission Council. 1990. *Leadership for a Changing World: The Future Role of Graduate Management Education.* Los Angeles, CA: The Council.

Miles, Raymond E. 1990. Commission Report: Implications for Assessment. *Selections*, Spring.

Mintzberg, Henry. 1989. *Mintzberg on Management.* New York: The Free Press.

National Commission on Excellence in Education. 1988. *A Nation at Risk.* Washington, D.C.

Ouchi, William G. 1990. Commission Report: Implications for Assessment, *Selections*, Spring.

Porter, Lyman W., and McKibbin, Lawrence E. 1988. *Management Education and Development: Drift or Thrust into the 21st Century.* New York: McGraw Hill.

Seaman, Ann. 1990. "The International MBA is Drawing Attention—and Students—to U.S. Business Schools. Which are Best?" *World Trade* October/November.

U.S. Congress. *Omnibus Trade and Competitiveness Act of 1988.* Washington, D.C.: U.S. Government Printing Office.

The CIBER Agenda[1]

BEN L. KEDIA

INTRODUCTION

In recent years, there has been a growing recognition of America's declining position in world markets and, therefore, the need to compete more effectively in the global marketplace (Young 1985; Hill, Hitt, and Hoskisson 1988; Dertouzos, Thurow, and Solow 1989). The United States, at one time, led the world in production and marketing but now faces a severe productivity decline in numerous industries. For example, American companies in automobiles, motorcycles, consumer electronics, steel, shipbuilding, apparel, earth moving equipment, lawn mowers, machine tools, zippers, chemicals, semi-conductors, micro-chips, software, banking, etc. are facing stiff competition (*Business Week* 1987; *Fortune* 1988). A quick glance at this list suggests that the decline cuts across a broad spectrum of industries rather than just being confined to the so-called labor-intensive industries where the United States has been traditionally vulnerable. The purely domestic U.S. firms also need to be concerned about competition from foreign firms in the U.S. market. The United States is still the world's largest market for products and services, and many foreign firms develop strategies to gain a market share in the United States, thereby causing a decline in domestic firms.

The effects of the loss of American competitiveness are readily apparent. Most importantly, it results in plant closings and job losses. It erodes the tax base and funds available for public services and national defense. The highly visible trade deficits, debtor nation status, declining value of the dollar, foreign ownership of capital and corporations, and increasing protectionist sentiments in Congress are also the result of the declining competitiveness of

65

U.S. industries. It affects every individual, firm, and community associated with these declining industries.

At the same time, national markets and economies are becoming increasingly global due to rapid advances in transportation, telecommunication, and information processing and its transmission. It is estimated that 25 percent of the global output of goods and services now moves across national borders. In recent years, the role of cross-border investments has increased significantly. External financial markets are now larger than any domestic financial markets (Aggrawal 1987).

In view of the effects of declining competitiveness and increasing globalization of the economy, one concern that supercedes everything else is that America must have a strategic objective of becoming competitive, not only at home but also overseas. Indeed the stakes in the "competitive game" are high. To play this competitive game, one needs more than just well-made products: one needs to know about the conditions of the "turf" and the capabilities and moves of one's competitors. Some of the competitors, not the least of which are Japan and West Germany, are veteran players.

In other words, international players must not only have expertise in the business arena, but they must also have knowledge of the global economic system, including international markets, and mastery of the skills needed to meet culturally diverse competitors on the global playing field.

Business schools in the United States have unfortunately failed in providing the necessary knowledge and skills to prepare students to function in a global economy. Traditionally, they have suffered from a national bias and orientation in the training of their students. In November 1979, the President's Commission on Foreign Language and International Studies found that one of the major reasons behind the declining U.S. international competitive edge was the lack of foreign language and geographical area expertise on the part of American businesses. The Commission suggested that, "Colleges and Universities must extend and improve their curricula in meeting the needs of foreign language and area expertise in international business." Similarly, numerous scholars have appealed for the internationalizing of business programs in order to prepare students for the global economy (Nehrt 1977; Dymsza 1982; Joyal 1982; Porter and McKibbin 1988). In addition, since 1974, the American Assembly of Collegiate Schools of Business (AACSB) has required that business schools address this international dimension in their curricula for the purpose of accreditation.

Despite the recognized need for internationalization of the business curriculum for nearly two decades, a recent survey by Porter and McKibbin (1988) found that very few business schools have actually internationalized their curricula. Nehrt (1987) conducted a survey of 548 business schools in the United States and found that while 20 percent of the business schools have actually made attempts to internationalize their curricula, another 20 percent of the schools have done nothing and the remaining 60 percent have agreed to internationalize their curricula. However, Nehrt warns that of the schools that have agreed to internationalize their curricula, the decision has not necessarily been implemented (86). Interestingly, 66 percent of the business schools responding to a survey by Thanopoulos and Vernon (1987) thought that they qualified for satisfaction of the AACSB requirement by mere inclusion of international material in their core functional courses.

THE CENTERS FOR INTERNATIONAL BUSINESS EDUCATION AND RESEARCH (CIBER) PROGRAM

To promote international business education, the Congress of the United States amended Title VI, Part B, Section 612 of the Higher Education Act of 1965 by section 6261 of the Omnibus Trade and Competitiveness Act of 1988. This amendment provided for the establishment of the Centers for International Business Education and Research (CIBER) Program. The purpose of the CIBER program is to provide federal support to institutions of higher education or combinations of these institutions, to plan, establish, and operate Centers for International Business Education and Research that will:

1. Be national resources for the teaching of improved business techniques, strategies, and methodologies that emphasize the international context in which business is transacted;
2. Provide instruction in critical foreign languages and international fields needed to provide an understanding of the cultures and customs of the United States trading partners;
3. Provide research and training in the international aspects of trade, commerce, and other fields of study;
4. Provide research and training to students enrolled in the institution, or combinations of institutions, in which a center is located; and

5. Serve as a regional resource to businesses proximately located by offering programs and providing research designed to meet the international training needs of these businesses (Federal Register 1990).

Programs and activities to be conducted by Centers for International Business Education and Research must include:

1. Interdisciplinary programs that incorporate foreign language and international studies training into business, finance, management, communication systems, and other professional curricula;
2. Interdisciplinary programs that provide business, finance, management, communication systems, and other professional training for foreign language and international studies faculty and advanced degree candidates;
3. Collaborative programs, activities, or research involving other institutions of higher education, local educational agencies, professional associations, businesses, firms or combinations thereof, to promote the development of international skills, awareness, and expertise among current and prospective members of the business community and other professionals;
4. Research designed to strengthen and improve the international aspects of business and professional education and promote integrated curricula; and
5. Research designed to promote the international competitiveness of American businesses and firms, including those not currently active in international trade (Federal Register 1990).

Programs and activities to be conducted by Centers for International Business Education and Research may also include:

1. The establishment of overseas internship programs for students and faculty designed to provide training and experience in international business activities; and
2. Other eligible activities consistent with the purposes and intent of the legislation.

In the two rounds of competition during 1989 and 1990, the U.S. Department of Education approved the establishment of sixteen Centers of International Business Education and Research in the United States. The institutions where CIBERs are established are, in alphabetical order: Bentley College in consortium with Tufts University, University of California at Los Angeles in cooperation with San Diego State University, Columbia University, University of Hawaii, University of Maryland, Memphis State University in consortium with Southern Illinois University at Carbondale, University of Miami, University of Michigan, Michigan State University, University of Pittsburgh, University of South Carolina, University of Southern California, University of Texas at Austin, Texas A & M University, University of Utah in consortium with Brigham Young University, and University of Washington.

The sixteen centers are experimenting with different approaches to internationalize their faculty/administration, academic programs, students, and thereby their colleges. They are also devising various strategies to work with local businesses and business executives to enhance their competitiveness. What follows is a brief discussion of some of these approaches, and more of my CIBER experiences at Memphis State University and Southern Illinois University. In a subsequent paper, we plan to examine the approaches of all sixteen centers in the hope of providing more useful and perhaps effective guidelines for internationalizing business schools.

Business schools are unlikely to be internationalized unless their key components are internationalized. These components include faculty and administration, academic programs, students, and executive education.

FACULTY AND ADMINISTRATION

One of the fundamental problems in internationalizing business schools is the lack of knowledge and/or interest on the part of faculty. Nehrt (1987) conducted a survey in 1984 of 53 of the largest doctoral programs in business in the United States that produced 92 percent of all doctoral graduates. He found that of the 1,690 doctoral students who had completed all of their coursework and would be graduating in the next one to three years, only 287 (17 percent) had had one or more international courses. In 1976, he had conducted a similar survey of 25 of the largest doctoral programs and found that 25 percent of doctoral students have had one or more international courses. To make the two survey results comparable, he selected the 25 largest programs from his later survey of 53 such programs; he found that only 15 percent of these students had taken one or more international courses.

Therefore, he concluded that the situation had deteriorated while the need had increased.

To encourage faculty to internationalize their curricula and to provide them some training for this purpose, in 1977 the AACSB launched a series of seminars and workshops for faculty, deans, and associate deans. By March 1986, 30 seminars/workshops had been conducted in various parts of the country and over 1,100 faculty members and over 50 deans and associate deans had participated in them. Nehrt conducted a survey of 1,071 participants of these 27 workshops/seminars in 1987. There were three types of workshops/seminars. It was found that depending upon the type of workshops/conferences attended, 57 percent to 83 percent of the participants had introduced new curricula, new courses, or added an international dimension to their core courses. Furthermore, over 80 percent of the participants in the workshops/seminars had shared their learning with colleagues, which implied a significant multiplier effect. Finally, over three-fourths of the participants were quite positive in terms of the effect of workshops/seminars on their own outlook in making them "think more internationally." In spite of the significant success of the AACSB workshops/seminars, Nehrt (1987) warns that the efforts of several individuals at each school are not likely to result in a real change in the school's curriculum, since the 1,071 participants represent an average of two faculty members per school (85).

Thus, it is clear that business school faculty are not in a position to truly impart international knowledge and vision, because most of them do not possess it. In view of their lack of training and experience, faculty tend to view the world through glasses polarized by their home-country experience. The most urgent need, therefore, is to internationalize faculty in order to internationalize schools of business. Faculty are trained in specialized functional fields such as accounting, finance, labor economics, organizational behavior, or marketing. Given their specialized training and experience, faculty may be neither confident nor knowledgeable enough to incorporate international content relevant to specific courses they teach. In addition to being unprepared to teach unfamiliar international material, faculty members are frequently torn between two fields, the functional field in which they tend to be evaluated for tenure and promotion and the international dimension of their functional field to which they may be expected to devote more of their attention under the increasing internationalization of business schools programs. Infusion of international topics and subjects into existing core courses require faculty retraining, which is often not easy to arrange. Furthermore, faculty involvement in internationalization requires them to give up some of what they do well to reallocate time and personal energy to "retool" in this area.

On the more positive side, many faculty themselves may realize that economies and businesses are increasingly becoming global and may respond to the internationalization calls from students, colleagues, and institutions. At Memphis State University, the interim dean of the college, having spent a month in Europe developing exchange and internship programs, became deeply interested in the internationalization of the college and became an ardent supporter of the purpose and the process. After getting involved in the internationalization process, many faculty report a professional rejuvenation and cite examples of how international issues have positively benefitted their research and teaching and have become even more committed (Serey, Lindsay, and Myers 1989). This suggests that faculty behaviors are modified not only by the needs of their students, curricula, and institutions, but by their own needs as well.

Faculty involvement is essential in any internationalization effort, but it is certainly neither necessary nor worth the time and expenditure involved to secure unanimous support. Instead, it may be far more valuable if the strategy attempted to focus on a few influential faculty members whose perceptions, values, and attitudes are congruent with the goals of internationalization and who act as "international product champions" (Alutto 1988; Serey, Lindsay, and Myers 1989; see Chapter 1 by S. Tamer Cavusgil). A few core faculty working in coalition and in a favorable environment can achieve a lot.

Serey, Lindsay, and Myers (1989, 2123) have provided the following excellent and comprehensive (if not exhaustive) list of suggestions which, if followed, could augment faculty interest, provide the needed basic training and experience, and move them toward internationalization:

1. Direct college development efforts toward establishing seed money for pursuing international programs, especially if local businesses perceive this as extending eventual market opportunities.
2. Champion course release time for faculty to actively pursue international retooling.
3. Encourage and award faculty development grants in the area of international business.

4. Initiate and actively promote cross-disciplinary dialogue. Understanding of many "business" issues such as trade friction or current business practices is greatly enhanced by drawing on the expertise of social scientists, philosophers, artists, and others who can contribute rich information about culture.

5. Encourage and reward faculty who apply for overseas sabbaticals, fellowships, or paper presentations.

6. Establish international background or interest as a primary or secondary faculty recruitment criterion.

7. Elevate the level of visibility of international issues to faculty and students by one or more of the following:
   • Invite guest speakers who have international credentials to class.
   • Encourage colleagues from across campus and within the business school, who are from other countries, to share their international business expertise.
   • Use funds allocated for distinguished speakers to invite experts with international focus.

8. Encourage and reward experimentation in course offerings. These might include summer offerings, non-credit courses, or management development sessions offered to the public.

9. Encourage internationally oriented consulting to broaden the experience base of the faculty. The effectiveness of reading and writing about international issues is limited unless faculty have the opportunity to travel abroad. This has the advantage of not only making international contacts, but permits a wonderfully broadening experience which carries over to students, colleagues and administrators.

10. Use existing faculty and administrators to develop both informal and formal faculty and student exchange programs. Often these programs are linkages with local businesses that have interests in specific countries or regions (e.g., the southeastern United States and Asia, due to textile manufacturing).

The CIBER at Memphis State and Southern Illinois Universities have followed some of these suggestions. For example, fourteen faculty members are involved in developing an international course in their own disciplines. Twelve faculty members will have participated in the University of South Carolina summer program for international retooling. Sixteen faculty members will have participated in the summer international faculty development program in consortium with the University of Lille (1991) and the

University of Grenoble (1992) in France. Nine faculty members have been awarded summer research grants to pursue international research. Two faculty members will spend a year as visiting professors in Asian and African universities. Two European faculty members will spend time with us as visiting professors, which will be followed by our professors visiting the same universities. A faculty associates program combining the faculty from business and arts and humanities has been initiated to promote cross-disciplinary dialogue. A professor from Germany and another from the former Soviet Union were invited as guest speakers to enhance the awareness of recent events in these countries. Attempts are being made to establish viable faculty exchange programs with universities overseas. Consideration is being given to steering the faculty development leave in the international direction. The outcome of all these activities is likely to be a group of core faculty interested, prepared, and ready to launch and sustain a major internationalization effort at our universities.

The process of internationalizing faculty is seriously flawed if it does not begin with the active leadership and direct involvement of the dean and department heads of business schools and even vice presidents, if necessary, for the setting of a general direction and the coordination of efforts. At most universities, faculty rewards such as tenure, promotion, pay raises, travel, honor (status), and other benefits are tied closely to research and publication in functional disciplines. Because of its emerging nature, international dimensions have a limited body of existing research and few publication outlets; hence, few faculty members are willing to dilute their professional efforts in an area that is comparatively unrewarded. Thus, the internationalization process needs to be recognized and encouraged by administrators in their hiring, tenure, promotion, travel, sabbatical, and other funding decisions.

Joseph Alutto, the present dean of the College of Business Administration at Ohio State University (1992), has emphasized the following four points with respect to the role played by a dean in a business school's internationalization efforts:

1. The dean must attach a high personal priority to the change and be seen as personally committed to the new course of action. At the same time, the dean must make it clear and convince the administrative staff, including departments and/or program chairs, that he supports changes in the direction of internationalization.

2. The dean must allocate personal time to the change efforts. This time allocation has a very important symbolic as well as practical value and should not be underestimated as an indicator of commitment to a new course of action. The dean will find it difficult to secure the complete commitment of others unless it is clear that the dean is willing to accept the costs involved in changes in personal patterns of behavior.

3. Perhaps the most important aspect of the dean's performance is that all key actors must understand that they believe in the importance of the outcome to such an extent that they are willing to risk their positions in order to ensure movement toward college objectives.

4. The dean must constantly educate all stakeholders about college needs and potential. These stakeholders include faculty, students, staff, university administrators, alumni, corporate sponsors, and politicians. Since specific stakeholders change over time, the dean must have an ongoing program of managing and influencing the perceptions of new stakeholders.

Therefore, it is crucial to obtain the full support of the dean in the internationalization process of a college. Ideally, faculty must also realize the importance of such efforts. By following the various strategies outlined earlier for faculty development and involvement, perhaps a core faculty group can be established to launch and sustain the college internationalization effort so as to make a real impact and create a permanent international culture.

ACADEMIC PROGRAMS

To achieve internationalization, academic programs in business schools should include two broad sets of foci: (1) functional areas of business such as accounting, finance, marketing, and management taught in a global context or including an international dimension; and (2) the environment in which international business is transacted, i.e. culture, customs, and languages of other nations. The CIBER agenda has particularly emphasized the need to include both of these foci in the teaching and training of students. It is important to examine strategies for incorporating each focus in the academic programs of a college.

For the purpose of internationalization, it is not uncommon for each university and college to attempt to capitalize on the world area opportunities unique to its location. For example, among CIBER institutions, San Diego State University has built The Japan

Studies Institute in response to the presence of prominent Japanese firms in Southern California. Similarly, the University of Hawaii, due to its proximity, has largely focused its efforts on the Pacific-Rim countries. The heavy influence of energy companies and agribusiness has oriented Texas A&M's international programs to these industries. The University of Miami has geared its program to Latin America and the University of Pittsburgh, influenced by its population base, is collaborating with central and eastern European countries. Again, on account of proximity, the University of Michigan has paid considerable attention to Canadian studies in its programs. The historical patterns of trade and investment with Europe and the recent influx of huge Japanese investment into Tennessee and Illinois, has directed the CIBER at Memphis State and Southern Illinois to emphasize Europe and Japan in its various programs.

There are basically three strategies for internationalizing business curricula. The first strategy is to require that every student take an introductory course in international business. A second alternative is to require that all student take an international course within their major area, e.g. marketing, finance, accounting, and management, or any international course from such a menu. A third possibility is to infuse relevant international business topics in traditional courses in business and economics. For example, a serious effort can be made to incorporate international aspects of accounting in the basic accounting course and to integrate relevant aspects of international finance in the corporate finance course.

There are, of course, pros and cons to each of these three approaches. In smaller colleges and universities, due to limited faculty resources and insufficient demand for more specialized international courses in each of the functional areas, a single introductory course in international business is perhaps a more viable alternative. Such a course could be taught in large sections, requiring few additional faculty resources. This strategy also has an advantage of integrating various international business subjects from several functional areas into a meaningful whole. However, to be effective, this strategy requires a faculty member who is well trained and who maintains a broad level of interest in international business.

The strategy of adding international business courses in each of the functional areas makes sense for schools with larger enrollment, sufficient resources, and greater commitment to the internationalization process. Adoption of this strategy requires that schools have international faculty experts in each of the functional areas capable of teaching specialized international courses. With a critical mass of specialized international business faculty resources and enhanced research posture in the field, such schools are likely to emerge as leaders in international business education.

The least expensive strategy in terms of faculty resources is the infusion approach. This strategy requires inclusion of international business issues in each of the existing core courses through a carefully planned and coordinated approach. These courses will continue to be taught by existing faculty, and such course changes would place little additional demand on fiscal resources. To be successful, this approach requires faculty retraining in the international dimension of their core courses. Unless such training is planned, coordinated, and executed carefully, faculty members may not be capable of incorporating international content in their courses or may be unwilling or uncomfortable in teaching the international material. Since the infusion approach does not require a commitment of large resources, this strategy is most commonly utilized. If actually pursued, it could be an effective or perhaps even an ideal strategy to truly integrate and impart international knowledge through existing courses. However, a number of researchers point to the finding that due to lack of interest, expertise, and/or time pressure the international component gets left out of the course content (Aggrawal 1989; Cavusgil 1991).

It is important to emphasize that these three approaches are not necessarily mutually exclusive and, depending upon institutional goals and resources, they can be combined in a profitable manner. For example, under the CIBER program at Memphis State University and Southern Illinois University, we have utilized different approaches. At Memphis State University, we have added new specialized international business courses in each of the functional areas and require that students take one course of their choice. On the other hand, Southern Illinois University has added a required introductory course in international business and has allowed the students to opt for advanced elective courses in the field. Our approaches are relatively too new to permit meaningful evaluation. Hopefully, with more experience, we will be in a better position to examine the merits and demerits of our approaches at a later date.

The CIBER agenda also requires instruction in critical foreign languages and area studies necessary to provide an understanding of the cultures and customs of the United States' trading partners. Traditionally, except as a component of general studies, these disciplines have not been integrated into professional business curricula. Furthermore, business curricula are, in general, already heavily "loaded" and do not have the necessary flexibility or additional room to include these disciplines except in a joint degree program or in an approved major or concentration where international business is the major focus of the degree, major, or concentration. Integration of these disciplines in curricula not only provides the necessary foreign language expertise but also enhances the understanding of historical, political, legal, and cultural environments within which international business is transacted.

The integration of foreign language, area studies, and business education is being emphasized to eliminate deficiencies pointed out by the American Council on Education (ACE 1983) that "many Americans are uninformed about other peoples and countries and poorly prepared for an increasingly interdependent world," and that "foreign languages and cultures are a mystery to many of our young people." Similarly, the Association of American Colleges (AAC 1989) devoted an entire issue of its publication to the topic of Internationalizing Higher Education through Business School/ Liberal Arts cooperation to emphasize that colleges are attaching greater importance to economic issues now than they did in the past.

Among the CIBER institutions, courses of study that have specifically established links among foreign languages, area studies, and business can be found at the University of South Carolina in its Master of International Business Studies (MIBS) program; in the International Business Education and Research (IBEAR) program at the University of Southern California, which offers an intensive twelve-month MBA to American and Asian executives; at San Diego State University in its undergraduate international business program; and in Southern Illinois University's Foreign Language and International Trade (FLIT) program. Memphis State University is in the process of developing an International Master of Business Administration (MBA) program which will incorporate foreign language, international studies, and overseas internship experiences into a professional business program. Similar efforts are underway at the University of Miami.

INTERNATIONALIZING STUDENTS

Preparing students to be effective in the global era is a matter not only of providing substantive academic programs but also of inculcating an attitude of understanding other people/cultures and knowing how to relate to them. For this purpose, students need to be exposed to different cultures to appreciate how these differences affect the way people think, solve problems, negotiate, respond to authority, value work, set work norms, and reward achievement. It is the combination of academic programs and exposure to foreign cultures that enhances student awareness and sensitivity to cross-country differences and their managerial implications, develops necessary skills to operate effectively in different environments, and provides a more global setting for decision making.

Having a greater number of foreign students on campus is one way of exposing U.S. students to foreign people and cultures. A critical mass of foreign students representing a number of countries rather than just one or two countries, is needed to promote the desired interactive effect on campus. To support this goal, it is important for universities to undertake trips to recruit foreign students and diversify their student body. Furthermore, American students need to be encouraged to participate and get involved in foreign students' activities and organizations such as foreign plays, films, lectures, and international fairs. At our own university, discussions are underway to establish a language floor in each of the student dorms, for students to be able to practice their language skills and learn more about the culture of that country.

A potentially important component of internationalizing students could be a well organized study abroad program. Not only can such a program broaden and transform students' intellectual horizons, but it can also immerse a student in the language and culture of a host nation. The combined experience will tend to shape the rest of the students' lives. Study abroad programs could be for a long duration, such as a year or a semester, or for a short period such as two to four weeks. To be sure, there are difficulties associated with study abroad programs, including of lack of financial support, transfer of credits, institutional support for organizing such programs. Also, recent technological advances have made it possible to bring much of the world to the campus through satellite communications; however, at least in the foreseeable future, these developments are unlikely to replace "being there."

There has been an increase in specialized short-term study abroad programs, especially in professional schools such as business. While such short-term programs cannot go very far in advancing language skills or immersing students in host-country culture, students perceive a positive value from such programs. Based on his evaluation of Northeastern University's short-term overseas programs, Sarathy (1990) reported that "the course has heightened their students' interest in international business affairs and education," and "many express an interest in seeking an international

business career path upon graduation." Similarly, Bracker, Brenenstuhl, and Gwinner (1989) have conducted short-term international
business seminars overseas during the past twelve years for over
1,000 students, and their evaluations suggest that "students' ability
and willingness to learn are materially enhanced in a real-world setting." Experience from study abroad programs is increasingly being
regarded as pertinent to career development. CIBER at Memphis
State and Southern Illinois universities is planning to provide similar short-term study abroad opportunities for their students.

Providing opportunities for an overseas internship is another
meaningful way to internationalize students. Unfortunately, overseas internship opportunities are likely to be limited, and managing such programs is highly complex. A project needs to be
identified for each participating student, that meets the need of a
host company and utilizes the student's particular skills in finance,
marketing, or management. Each project must also result in a
report. There are several requisites for managing such a program:
an expert facilitator to negotiate arrangements, a mentor in the
host company, and faculty guidance in preparing a suitable report.
The role of coordinator becomes critical in managing such a labor-
intensive program. At most institutions, internships are arranged
on an ad hoc basis and, in general, demand greatly exceeds the
internship opportunities.

One of the CIBER institutions that has successfully integrated
experiential learning into a meaningful curriculum is the University of South Carolina, which requires a six-month foreign internship for its Master's degree in International Business Studies (MIBS).
Similarly, Southern Illinois University at Carbondale has integrated
the overseas internship experience in its undergraduate Foreign
Language and International Trade (FLIT) program. At Memphis
State University, we are planning to incorporate internship experience into our proposed International Master of Business Administration (IMBA) program.

EXECUTIVE DEVELOPMENT

Managers have recognized that they must "act locally while
thinking globally." This means that they should know the language, customs, institutions, government relations, social values,
and "corporate culture" of the various countries in which the company operates while thinking globally in overall strategic terms.
Thus, executive development has become a major business school

function. Internationally experienced executives, in turn, can help business schools with overseas internship opportunities, guest lectures in classrooms or conferences, applied research opportunities and/or research sites, and by serving on the International Business Advisory Board.

CIBER at UCLA's Advanced Executive Program focuses on "Competing in a Global Environment." The program attracts executives from the United States as well as other countries. The international participants lend an essential "real world" perspective to the international issues discussed.

The University of California at Los Angeles also has an International Business Roundtable (INTABLE) which brings senior executives in international business to (1) explore critical international business issues, (2) exchange information, experience and expertise, and (3) initiate, sponsor, and disseminate state-of-the-art research. Four Roundtable sessions are held each year, and topics are decided by a survey of member interests. INTABLE members hope to find innovative opportunities and effective solutions to the challenges presented by a rapidly changing global economy.

Similarly, CIBER at the University of Michigan offers "Strategies for Global Competition." This seminar addresses the need for managers to think globally. The objective of the program is to prepare managers and executives who have global competitors, as well as those with foreign operations, to be aware of their competitors and to be more effective in domestic and foreign markets. The intention is to develop an understanding of global competition, financial issues in overseas operations, and organizational strategies for joint ventures and strategic alliances. There are also programs on "Managing International Joint Ventures," "Negotiating with the Japanese," and "Doing Business in Newly Industrialized and Less-Developed Countries." The University of Michigan also provides briefings for companies, state development agencies, and trade missions planning business in Southeast Asia. In addition, the University conducts orientation programs for corporate personnel to be assigned to ASEAN (Association of South East Asian Nations) or other regions of the world.

The CIBER at Memphis State University and Southern Illinois University has offered executive programs for "Building Business Partnerships with Japan" and "European Integration of1992." In cooperation with Arthur Andersen & Company, we have also offered a one-day major conference on "Competing in the Global Marketplace" for area businesses. Another conference on Japan was offered in Carbondale for academics and executives.

CONCLUSION

As with the introduction of most organizational changes, the internationalization of business school programs cannot be expected to be a totally smooth process. One needs to begin by determining how much change is required and what the appropriate time frame is for changes, given the level of commitment at the college and institutional level. What are the financial and human resources required, and what is available? Is it better to get a small group of faculty involved, or to encourage most faculty to diversify in the international area? The answers to these questions will depend upon the possible mission a business school might adopt with respect to internationalization. Arpan (see Chapter 2 by Jeffrey Arpan) has outlined three possible missions: Global Awareness, Global Understanding, and Global Competence. Each succeeding mission involves a greater commitment of resources and enhanced focus of the school on internationalization. It is also important to examine the facilitating factors necessary for achieving the goal. These include reaffirmation of internationalization as high priority, the dean's commitment and support, a more supportive reward system, allocation of necessary resources and funds, free exchange of information, participation in internationalization workshops, and review of teaching loads.

The United States has entered a global era, and it is the responsibility of education to prepare people for the world in which they will be living. Business schools in the United States have often fallen short in fulfilling this mission. In this chapter we have outlined some of the strategies that could be utilized for internationalizing business schools. To be sure, internationalization is likely to be a slow process; therefore, long-term commitment is essential toward making significant changes to educate students who are more capable of managing in a global economy. The CIBER program has provided the necessary agenda and financial support to enable us to seek this objective.

NOTE

1. The author would like to thank Robert Berl, Rabi Bhagat, Tonna Bruce, and Thomas Miller for their helpful comments on this article.

REFERENCES

Association of American Colleges (AAC). 1989. *Liberal Education*, May–June. Washington, D.C.: The Association.

American Association of State Colleges and Universities (AASCU). 1985. *Guidelines on Incorporating an International Dimension in Colleges and Universities.* Washington, D.C.: The Association.

American Council on Education (ACE). 1983. *What We Don't Know Can Hurt Us: The Shortfall in International Competence.* Washington, D.C.: The Council.

Aggrawal, R. 1987. "The Strategic Challenge of the Evolving Global Economy," *Business Horizons* 30 (July/August): 38-44.

_____. 1989. "Strategies for Internationalizing the Business Schools: Educating for the Global Economy." *Journal of Marketing Education* (Fall): 59-64.

Alutto, J. 1988. "Case Discussion: A Framework for Introducing International Perspectives in a School of Management." Unpublished paper, State University of New York at Buffalo, 113.

Bracker, J.; D. Brenenstuhl; and R. Gwinner. 1989. "Experiential Learning in the International Environment." *Journal of Teaching in International Business* 2: 37-48.

Business Week. 1987. "Can America Compete?" 20 April, 44-69.

Council on International Educational Exchange (CIEE). 1988. *Educating for Global Competence.* New York: The Council.

Dertouzos, M.; Thurow, Lester; and Solow, R. 1989. *Made in America.* MIT Press.

Dymsza, W. A. 1982. "The Education and Development of Managers for Future Decades." *Journal of International Business Studies* 13, no. 3 (Winter): 9-18.

Federal Register. 1990. "Department of Education." 31 January, 55: 21, 33-38.

Fortune. 1988. "Entering an Age of Boundless Competition." 28 March, 39-45.

Hill, C. W.; Hitt, M. A.; and Hoskisson, R. E. 1988. "Declining U.S. Competitiveness: Reflections on a Crisis." *Academy of Management Executive* 2, no. 1: 51-60.

Ito, B., and Hamada, T. 1987. "East Asian Studies Curriculum Development: Preparing Engineers for the Pacific-Rim Challenge." L. P. Grayson and J. M. Biedenbach eds. *Frontiers in Education Conference Proceedings.* Terre Haute, IN: Rose-Hulman Institute of Technology.

Joyal, D. L. 1982. *Trends and Developments in Business Administration Programs.* New York: Praeger.

Nehrt, Lee. 1987. "The Internationalization of the Curriculum." *Journal of International Business Studies* 18: 83-90.

_____. 1977. *Business and International Education.* Washington, D. C.: American Council on Education.

Porter, L. W., and McKibbin, L. E. 1988. *Management Education and Development.* New York: McGraw-Hill.

Presidential Commission on Foreign Language and International Studies. 1979. *Strength Through Wisdom: A Critique of U.S. Capabilities.* Washington, DC: U.S. Government Printing Office.

Sarathy, R. 1990. "Internationalizing MBA Education: The Role of Short Overseas Programs." *Journal of Teaching in International Business* 3, no. 4: 101-18.

Serey, T.; Lindsay, W.; and Myers, M. 1989. "Internationalizing Colleges of Business: Applying a Strategic Planning Framework." *Journal of Teaching in International Business* 2: 5-25.

Thanopoulos, J., and Vernon, I. R. 1987. "International Business Education in the AACSB Schools." *Journal of International Business Studies* 18: 91-98.

Young, J. 1985. "Global Competition: The New Reality." *California Management Review* 3: 11-25.

International Business Education Centers and Programs: The Federal Role

SUSANNA C. EASTON

BACKGROUND

The International Education Programs of the U.S. Department of Education trace their origins to the passage of the National Defense Education Act (NDEA) in 1958. This legislation, a response to the launching of the first space satellite, *Sputnik* by the USSR in 1957, marked the initiation of federal involvement in a national campaign to improve instructional programs at institutions of higher education throughout the United States. Specifically, the NDEA authorized funding efforts to improve the teaching of the sciences, mathematics, and foreign languages.

Title VI of the National Defense Education Act focused primarily on strengthening the study of "critical" or uncommonly-taught languages, and the study of the geographic regions of the world where such languages are spoken. The legislation authorized the establishment of language and area centers at institutions of higher education in the United States, included foreign language fellowships, and funded research and the preparation of teaching materials in the uncommonly taught languages. For the next twenty-one years, from 1959 to 1980, over $220 million was expended for these activities.

By 1980, only Title VI of the NDEA was still receiving annual appropriations while other parts of the law were gradually phased out or incorporated into other pieces of legislation. In 1980, Congress permitted the NDEA to lapse, and the remaining international education programs were transferred as Title VI, Part A, to the Higher Education Act as part of the 1980 Education Amendments.

In response to changing economic conditions, Congress at that time also added a new section, Part B—Business and International Education Programs—to the legislation.

THE BUSINESS AND INTERNATIONAL EDUCATION PROGRAM

The purpose of the Business and International Education Program is to provide matching funds to institutions of higher education to accomplish two objectives. The first is to increase and promote the nation's capacity for international economic enterprise through the provision of suitable international education and training for business professionals in various stages of professional development. The second is to promote institutional and noninstitutional education and training that will contribute to the ability of United States business to prosper in an international economy.

Before Title VI, Part B, was enacted in 1980, the Congress held a series of hearings to determine the extent of the need for the new legislation. The testimony was summarized in the opening paragraphs of the law in a section entitled "Findings and Purposes." It is in the context of these findings that the Department of Education administers the International Business Education programs:

- The future economic welfare of the United States will depend substantially on increasing international skills in the business community and creating an awareness among the American public of the internationalization of our economy;
- concerted efforts are necessary to engage business schools, language and area study programs, public and private sector organizations, and United States business in a mutually productive relationship that benefits the nation's future economic interests;
- few linkages presently exist between the manpower and information needs of United States business and the international education, language training and research capacities of institutions of higher education in the United States, and public and private organizations; and
- organizations such as world trade councils, world trade clubs, chambers of commerce, and state departments of commerce are not adequately used to link universities and business for joint venture exploration and program development.

The purpose of the Business and International Education program is to improve the teaching of international business at the recipient institution, and to provide export assistance to the local business community.

The following activities are authorized:

- improvement of the business and international education curriculum of institutions to serve the needs of the business community, including the development of new programs for mid-career or part-time students;
- development of programs to inform the public of increasing international economic interdependence and the role of American business within the international economic system;
- internationalization of curricula at the junior and community college level, and at undergraduate and graduate schools of business;
- development of area studies programs and interdisciplinary international programs;
- establishment of export education programs;
- research for and development of specialized teaching materials appropriate to business-oriented students;
- establishment of student and faculty fellowships and internships or other training or research opportunities;
- creating opportunities for business and professional faculty to strengthen international skills;
- development of research programs on issues of common interest to institutions of higher education and private sector organizations and associations engaged in or promoting international economic activity; and
- the establishment of internships overseas to enable foreign language students to develop their foreign language skills and knowledge of foreign cultures and societies.

To ensure that the proposed services to the business community were consistent with business objectives, the authorizing legislation included the following stipulations:

- Each application must be accompanied by an agreement between the institution and a business enterprise, trade organization, or association engaged in international economic activity.
- Each application must include plans to provide appropriate services to the business community to expand its capacity to engage in commerce abroad.

To qualify for funding all applicants must meet two other requirements:

- The institution must provide fifty percent matching funds from other than federal sources, and
- the institution must guarantee that federal funds will be used to supplement, and not to supplant, other funds.

In the last decade, Federal expenditures for this program averaged above $3,000,000 annually. Approximately forty projects are funded each year at an average $72,000 per project per year. Since 1982, over 155 institutions have received these awards, with many applicants receiving grants for several two-year funding cycles.

CENTERS FOR INTERNATIONAL BUSINESS EDUCATION AND RESEARCH

The need for additional federal support to assist university efforts to improve the teaching of international business subjects was again recognized during the passage of the Omnibus Trade and Competitiveness Act in 1988. While this bill addressed primarily commercial rather than educational issues, one chapter of the legislation amended Title VI, Part B, of the Higher Education Act to permit the establishment of new "Centers for International Business Education." These centers are intended to:

- be national resources for the teaching of improved business techniques, strategies, and methodologies that emphasize the international context in which business is transacted;
- provide instruction in critical foreign languages and international fields needed to provide an understanding of the cultures and customs of United States trading partners;
- provide research and training in the international aspects of trade, commerce, and other fields of study;
- provide training to students enrolled in the institution or institutions in which a center is located;
- serve as regional resources to local businesses by offering programs and providing research designed to meet the international training needs of such businesses; and
- serve other faculty, students, and institutions of higher education located within their region.

The Centers for International Business Education and Research (CIBER) agenda has far exceeded its promise in producing a unique and unparalleled impact on international business education in the

United States. As of October 1992, twenty-three CIBERs were in operation and received over six million dollars annually in governmental support. It is impossible within the confines of this chapter to share the richness and breadth of these programs, located at the nation's most prestigious institutions of higher education. What follows is an overview of CIBER activities, which we have categorized here under a series of definable goals.

CURRICULUM DEVELOPMENT AND COURSE ENRICHMENT

For the CIBERs, curriculum development at the undergraduate, masters, and Ph.D. level is a requirement. New courses have been introduced, either as electives or as core courses, the latter reflecting a core course modified to accommodate its international dimension by inclusion of international modules. Concentrations and minors in international business have been strengthened and created. Undergraduate degree requirements were revised to include international business courses or clusters of courses for all business majors. Faculty and administrators have begun to adopt a more integrated approach to international business education; increasingly, courses are being team taught by business and international studies faculty to reinforce the interdisciplinary nature of the curriculum. Methods of instruction utilized include guest lectures by practitioners, workshops, seminars and mini-courses. Course development grants continue to be awarded to faculty members interested in creating new courses or programs based on the curricular gaps identified by the centers. Transportable modules and cases that can be used to internationalize existing courses or as components of new international courses are being introduced. Some CIBERs have opted to develop joint business and foreign area curricula, such as East Asian or Latin American studies, or joint degree programs with law or engineering schools to provide cross-disciplinary training and develop specialists with unique expertise.

FOREIGN LANGUAGE INTEGRATION

One CIBER response to the need to integrate foreign language study into the business curriculum has been to emphasize the teaching of a commercial or business version of the language to students. "Mini courses" in commercial German, Japanese, Spanish, and three other languages open to practitioners as well as students, are being offered, some during evening hours. These courses focus on the business culture, economy, and commercial vocabulary of a particular country or geographic region. Several centers, however, have found it difficult to provide appropriate language training for the business community; this issue will require further study. One of the centers has therefore commissioned a study of the applicability of the immersion/multiliteracy method and its potential popularity with the business practitioner. This study, designed in conjunction with the language faculty, would be conducted by an MBA market research class and would help the centers understand the nature and extent of demand for different types of language delivery systems.

At the undergraduate level, many centers have promoted an International Business-Foreign Language concentration or double major as an interdisciplinary offering of the colleges of business, and arts and humanities. For many MBA and Ph.D. students, overseas study and internship provisions to gain mastery of a foreign language are a required part of the curriculum. One option developed by a CIBER, the International Management Fellows Program, is a twenty-four-month certificate program that provides intensive language/culture training in the student's first summer. A second summer and the subsequent fall are spent overseas combining a three-month internship with coursework in the target language at selected overseas MBA programs.

As for U.S.-based language instruction, among the most interesting instructional innovations have been computer-driven interactive foreign language course modules. One CIBER has developed a Macintosh Hypercard program for Business German—an interactive, graphics-based tutorial written entirely in German. Others have developed interactive programs using televised foreign language news broadcasts or TV soap operas to familiarize students with contemporary usage of the foreign language.

STUDENT DEVELOPMENT

The development of a cadre of trained specialists is a goal of every CIBER. One way to enhance this training is to develop international internships. In reinforcement of their belief in the interdisciplinary nature of international business, the CIBERs are advocating that students need to learn not only the technical business skills learned from on-the-job experience, but also the interrelationships between national policies, culture, language and business practices. Several business programs, in recognition of this valuable learning exercise, have mandated internships as a compulsory or key element for undergraduate and MBA students. Every effort is being made to extend internship opportunities to as many countries as possible. Such overseas experiences range in time span from six months to a year.

Overseas study programs, as opposed to internships, are another unique way for students to experience first-hand the complex interactions between business, culture, language and the political environment. At the undergraduate and MBA level, overseas experiences of six months to one year are recommended.

Most CIBERs fund doctoral student research, including research abroad, and offer travel grants. Undergraduates and MBA students, too, receive support to conduct research projects on international business issues. Under the auspices of the centers, students participate in major conferences. Monthly debates—informal gatherings to debate pivotal issues in international business—in and out of the classroom setting, have also been developed.

One of the centers has established an International Mentors program, staffed by internationally oriented faculty, to advise business, area studies, and modern language students on internships, study abroad programs, and other curricular and career matters. Some centers have formed advisory groups and sponsor International Career Days that include presentations on career opportunities in international business.

FACULTY DEVELOPMENT

Faculty members are funded through the centers for international research and travel. Travel abroad is undertaken to attend conferences and present papers, to work with faculty members on research projects, or to accompany student groups. Funding to participate in language programs to visit governmental and business officials, or to experience another culture, are all offered with the intent of enhancing the faculty's international expertise.

Several CIBERs now have well-established programs responding to the faculty's need to acquire international expertise. Programs like the Faculty Development in International Business (FDIB) or the Pacific-Asian Management Institute (PAMI) have received national recognition. Most centers have begun to conduct training programs for faculty from regional colleges. Some of these are held at overseas locations, and many on the involve teaching faculty are from CIBER and non-CIBER institutions.

Most centers have also designed professional development opportunities for foreign language faculty. As an example, one center has implemented a two-week intensive training program in commercial German. This program trained thirty language instructors from a variety of U.S. institutions in the use of contemporary methods for teaching German to business and economics students. Participating language instructors were also exposed to basic management concepts and principles in the course of the program.

The CIBERs host an annual conference for language faculty; participation at national meetings on the teaching of languages for business or professional use by CIBER faculty is also encouraged.

SEMINARS AND CONFERENCES

Conferences and the presentation of papers at professional meetings are an effective way to disseminate CIBER expertise. CIBER-sponsored conferences are designed to attract a broad segment of faculty, national business leaders, and the regional business community. Some of the major issues addressed in the last year include:

- Germany, post-reunification
- Asia-Pacific business outlook
- The role of U.S. business in Europe after 1992
- U.S. competitiveness in the global marketplace with a special emphasis on the service sector
- The North American Free Trade Agreement (NAFTA)
- Business environment in the international arena: overcoming legal and institutional impediments to sound environmental practice in industrializing economies
- Doing business in Eastern Europe

Many of these conferences were jointly sponsored with national or regional business groups and governmental agencies. Activities like these help foster a partnership between the educational, business, and public sectors.

INSTITUTIONAL COLLABORATION

Diverse collaborative activities between CIBERs and other units on campus are undertaken. These units include language departments, area studies centers, and professional schools. These collaborative efforts have produced new team-taught international business courses; one such course was taught by professors from business, political science, and law. This course was offered in an Asian studies undergraduate degree program designed for business and international relations students as a dual major. In addition, CIBERs sponsor interdisciplinary faculty workshops where faculty representing diverse fields can study an issue from a variety of disciplinary perspectives. One center has faculty members designated as "area chairs" for each of the main geographical areas of the world, to bring together the resident experts in small study groups.

A welcome development has been the publication of newsletters on a regular basis by the CIBERs. While most of these newsletters provide an account of international business related activities taking place on campus, and therefore serve as an outreach tool for the center, one center publishes its newsletter jointly with the District Export Council. This newsletter was created to help regional businesses meet the challenges of competing in the global marketplace by improving their access to information, local expertise, and educational opportunities. It addresses the concerns of companies with and without export operations, and supports cooperation and greater visibility of international business service providers, both nonprofit and commercial. Yet another center's quarterly *Latin American Business Advisor*, has chosen to concentrate and cover all of Latin America.

Some centers have produced videotaped summaries of conferences for loan/sale to interested institutions and have developed an inventory of international business videotapes and films. This is an excellent tool to facilitate the dissemination of information.

Interinstitutional collaborative efforts include joint conferences, joint research projects and joint publications, as well as the sponsorship of faculty seminars and arrangements for overseas experiences.

OVERSEAS EXCHANGES AND LINKAGES

Faculty and student exchanges with foreign institutions or agencies afford an invaluable exposure to a foreign environment. In the context of current happenings (1992), special emphasis has been placed on fostering exchanges with the European Community, central Europe, the Commonwealth of Independent States, and the rapidly developing ASEAN countries. Increased attention is being given to the development or expansion of institutional linkages between U.S.-based CIBERs and foreign universities. For example, the U.S. Agency for International Development recently provided $1 million to establish linkages between CIBER institutions and business schools located in ASEAN countries. Another major initiative is the Pacific Asian Consortium for International Business Education and Research (PACIBER), which links CIBER and non-CIBER institutions with twelve Asian business schools.

RESEARCH ACTIVITIES

Research is an integral part of every business school's response to the challenge of staying competitive in an increasingly global market environment. Some of the major research efforts undertaken include the following topics:

- Restructuring for a competitive America
- New export opportunities for the U.S. telecommunications industry
- The export potential of medical equipment to the European community
- The impact of ISO 9000 standards on the competitiveness of U.S. exports
- The implications of NAFTA and the creation of global trade blocs
- Development of an international trade information system for use by researchers and the international business community
- Development of decision support systems for international business executives on international market entry and expansion.

PUBLICATIONS

All CIBERs sponsor faculty research on issues of competitiveness, resulting in case studies, research monographs, and refereed papers. To disseminate research in progress, most CIBERs issue collections of occasional papers. In addition to numerous books edited or published by individual CIBER faculty members, a number of collective CIBER efforts deserve special mention.

One center has produced a series of resource books for faculty and administrators interested in internationalizing business education. These resulted from the Roundtable on Internationalizing Business Education, which gathered leading experts from eight CIBERs, the Academy of International Business, and several other

North American and international educators. The first publication, a twenty-eight-page booklet, *Internationalizing Business Education: Issues and Recommendations by Leading Educators*, has been distributed to all business schools in the United States. The second publication is the book you are holding: *Internationalizing Business Education: Toward Meeting the Challenge*, incorporating the edited contributions of the twenty-three educators who had gathered for the Roundtable.

Also of particular interest to business educators will be two volumes featuring contributions from leading international business experts worldwide. Volume one, *The State of International Business Inquiry*, is in press, to be followed by the *Institutional Status of International Business*.

Several centers have also launched new serials. An example is the new *Journal of International Marketing*—a refereed publication covering issues of interest to international marketing specialists.

EXECUTIVE EDUCATION

Intensive education programs for managers focused on a particular geographical area, or on an international issue of particular contemporary relevance, are among the most popular and highly sought executive programs. Some CIBERs sponsor overseas programs to facilitate interactions between U.S. executives and their foreign counterparts, interspersed by briefings from government and nongovernment officials. Other CIBERs offer short domestic programs that apply business theory to "real time" situations which encourage managers to generate solutions to problems encountered in international situations. Many of these executive training programs are of international renown and generate substantial income for the CIBERs.

OUTREACH TO THE BUSINESS COMMUNITY

The CIBERs have established linkages to the business community through a variety of formats. These include organizing evening courses on international trade and culture sponsored by regional institutes, modular courses focusing on country-specific topics of interest to business professionals, or topical courses on current and projected trends in global business. Executives in Residence are often utilized. Monthly seminars for faculty, students and business practitioners are conducted with speakers from government, industry and academia. These seminars address the increasing globalization of business and focus discussion on its implications for the U.S. economy. Recent topics have included issues such as the pending economic integration of Europe, and the impact of the proposed North American Free Trade Agreement on U.S. competitiveness. Speakers' bureaus and listings of international business practitioners willing to speak to executives have been drawn up. All CIBERs provide speakers for community groups, trade associations, chambers of commerce, and other business forums where "going international" can be brought before potential new exporters.

One center has initiated an annual Summer Institute for Global Business Development Professionals. This week-long intensive training program is aimed at strengthening the advisory capabilities of export assistance agencies. Another CIBER is collaborating with the U.S. Foreign Service to provide training to Foreign Service officers on issues affecting U.S. competitiveness.

Outside their own academic confines, the CIBERs have worked successfully with the World Trade Associations, District Export Councils, state professional associations, and small business development centers. Several centers have received funding to provide management assistance to East European executives under the auspices of the U.S. Agency for International Development. This training, in turn, should open these regions to U.S. markets.

State Government Linkages

These linkages involve working with state and local government organizations to develop an export educational program, to promote exports, and to attract direct foreign investment into the state. One center has offered business-oriented training programs for foreign service officers in order to increase their awareness of business transactions and economic issues. Faculty from many centers serve on District Export Councils and the advisory councils created by state governments. One center also serves as the only state-sponsored international trade specialty center in its region.

Conclusion

The national legislation that created the Centers for International Business Education and Research mandates a leadership role for CIBERs in the following areas: they must serve as national resources for the teaching of international business; they must foster curricular innovations in business, area studies, and foreign languages; they are required to engage in research on issues related to our nation's competitiveness; and they must provide outreach to the business community. To accomplish these objectives, the CIBERs address a variety of audiences: students, business and non-business faculty, business executives, local and federal government officials, and the general public. Each of the CIBERs has also chosen its own model of internationalization and has developed some unique characteristics and specialized expertise, shaped by institutional history and faculty initiatives. Our challenge for the next three to five years is to encourage further synergism among the CIBERs while preserving each CIBER's unique mission and status. The legislation authorizing CIBERs has created enthusiasm and an ambitious agenda among the nation's most prestigious universities. It is gratifying to be involved in this national effort to achieve excellence in international business education.

Business Community Links: The International Business & Banking Institute

ROBERT GROSSE

INTRODUCTION

The organization described in this chapter is attached to the business school at the University of Miami and was created for the express purpose of focusing attention and activities on international business. More specifically, this new nontraditional organization, the International Business & Banking Institute, is designed to create and sustain significant *collaboration between the business school and the local international business community*. The primary goal of this chapter is to show the manner in which this kind of organization is a valuable vehicle for cooperation with business, considering two perspectives—what the firms can offer to the school, and what the school can provide to the firms.

Further, this chapter provides a history of the institute, explaining how it came into being and how it was developed over the first few years. The structure and functioning of the institute's Executive Advisory Board is then explained, to demonstrate how the institute forms a fundamental part of the relationship between the school and the business community. The following section describes how overseas opportunities for professors and students have been developed through the years. After pointing out some of the key limitations of its organizational structure, some lessons are drawn from this experience for other schools in other contexts.

HISTORY

The University of Miami has operated a center for international business research since 1982. In that year, the R.J. Reynolds Corporation made a five-year, $50,000 grant to the School of Business

99

Administration to support international business. The dean asked Professors Kujawa and Grosse to form an organization under the Business School umbrella that would focus faculty interest on international business issues. As initially defined, the two kinds of activity that would appropriately fit into this new organization were academic research and executive programs in international business. The organization was named the International Business & Banking Institute (IBBI).

It was clear from the outset that, even with the funding from R.J. Reynolds, the institute could not proceed beyond the basic infrastructural costs of buying furniture for its three assigned offices and hiring a half-time secretary. So the two founding professors began a round of visits to local offices of international companies and banks, seeking additional sponsors whose firms could financially support IBBI. With this additional help, the institute would be able to buy student assistance, publish papers, and begin to modestly support faculty research projects.

This thrust was developed by Professors Kujawa and Grosse and accepted by the dean. The first step was to identify the firms that would most likely be interested in an affiliation with the University on the subject of international business. Because the banking industry is the most clearly defined international business in Miami, with literally 100 banks competing in IB there, we began with major money center banks and banks headquartered in the local area. In addition, more than 100 industrial firms have Latin American and/or Caribbean marketing offices (and some have regional headquarters) in South Florida—so these firms, too, formed part of the target group.

We chose to pursue firms with the idea of attracting the general manager of the international office in Miami to join the Board of Advisors of IBBI, each manager's firm contributing an annual sum of between $2,500 and $10,000. These figures were simply based on the minimum amount that appeared to compensate the effort of recruiting the firms and a maximum amount that appeared likely to be offered, based on the school's previous fund-raising experiences. The goal was to have a permanent board of about a dozen firms, representing a range of industrial sectors and nationalities, with the common thread of an international business focus.

Please do not get the idea that this process was easy, or that establishing goals and limits on the scope of activities of the institute was a simple task. Over the course of about two years, we recruited board members, polished our statement of objectives of the institute, and began to produce research papers that were distributed around the local international business community. Perhaps the most important steps in gaining access to the firms were our organization of an executive course for international bankers and our production of a series of *Discussion Papers*.

THE DISCUSSION PAPERS

The *Discussion Papers* are a series of academic articles that are published semiannually and distributed to about 250 of the international banks, multinational companies, and other international firms in South Florida, as well as to about seventy-five academics in IB around the world. These papers were initiated in 1982 as a means to make the institute and its work known to a wide range of potentially interested firms, and also to disseminate the papers to other academics who would not see them otherwise until published in journals or books much later. (The series is *not* copyrighted, so that publication as a discussion paper does not preclude subsequent publication in an academic journal or other publication.) The discussion papers are reviewed by two professors at the University of Miami and sometimes elsewhere; depending on the reviews, they may be published. This process assures a good degree of quality control over the papers and still offers the authors a chance to receive quick feedback on their work. (The review process typically takes about four weeks.)

About six to ten *Discussion Papers* are published annually, and the most current ones are distributed once each academic semester, to the audiences noted above. We developed a system of enlisting the help of a professor (beyond the institute's director and associate director) to act as editor of the *Discussion Papers*; his job is to send out the papers for review and to communicate with authors about the results of this process. The institute then prints and distributes the papers twice a year. This vehicle at once lends major academic credibility to the institute in the eyes of professors in the school and creates visibility in the international business community.

INTERBAN

The one executive course that was initially offered through the institute is the Latin American bankers' course, INTERBAN. This course actually predated the institute by three years, but it has been offered under the aegis of IBBI since the institute's formation. Professors Kujawa and Grosse designed this course jointly with members of the local international banking community. With their help the course was organized and marketed throughout Latin America for the first time in 1979. INTERBAN has become known as a joint venture between the University of Miami and the international banking community since that time. This project added to the positive visibility of the institute, as well as generated some additional revenues for it.

The importance of INTERBAN to our efforts to stimulate business community support should not be downplayed. This course is sponsored annually by about twenty international banks in Miami, along with the institute. Meetings with sponsor banks during the year maintain a high level of contact, typically with two or three people from each bank. Thus, community appreciation for the institute has grown along with the success of the Latin American bankers' course. Several members of the Advisory Board came from the group of INTERBAN sponsor banks.

The initial course in the week-long INTERBAN program was presented in 1979 was an interesting combination of practitioner topics and academic themes that relate to the problems facing international bank managers. Over the years, a successful (highly positively evaluated) team of instructors from both the University of Miami and the local international banking community has been put together. In addition professors from other universities in three countries teach as part of the total course. Each year, the banking community joins with Professors Grosse and Kujawa to refine the program and provide significant input into the course. Along with their input on course content, the bankers are a major vehicle for promoting the course on their own visits to Latin American banks. The sponsor banks distribute brochures to colleagues in Latin America and have proven very effective as marketers of our program in their dealing with Latin American bank executives.

The Latin American bankers, in turn, have been quite enthusiastic about the course. INTERBAN offers both training in areas of importance to them as bankers and the opportunity to meet with members of the Miami international banking community and to learn about the U.S. banking market while they are physically in the United States. The ability to interact with the local community of international bankers cannot be overstated as a reason why the Latin American bankers are so satisfied with their experience in INTERBAN. Both the high quality of instructors as judged by the Latin American bankers, and the opportunity to learn firsthand about the international banking community of Miami, are probably the two principal reasons for success of the program over the years. INTERBAN now has over 600 alumni throughout Latin America and the Caribbean.

It should be emphasized that our development of this program, as well as other executive programs more recently, has been guided by the creation of a business advisory group during the planning stage of each program. By bringing together senior executives from the kinds of firms that we want to attract to each program (e.g., bankers, country managers, Latin American company presidents), a fair consensus of opinion can be created and, equally important, the firms develop a sense of commitment to the program such that they help in marketing it. The time and effort spent in organizing these advisory groups has been more than repaid through the successes of the programs.

With these steps in place, we established credibility and experience in dealing with company and bank managers that enabled us to recruit half a dozen firms to join R.J. Reynolds on the board over the first two years of IBBI's existence.

I am sure that this presentation does not convey the starts and stops that occurred as IBBI was developed over the first two years. Moving from total dependence on the R.J. Reynolds contribution to diversifying our financial base was a difficult and slow process. In the end it was the combination of our joint venture executive program in international banking and our production and dissemination of the discussion papers that seemed to be key factors in our ability to attract corporate support. Even this assessment may be incomplete, since it is quite possible that some of the firms that joined us have done so primarily to demonstrate their support for a local university rather than to participate in these two activities.

RELATIONS WITH EXECUTIVE ADVISORY BOARD MEMBERS

Relations with the business people that join IBBI's Executive Advisory Board, range from once-a-semester meetings with the entire board to much more frequent contacts with those members who participate in the Latin American bankers' course and other seminars and courses offered at the University. It was our intent that board members be given maximum opportunity to participate in University activities that appealed to them with minimum demands on their time; so the board meets twice annually for an hour-and-a-half breakfast session. The professors who direct the institute discuss projects underway and those recently completed. Board members offer comments and suggestions about new directions for applied research and executive programs.

The board meetings have turned out to be fascinating interchanges of ideas and experiences among the business leaders and professors. At least a dozen research projects were spawned in that forum over the decade of IBBI's existence. Often, a project suggested by a board member has subsequently been financed by a grant from another source, such as a corporate foundation or the U.S. Department of Education. Major projects of this sort include: a study of the economic impact of the tourism industry in the Caribbean; a study on the market positioning of countries as tourist destinations in that region; a series of studies on Latin American debt, the secondary market in sovereign loans, debt/equity swaps, and so on; a study of the impact of democratization in Argentina and Brazil on economic policy in those countries; and a study of economic integration in the Americas. The point here is that, without a doubt, the managers are well ahead of the academics in thinking about some of the key international business problems of the day; and also that the interchange of thinking between decision-makers and academics clearly is stimulating and useful to both kinds of participants in these discussions.

Beyond the semiannual board meetings, the institute invites board members to attend lectures at the University when they appear potentially interesting to them. Occasional lectures by CEOs of major corporations gave us the opportunity to invite board members to lunches or breakfasts of twenty to thirty people. Similarly, we promote public lectures at the university, presented by visiting professors to the Executive Advisory Board members. In sum, we try to keep in touch with the board on a regular basis (in addition to sending them the discussion papers twice a year), such that they are not committed to numerous meetings but so they feel that information is being conveyed, and opportunities are being offered on a regular basis.

ADVISORY BOARD INTERACTIONS
WITH THE BUSINESS SCHOOL

The Advisory Board members are regularly introduced to opportunities to become more involved with the Business School, as discussed above. One avenue for added interaction is through the program of student internships. Each firm whose Miami-office general manager is on the board is offered the opportunity to receive one or more student interns for a semester or summer. The internships are arranged either for academic credit or for compensation, depending on the student's interest and of course the firm's willingness to pay. In fact, both arrangements have worked very well; and the firms appreciate that IBBI organizes the process of sending potential interns to them and that IBBI conveys a sense of "quality control" over those students who are introduced to them.

This process is certainly within the ordinary scope of the student placement office, which regularly places dozens of students each semester in business internships. However, the process in this instance is tailored to international business needs by choosing students with language skills and other characteristics that go beyond the normal internship requirements. Fortunately, the firms' evaluations of their internship experiences have been quite positive, thus generating more goodwill for the institute.

To date, the Executive Advisory Board members have not become heavily involved in business school activities. This seems to be due to the heavy demands on their time that members face in their regular work—including travel to Latin America and elsewhere often for 30 to 60 percent of the time. For this reason, we believe that the semiannual meetings of the board, along with occasional one-time invitations to address a class or participate in some other school forum, constitute an appropriate level of time commitment.

OVERSEAS OPPORTUNITIES

The Executive Advisory Board members have been able to help University of Miami faculty members pursue overseas activities in several ways. First and foremost, these people are executives in major international firms that are of interest to our faculty. When one of our professors wanted to study a particular aspect of the EXXON coal mine joint venture with Colombia's government, the board member from EXXON arranged interviews and other help directly for that professor. When another professor undertook a study of technology transfer in international banking, the board members from Citibank and Bank of America, each with affiliates in several Latin American countries, arranged for meetings with the local office managers of those banks in several Latin American countries. Similar help in making available information about their own firms and about other international firms in Latin America, has greatly benefitted our faculty members over the years.

A second type of overseas activity that has resulted from dealings with our Advisory Board members is executive training seminars.

Both in Miami and Latin America, quite a few of our professors have lectured in executive programs on all kinds of topics—due specifically to the advice of board members who requested our participation. While this is not a primary goal of the institute, it certainly generates goodwill among both faculty members and from the participants in the program.

Yet another kind of overseas activity that IBBI's Advisory Board has helped to develop are student internships abroad. In addition to recruiting students for their own offices in Miami, several of the board members' firms have hired our students as interns in Latin America, frequently hiring a native of that country who is studying at the University of Miami. In several cases, they have hired our graduates to full-time employment.

In sum, the range of overseas activities that can be fostered by our links with the Executive Advisory Board have been *limited* mainly by our *somewhat limited* requests for help. The firms have almost routinely been willing to provide information, hire interns, and arrange meetings with their own firms' people overseas when we ask.

LIMITATIONS ON IBBI's EFFECTIVENESS

A main strength and perhaps the main weakness of the International Business and Banking Institute is its relative independence from the School of Business. Since the institute's entire budget comes from corporate contributions, executive programs, and external grants obtained, it does not have to seek constant approval for its activities from the dean or some other administrator of the school. On the other hand, without such a link, the dean does not see the institute as an integral part of his domain; hence a potential dysfunctionality exists. This tension has persisted through the entire life of the institute.

The result of this independence is that IBBI operates according to the self-imposed goals of its leaders, with the final approval for specific new activities and for the organization's continued existence, resting with the dean. The initial establishment of goals was approved by the dean in 1982, and since those goals have not changed, no direct challenges to the institute's existence have arisen. Still, faculty complaints about the autonomy of the organization surface from time to time, and a never-ending effort is required to promote IBBI *within* the School of Business.

Since not all of the school's international business effort is operated through IBBI, the limitations of the institute do not limit the school's achievements. For example, the development of the Masters in International Business program was spearheaded by the new dean, managed by Professor Kujawa (who wears another hat as Senior Fellow of the institute), and carried out by a team of more than two dozen faculty members in the school. IBBI, as an organization, had nothing to do with the new degree program, but its leaders each played a part in it, and the school pursued that key international business objective quite successfully. This coexistence of a multitude of efforts that relate to IB in the school is a hallmark of the program, which seems to function quite well. No individual is held out as "Mr. International" for the whole school. Rather, about half a dozen professors have international business titles (Director of IBBI, Director of MIBS, Associate Dean for International Programs, Director of the undergraduate IB major, etc.)

Thus, the limitations on IBBI's activities are primarily its charter to focus the faculty's interest in IB research and to operate a small number of executive programs. The limits to its effectiveness in achieving these two goals are partly the limits of the leaders of IBBI and partly the relative autonomy of the institute from the school.

LESSONS FROM THE IBBI EXPERIENCE

After directing the International Business & Banking Institute for five years and participating in its leadership from the beginning, I feel, for several reasons, that the effort was eminently worthwhile. First, it helped to create links with the local international business community that probably would not have occurred otherwise. Second, it provided financial support (through recruiting board members and operating executive programs) for research done by the institute's leaders and other faculty members as well. And third, it has been rewarding to be associated with a major success story at the University of Miami.

This kind of institute could be viable at another school if it existed in an environment with numerous firms involved in international business. For a school located away from a concentration of business activity, this kind of venture would probably be difficult to undertake. However, even in a context with limited IB interest, if a handful of firms can be attracted to support the venture, it is adequate to form the financial and goodwill bases that are needed.

We found that large, well-established international firms were the primary candidates that responded to our overtures for membership on the board. As much as small export/import firms and other small IB participants in our area like publicity, and although quite a few of their leaders participate in community activities, we found that small business had virtually no interest in contributing to our institute. Conversely, once we had attracted a couple of major money-center banks to the board, it was relatively easy to convince other large multinational and local banks to join us.

The main lasting output of the institute has been the series of discussion papers, which are distributed literally around the world to academics and locally in the IB community. This kind of activity is viewed favorably within the University as an appropriate use of effort (i.e., to justify the institute's existence, *not* to gain promotion or tenure). These papers continue to be generated at a rate of about six to ten per year, with about a quarter of them written by non-University of Miami authors. This output is a valuable service to the international business community and to the IB professors who write and read the papers as well.

Our two annual executive programs, and occasional one-time programs, continue to generate additional financial support which enables IBBI to offer summer research grants to faculty members who write papers on IB issues. This support overall has produced four or five of the discussion papers each year for the past five or six years.

The International Business & Banking Institute has achieved a level of activity that is fairly well self-sustaining at this point. It should be able to continue at this level indefinitely, with continued leadership. Hopefully, it offers a useful example of business community links that can be emulated by other schools in other contexts.

The creation of the Executive Advisory Board has paid rich dividends, including financial support from the members' firms, counsel from the members on research initiatives undertaken through the institute, student internships in the firms, and access to information about these multinational firms that has been useful in academic research projects. Beyond these important outcomes of our experience with the board, the many personal friendships developed with board members should not be undervalued; they are truly a welcome and unexpected dividend received by all of us professors involved in the institute.

Development of a Research Center:
The National Center For Export—Import Studies

MICHAEL R. CZINKOTA

INTRODUCTION

This chapter provides an overview of the author's experience in developing, funding and maintaining a research center with an international focus. The specific focus will be on the initial five years of the Center at Georgetown University, since it is the start-up phase which is of primary concern here. While circumstances and times will be different for any particular reader, it is hoped that perhaps some of the experiences reported here may be of use to colleagues contemplating similar endeavors.

THE SITUATION

The School of Business Administration at Georgetown University was in the throes of a new orientation in the late 1970s. A new dean had the vision of drawing the school into citywide, if not national prominence. Given the university's location in Washington D.C., these two goals were seen as highly complementary.

To achieve the objective, a MBA program had been designed, with an international orientation being a key differentiating dimension from competing programs. Existing internationally known resources at the university, such as the School of Foreign Service, the School of Languages and Linguistics, the Center for Strategic and International Studies, and the Center for Contemporary Arab Studies, provided the backdrop to this decision. The emphasis of the American Assembly of Collegiate Schools of Business (AACSB) in internationalization helped as well.

In addition to internationalization of the curriculum, an internationalized research thrust was also planned. All these efforts were to be carried out by a faculty of thirty (envisioned to grow), with the minimal consumption of resources.

As a newly minted Ph.D. from Ohio State, Georgetown's desire to grow, to internationalize and to achieve preeminence was very attractive to me. I joined the faculty after completing my dissertation in international marketing, being the only member trained in marketing and the international business field. However, a large number of colleagues had either been foreign born, or had taught abroad. Virtually all of them were highly enthusiastic about the oncoming transformation of the business school.

The dean had envisioned several research centers, which were to be developed by faculty members, ranging from a Center for Business-Government Relations over a Center for Entrepreneurship, to an International Business Center. Funding for all this research was to come from the business community.

THE BEGINNING

I offered to "run" the International Center, as it was described on paper. The issue of teaching versus research versus service was never raised, since, in view of the small size of the faculty, we all had to teach our six-course load during the year, and the center would provide room for both research and service.

The first six months passed quickly, with various mission statements being drawn up and discussed with members of the Deans Advisory Board. After many meetings, the agreed-upon components were: The center would "study international trade issues. It would strive to expand the existing body of knowledge on international trade and to foster communication among the business, policy, and academic sectors of the international trade community." The center was christened the National Center for Export-Import Studies (even though, for years to come, the dean would always place imports first when talking about the center).

Now all we had to do was wait for the funding. Yet, for some reason, that funding never materialized. Popular opinion had it that the recession was making it very difficult to raise money, but old hands confided that fundraising was always tough. The key issue appeared to be one of credibility. Very few firms were willing to invest money in a paper concept. Many, however, indicated that they might look more favorably upon an ongoing operation.

In the meantime, as for most new Ph.D.'s, there were many articles inside me waiting to be written. All of them dealt with exporting. Many of them were published with a headnote that made reference to the center.

A CONFERENCE

With the help of some colleagues, we planned a conference in 1981. Perhaps a meeting of academicians similarly interested in international marketing and trade could provide us with some more insights, research, and visibility. Since there was no funding, we had to charge a conference fee, and pay for the printing of flyers. The response, however, was great. Together with George Tesar, from the University of Wisconsin-Whitewater, who shared my international marketing interests and also had an export research background, and two student assistants, we organized the first international symposium on export research, focusing both on export management and export policy. Forty researchers from the United States, Canada, England, Ireland, and Sweden participated in this first meeting. The intimacy permitted for an excellent exchange of ideas, fruitful presentation of substantial research, and the subsequent publication of two books.

Further encouragement came from another quarter. In search of funding, I learned from a colleague in the law school, Gary Hufbauer, that the National Science Foundation offered grants for research in the field of international trade. Under his guidance I prepared two sub-proposals on exporting which were incorporated into his grant application. The application was funded, and provided $14,000 for my research components. Small as the grant was, it established important credibility within the university—ever sensitive to overhead charges and outside funding.

A RENEWED EFFORT TO RAISE FUNDS

In 1982, a new push toward fundraising was undertaken. Rather than ask for donations, however, the plan was now to establish which international trade issues were of interest to companies. By doing work in these areas, one could then ask firms for an annual membership fee rather than a donation. Visits to the government relations offices of large multinationals helped in identifying areas of major importance to these firms such as countertrade, export controls, and export trading company issues. For each one of these areas, a specific research agenda was developed and submitted to firms for funding. Various faculty colleagues assisted in the research planning with hopes of obtaining funding for their own research activities. These faculty efforts were augmented by center fellows—individuals drawn from the business and policy communities who were in search of university affiliation. Concurrently, a corporate advisory board, which assisted in evaluating research proposals, was formed. These efforts resulted in the signing up of seven firms, each of which contributed either $5,000 or $10,000. Even though not spectacular, the funds obtained assisted greatly in further involving faculty colleagues. Suddenly, long-planned research trips became feasible, and typing support and magazine subscriptions became a reality. What had been passive faculty support was converted into proactive research involvement. Proposals were written independently, or in response to research agenda circulated among the faculty.

BROADENING CENTER ACTIVITIES

The research conducted was published in staff papers that were provided to the sponsors, and submitted to academic journals. Several individual research projects were then grouped together to produce, with the collaboration of outside individuals and institutions, an ongoing conference program. These conferences either had a topical focus (e.g., export controls) or a regional orientation (e.g., U.S.-Latin American trade relations). Special care was taken in these conference efforts to intermingle academic and business efforts in order to provide a balance between theory and practice. Relevant topics combined with judicious selection of conference sites, either in Washington D.C. or foreign locations such as Rio de Janeiro, continued to maintain the interest of sponsors, broaden the center's international contacts and enhance its visibility. As a result, corporate funding covered most conference expenditures and permitted for further travel and research grants. Furthermore, the opening of all local seminars to our MBA students on a first-come, first-served basis, greatly enriched the international and timely content of our teaching.

By 1983, center staff had grown to four full-time members and the in-depth involvement of several faculty members and part-time outsiders. By linking up with the Fulbright program, several grantees from abroad were supplied with research space in exchange for lectures and one research paper. In addition, four students were receiving tuition stipends (paid for with outside funds) in exchange for work at the center.

Research papers were published at the rate of one per month. Faculty members were involved in every conference and were able to fulfill their research requirements. Travel to various conferences and meetings was funded.

Center activities now expanded to also include teaching. Several times a year, in-depth seminars were offered to the business and policy community. The seminar series lasted for one week at a time, but was subdivided into half-day and full-day sections addressing issues such as countertrade, export controls, export financing, export promotion, export trading, international human resources management, international taxation, and international licensing. Corporate sponsors were able to send attendees to these seminars as part of their membership benefits. Outside individuals and firms were able to sign up for sections of interest, which were taught by Georgetown faculty members or center fellows. Offered through the School for Summer and Continuing Education, attendance at these seminars awarded participants with a certificate of completion. For the teaching faculty, the seminars offered a welcome opportunity to interact with the "real" world, and to enhance faculty salaries. On a space-available basis, selected MBA students were also able to take the seminars on a complimentary basis.

Teaching programs were also specifically designed to fulfill corporate and institutional needs. With one Georgetown faculty member, Ilkka Ronkainen, taking the lead, several one-week programs on international business were developed for corporations and government departments. Even though the preparatory effort for each of these programs was high, annual contracts and frequent repetition of these courses made them easy to manage and highly desirable for the teaching faculty. Within a year, these programs made important funding contributions to the center.

INCREASING CENTER OUTREACH

On the advice of our corporate sponsors, center activities began to focus more on outreach to the business and policy communities. Special briefings were introduced, offering the opportunity for executives to meet with U.S. policy leaders and address specific business concerns. Such briefings were conducted with the Secretary of Commerce, the U.S. Trade Representative, the Secretary of the Treasury, and other high-ranking U.S. government officials. Only sponsoring members were invited to these briefings.

Roundtables were organized to focus on "hot" issues. These discussion sessions generally consisted of afternoon meetings, with a tightly defined focus on a current event, at which speakers from the business, policy, and academic communities explained their viewpoints and answered questions for the audience. Generally, these meetings were attended by fifteen to twenty-five executives from member companies, or from prospective member firms. Each meeting was followed up by a printed forum summary of eight to ten pages, which was distributed to the press and firms.

A newsletter, *The Trade Analyst*, was initiated on a bimonthly basis. It reported current events in Washington, carried the analysis of one or two current trade issues by a faculty member, featured an interview with a trade newsmaker from either business or government, and listed newly available center publications. Initially distributed without charge, non-members were urged to subscribe to the newsletter. Together with the sales of books and staff papers, publication income soon made a positive contribution to center income.

The center staff also became involved in the public policy process through the writing of editorials, frequent interviews with the media, and testimony at congressional hearings. Copies of these activities were forwarded on a regular basis to member firms to demonstrate the fact that their money was well spent.

FUNDING STATUS

By 1984, the center was supported by the annual membership dues of twenty-five organizations. Further efforts at grantsmanship resulted in the sponsorship of innovative teaching of export trading, by the U.S. Department of Education. As a result, a special MBA course on Export Trading Companies was offered to our students and computerized teaching modules were developed for self-instruction by firms. Income from publications and conferences made additional important contributions to operating funds. A lowering of membership fees for smaller-sized firms yielded a few more "subscribing" members. In addition, in-kind contributions were obtained, mainly from airlines, in order to support travel to international conferences cosponsored by the center. This availability of complimentary tickets enabled the center to make travel grants available to conference participants.

Throughout this time, direct university support consisted of generous space allocation and, of equal importance, internal university recognition for center programs. The president of the university attended several center functions. Center activities were prominently featured in the quarterly reports by the dean and the annual report of the university. This recognition brought with it credibility for the center, which in turn motivated more faculty members to participate in center activities or volunteer for new programs.

A RESEARCH NETWORK

Over time, the center was able to develop various research links with other universities and research institutions worldwide. In some instances, research funding was provided to individuals abroad. In most cases, however, the linkage focused mainly on the exchange of research materials and the development of collaborative research projects. The latter was of particular use in conducting comparative case-study-based research across countries. Even though the findings were highly useful in teaching, the corporate community did not support such efforts with much funding.

SOME COMMENTS

The author left the center in 1985 for a sabbatical and a subsequent leave of absence which was spent in the international trade area with the federal government. From a retrospective point of view, some summarizing comments may be helpful:

- A center is a good way to focus faculty attention on a particular issue or area.
- Ideally, some seed money should be available to cover initial expenses.
- To succeed, an internal champion is needed who will be able to deliver hands-on involvement and interact knowledgeably with the business community.
- Funding for research is difficult to obtain, particularly for a start-up venture. However, if the activities are of interest to potential sponsors, they will contribute.
- Obtaining funding is easier for a center with an established track record than for a good concept on paper.

- A focus on "hot" current issues is highly desired by the business community but less desired by faculty. A mix of short-term and long-term research seems therefore advisable.
- Any building effort has to be supported by the faculty. Such support is more easily obtained when faculty members are directly involved in center activities, and are able to see the center as a support mechanism that allows them to carry out their own desired activities, rather than merely an inside service activity which consumes much time with planning and discussion.
- Center efforts should also be linked to the primary teaching mission of the university. Not only will such linkages demonstrate the value of center activities, but they will also serve as a key motivator to students, and make them important contributors to a research program.
- Developing a center can be enormous fun—as a matter of fact, it has to be fun for the principals involved. Only in this way can the efforts expended be justified.

The popularity of "quick-fix" literature today makes it appropriate and, I hope, helpful to conclude with a brief, admittedly subjective list of Do's and Don'ts:

Do research on "client/audience" needs
Don't simply follow your own research preferences

Do regard funding expectations by others with a grain of salt
Don't expect the money to start pouring in

Do recognize that the step toward implementation is extremely important
Don't stay forever at the paper concept level

Do use center activities as a catalyst for colleague involvement
Don't be turned off by their sometimes only gradual participation

Do focus on the usefulness of your end product
Don't expect academic bustle to be useful for its own sake

Do submit your work to the test of the market, be it for publication or funding
Don't become too internally focused

Do involve people, many like it
Don't try to do everything yourself

Do recognize that business interests may not always track with academic ones
Don't forget that you are a member of the academic tribe

Do share the glory and rewards—memories are long
Don't forget to keep some for yourself—memories are short.

A CIBER-Maryland Perspective

ROBERT E. SCOTT

INTRODUCTION

CIBER Maryland was established on 2 January 1990, on the College Park campus of the University of Maryland (UMCP). This chapter describes the analytic foundations and educational principles that have influenced the planning and development of this center. The three primary responsibilities of CIBER Maryland, common to all of the national centers for international business education which are being supported by the U.S. Department of Education are: education, outreach, and research in international business. Two unique features of CIBER Maryland are emphasized in this discussion: our links with the World Trade Center Institute in Baltimore, and with the eleven campuses of the University of Maryland System (UMS).

BACKGROUND

U.S. foreign trade and foreign direct investment by U.S. firms have been increasing much more rapidly than total domestic output and investment. Between 1970 and 1990, U.S. foreign direct investment grew by 11 percent per year, in real terms. U.S. imports grew at an annual rate of 7 percent, and exports by 5.5 percent. During the same period, the rate of growth of real output averaged only 2.7 percent.[1] Most U.S. foreign trade and investment is carried out by very large firms. U.S. and foreign-based multinational companies (MNCs) are involved at one end or the other of 75 to 90 percent of all U.S. merchandise trade in 1987. A large and growing share of this commerce takes place between divisions or affiliates of the same firm, which is know as intra-firm trade. In 1987, 49 percent of all U.S. merchandise exports and imports constituted intra-firm

119

trade. This percentage increased by 5 and 10 percentage points, respectively, between 1977 and 1987.[2]

These characteristics of U.S. trade patterns have important implications for U.S. business education. Trade is expected to be a major engine of U.S. economic growth in the 1990s. U.S. firms that wish to share in this growth will expand their international operations or form joint ventures or other ties with foreign firms in order to increase their exports. This will reinforce the 1980s trend toward greatly increased flows of foreign direct investment, both into and out of the United States and other developed and developing economies. Furthermore, with more and more trade taking place *within* the firm (i.e. *among* units of the same firm), managers will become increasingly concerned with internal organizational issues such as transfer pricing, information and communication systems, and optimal decision-making structures. Therefore management curricula must be revised to emphasize these aspects of international business.

The public policy environment of international business will also change, for several reasons. First, U.S. government agencies are getting more involved in trade promotion. Second, U.S. firms will have increased exposure to foreign governments that are inherently more interventionist. Finally, the trade and industrial policies of our trading partners are also growing in scope, complexity, and impact.

Given the increasing importance of trade in determining the levels of output and employment, governments can be expected to devote an increasing amount of attention and resources to trade-based development strategies. Federal, state, and local government agencies in the United States will place greater emphasis on attracting and supporting MNCs, especially those in the manufacturing sectors. Manufacturing will receive special attention because goods trade represents the vast majority of nonfinancial trade flows. Service transactions are only a small (and relatively stable) segment of total trade. In addition, government opportunities to influence trade in agricultural and natural resource products are limited. Thus the manufacturing sectors will be the primary targets for government trade promotion efforts in the future.

As U.S. businesses get more involved in trade, investment, and production in other countries they are likely to find themselves interacting with foreign governments that are much more interventionist than government agencies in the United States. The United States has much lower levels of government ownership of manufacturing industries than many other countries in Europe and the developing nations. Many of these countries also have far more extensive systems of social regulation which embrace, for example, more comprehensive job rights including extended plant closing, retraining, and community settlement requirements. Furthermore, legal and administrative philosophies in other countries will often differ greatly from those that prevail in the United States. Thus U.S. firms will find a greater degree of foreign governments' involvement in private economic activity than is in the United States, despite the worldwide trend toward increased privatization of state industries.

Activist government policy models, which diverge radically from the GATT-based emphasis on liberal free trade patterns and reductions of tariff and nontariff trade barriers, are being rapidly developed. Western Europe, in particular, is becoming much more aggressive in its search for policies to help its own firms become more competitive in the world economy. For example, the EC has recently agreed to sharply restrict imports of Japanese autos, *including those Japanese autos assembled in Europe*, for ten years. Such policy developments will challenge governments in other developed nations to respond with new policy initiatives of their own.

As a result of these changes in the trade, investment, and public policy environments, both management education and techniques for managing in a dynamic external environment within firms involved in international business, must change in the future. The next generation of managers must be capable of managing in a truly international context. International management thus must include the capability of interacting with multiple government policy regimes in a dense matrix of production cost differences, and a wide range of production and logistical/organization possibilities.

CIBER Maryland emphasizes the interaction between management processes and the policy environment. We are able to do this because of the large number of nationally recognized policy analysts in economics, public affairs, and other related social sciences, as well as in the College of Business and Management, on our campus. These advantages are, in turn, related to our location in the Washington, D.C. area. These perspectives have influenced the design of our programs in ways that are illustrated with the following selected examples of CIBER Maryland educational, outreach, and research activities.

EDUCATIONAL PROGRAMS

The University of Maryland in College Park has been designated by the state as the flagship campus of the eleven-campus system. We are also the only comprehensive National Research University (as defined by the Carnegie Foundation) in the National Capitol Region. One part of the CIBER Maryland mission is the internationalization of business education throughout the Mid-Atlantic region. The development of these programs was influenced by two observations about the international business environment, which are reflected in a general principle of management education that guides our curriculum development work. The observations, which are derived from our analysis of the U.S. environment for international business, are:

- International competition is now a key concern of managers in many firms, even those that operate only in the United States. The increasing interpenetration of the global economy, through the increased flows of both goods and capital, means that in many industries, especially those involved in merchandise trade, no firm can avoid international competition in its own home market. These developments are forcing more firms to develop production and marketing strategies that include an international perspective. Although it is still true that "all business is local," it is also equally true that "all business is international."

- The international dimension is a new addition to the public policy environment of most business firms. In the 1970s and 1980s, most major businesses developed mechanisms for managing their public policy environments, including both scanning and participation in issue and electoral politics (e.g., development of corporate Political Action Committees). The emphasis in the 1990s, in this field, is the international dimension. This includes the policies of home-country governments vis-a-vis their own multinationals, as well as the policies of MNC host countries and the collective policies of groups of countries, such as the OECD Code of Conduct and the international shipping conferences.

We have distilled from these observations a general principle that guides our efforts to internationalize the management curricula:

Because international considerations arise in virtually all management contexts, international business education should not be separated from the core curriculum, or from the traditional management education disciplines. Of course, all international faculty must have an academic base, but to the extent possible, we should avoid the idea that international business is *separate* from other management areas; it is in fact a *part* of all areas. Students with special international interests are better served if they are given an academic base in a traditional management discipline, with additional international emphasis.

The challenge of multinational management is to develop procedures and processes for dealing with multiple actors (both public and private) and multiple production possibilities in a global economic environment. The environment both determines the firm's production and marketing possibilities, and can itself be influenced by business actions, as illustrated by events such as the Exxon-Valdez disaster. All aspects of the firm's management, including financial, personnel, accounting, and information systems, are affected by the internationalization of the economic environment. As a result, *international issues must be considered throughout the management curriculum and we should avoid overemphasis on specialized international courses and departments.*

In this regard it is important to point out that international students, in particular, are often poorly served by participating in specialized international business programs. The programs themselves often benefit greatly from the availability of native experts from different countries. However, the content of these programs is often of little benefit to the foreign students, who often could gain more from greater exposure to a traditional U.S. management curricula (for example, an MBA program).

This principle is reflected in the design of CIBER-Maryland international business education programs. Three examples will illustrate our approach.

1. INTERNATIONALIZING THE CORE CURRICULUM

We are developing a series of brief workshops on the integration of international issues in the core business disciplines for faculty from throughout the University of Maryland System (UMS) and for other colleges and universities in our region. The first workshop, which was offered in the summer of 1991, featured national experts such as Michael Czinkota of Georgetown, and Susan Douglas of New York University, and brought together a small group of faculty members to discuss strategies for integrating international issues in core marketing courses. A one-day workshop on the internationalization of core finance courses was offered in May 1992. Workshops for other disciplines will be developed in the future. These workshops are part of a broader effort to strengthen international modules in many of the required core courses at both the undergraduate and graduate levels throughout the UMS. The unique feature of these workshops is their emphasis on integrating international examples throughout the core curriculum, to avoid compartmentalization of international issues into syllabus topics and sections that are all too easily cut or dropped.

2. COMBINING BUSINESS AND FOREIGN LANGUAGE STUDY

We have recently introduced a new program in International Business and Foreign Languages (IBFL) for undergraduates at UMCP. This program is not a substitute for our undergraduate business curriculum, but an addition to it. The IBFL program is essentially a highly structured double major designed to combine the basics of an undergraduate degree in international business with its standard disciplinary foundations. The program develops foreign language skills, with a commercial emphasis. Initially, the program was developed for the Spanish Language option. It has now been expanded to include French, Chinese, Japanese, Russian, and German. Additional support has been received from a private foundation for the development of a computerized International Business Negotiation Simulation program for use in undergraduate business and language courses; this simulation is based on a model developed in the Department of Government and Politics at UMCP.

The structure of this program reflects our understanding that language and area studies are important aspects of International Business education, but in ways different from what is commonly understood. The point of such programs is not that students become proficient linguists or area specialists for their own sakes, but to provide a basis for understanding and operating within other cultures. Just as few schools offer "managing in the XYZ industry" courses, so few should offer "managing in country A or region B"—*but*, just as most students should learn something about some major industries, so those with international interests should also learn something about some other parts of the world (including language training), without becoming area specialists.

3. FACILITATING SYSTEM-WIDE INTERNATIONALIZATION

CIBER Maryland cosponsored a roundtable discussion on *Opportunities for Inter-Campus Cooperation* with the University of Baltimore's Business School at the UMS International Faculty and Administrator's Association (IFAA) meeting in the fall of 1991. Representatives from the five UMS business schools participated in a discussion of international programs and plans, culminating in the cosponsorship of the NTUN video-conference on business in the former Soviet Union on November 7 by CIBER Maryland and Towson State University. The IFAA provides continuing opportunities for formal and informal cooperation on internationalization programs. One of the initial activities of the IFAA was the establishment of a task force that developed plans for a Study in Mexico program. As a result, the UMS is going to establish and staff a permanent facility in Mexico City and arrange exchange programs with the Universidad Nacional Autonoma de Mexico (UNAM) and El Institute Technologico Autonovo de Mexico (ITAM) beginning in 1992. Funding for this project will include resources from the Debt for Development Coalition, Inc. of Washington, D.C.

OUTREACH PROGRAMS

Our outreach activities take advantage of two key sources of competitive advantage for the Mid-Atlantic economy: the port of Baltimore and its associated business community, and the engineering/research community in the Washington, D.C. area. The research community is undergoing a transition from a government orientation (linked to defense and health research) to a private market orientation in the wake of the federal budget crises of the late 1980s. As a result, for example, Maryland has become a leading exporter of medical equipment within the last five years. The state of Maryland has been very aggressive in its support of international trade, through technology leadership, as reflected in the rapid growth of support for the Maryland International Division of the state Government and the Maryland Biotechnology Institute in the UMS.

CIBER Maryland outreach programs are designed to bring together academics and practitioners from businesses with significant export market potential in the rapidly evolving high-tech markets, in which access to current information and effective management practice is critical. Three examples will illustrate some of the unique features of this program:

1. WORLD TRADE CENTER INSTITUTE

Our most significant vehicle for outreach with both business and government officials has been a series of collaborations between CIBER Maryland and the World Trade Center Institute (WTCI) in Baltimore. The WTCI is a private association of business and government leaders from the Mid-Atlantic region, which receives significant support from the state of Maryland. The WTCI organizes three types of programs: (1) country programs, (2) industry programs, and (3) trade training programs. The WTCI programs bring together business executives, academics, and other analysts with actual international business experience for each event. CIBER Maryland works with the WTCI in developing and presenting some of its programs. A series of jointly sponsored short programs on the proposed U.S.-Mexico Free Trade Agreement and U.S. business opportunities in Mexico have been very popular with the business community. The WTCI is developing workshop programs on Japan and Russia. Meetings have also been held on business opportunities in industries such as information technology and biotechnology.

2. WORLD TRADE WEEK

CIBER Maryland also worked with the WTCI in developing plans for the *World Trade Week*, which was held in Baltimore 20-24 May 1991. In addition to participating in the overall planning and marketing of this program, we organized a panel discussion on *"Maryland in the Global Economy: Recovery and Long-term Growth through Export Opportunities"* attended by representatives from business, government, and academia. Both institutions will continue to work together in developing material for future World Trade Week programs, which will become an annual event in Baltimore.

3. BUSINESS ADVISORY COUNCIL

CIBER Maryland is establishing an International Business Advisory Council (IBAC). In contrast to the University of Miami and Georgetown models (see papers by Robert Grosse and Michael Czinkota in this volume), which have set up advisory councils composed primarily of representatives from larger firms, IBAC will include executives from both small and large firms in the Mid-Atlantic region. This decision is based on the fact that small- and medium-sized firms are significant exporters in this region, and some of these firms could join the ranks of the leading MNCs in the future if they continue to grow rapidly.

Links with large multinational firms are also important components of the CIBER Maryland outreach program. Our group participated in a collaboration with Westinghouse, Enterprise Development Corporation, and IBM to develop plans for an international communications and teleconferencing center to be located in downtown Baltimore. This project resulted in a proposal to the Baltimore's office of economic development to upgrade the power plant facility on the inner harbor for this purpose.

RESEARCH PROGRAMS

International research issues that have been identified by our faculty, in consultation with practitioners associated with our education and outreach programs, are addressed through competitive research grants and through a series of core research projects. Results of this research are disseminated through a CIBER Maryland working paper series, research seminars and conferences, and publications in academic journals.

1. INTERNATIONAL RESEARCH AND INTERACTION WITH THE BUSINESS COMMUNITY

The research competition illustrates another aspect of the CIBER-Maryland educational philosophy. Internationalization forces academics and managers to break down traditional disciplinary limits and encourages them to become interdisciplinary "boundary spanners." Our criteria for award of research grants include use of interdisciplinary research techniques. We received twenty-one proposals for summer support for international business research, including a number from nonbusiness disciplines. Support was provided to an anthropologist who was conducting a case study of cross-cultural management in a U.S./Mexican joint venture (using participant/observer techniques) in Mexico City, and to a graduate student in public policy doing research on nontariff trade barriers in Argentina.

Within UMS business schools, support has been provided for a wide variety of projects. One member of the management faculty in our College is conducting a "Global Study on Corporate-Subsidiary Relations within Multinational Corporations." A paper that resulted from this project received the Academy of Management's 1991 Best Paper Award in Business Policy and Strategy. A graduate student from the same department is conducting a study on the "Strategic Use of Public Policy in Global Competition: An Evaluation of the Export Trading Certificate Program of the U.S. Department of Commerce." A member of our business law faculty is studying commercial law reform in Hungary and Poland. Business faculty from other UMS campuses are being supported for projects on firm strategies in post 1992 Europe and on the export patterns of small to medium-sized manufacturing firms.

2. CORE RESEARCH ON INTERNATIONAL BUSINESS

Lee E. Preston, CIBER Maryland Director (1990-1992), has just completed a book with Duane Windsor (Rice University) on *The*

Rules of the Game in the Global Economy: Policy Regimes for International Business, which has been accepted for publication by Kluwer Academic Publishers (forthcoming, 1992). Planning work for a follow-up conference in 1993 is underway.

The information technology industry is the focus of a project being developed in our information system department. This project will examine the links between information system theory and international management systems. It will explore international information technology issues that offer a significant opportunity to impact actual business practice, through case studies of a small set of progressive companies.

Other core research projects include: (1) case studies of the effects of trade and protection on domestic industries; (2) international consumer protection legislation and dispute resolution mechanisms in the ASEAN countries; (3) international banking, foreign direct investment and financial market integration among the developed nations; and (4) the structure and international competitiveness of the Mid-Atlantic economy.

CIBER-Maryland is developing a number of other education, outreach, and research programs, including domestic and foreign internships and research projects on Russia and other Eastern European countries that reflect the principles outlined above. Further information on these programs is provided in our project report and periodic "CIBER Updates" which are available on request from our office.

NOTES

1. Foreign direct investment in the United States grew by only 1.7 percent per year between 1970 and 1990. It was severely depressed in the early 1980s by the high value of the dollar, despite the rapid increase in foreign holding of *all* U.S. assets (including other equities and government debt) during the 1980s. All data in this paragraph are measured in flow terms and are from the U.S. balance of payment and national income accounts, from Citibase.

2. Trends in U.S. merchandise trade are reviewed in R. E. Scott, "The Role of International Business in the Maryland Economy," CIBER Maryland Occasional Paper #6 (May 1991). Primary sources for the data discussed in the text are provided there.

Internationalizing The University and Building Bridges Across Disciplines

MICHAEL G. SCHECHTER

I am a committed internationalist, trained in political science rather than in business, and have spent the past six years working on the internationalization of the Michigan State University (MSU) campus encouraging the requirement of foreign languages, strengthening area studies, supporting faculty development activities, and encouraging analogous activities across the country (Schechter 1990a). I have two messages for business faculty. While the first covers old ground, I am, however, hopeful it contains some ideas with which business educators may be unfamiliar. These address the issue of the internationalization of universities, not simply colleges or schools of business, and not simply the curriculum. The second focuses on how to overcome what I call the "two cultures" problem of building bridges across disciplines or campuses.

INTERNATIONALIZING OF UNIVERSITIES: LESSONS FROM THE PAST

First, I would like to share a number of lessons derived from my involvement with institutional internationalization.

LESSON ONE: DEVELOP A COMPREHENSIVE AND RELEVANT PLAN

Few institutions have plans, even when they have a Center for International Programs and/or across-the-campus committees to oversee internationalization activities. Of the few institutions that do have plans, few are comprehensive, i.e., they discuss how to internationalize all aspects and all disciplines. By aspects, I mean

129

faculty research (not simply conducting research abroad, but conducting research statewide about things foreign); university outreach activities that extend not merely to the business community, but to the general public, too, about issues such as the implications of foreign investment for their communities; student life and career placement; and curricular matters as well as faculty development.

LESSON TWO: HAVE A METHOD IN PLACE FOR ASSESSING PROGRESS

An institution must be able to gauge how far it has gone *and how far it still has to go*. To achieve this, one can, for example, simply administer a subset of the Education Testing Service's International Affairs Knowledge Test (Hembroff, Knott, and Keefe 1990). We, at MSU, did that in 1990 and discovered that indeed we had made progress in terms of students' international knowledge. However:

1. we realized that the test did not deal with concepts of provincialism and ethnocentrism, much less cultural sensitivity;
2. we were mystified by some of the findings, including the fact that our undergraduate business students still seemed to have less international knowledge than almost any other undergraduates on our campus, despite internationalization of their curriculum through infusion efforts, and the fact that the College of Business students were generally among our academically strongest students;
3. it was clear we still had a long way to go to take pride in our accomplishments in this arena; and
4. we had to face the empirical evidence of the survey that students' out-of-the-formal-classroom activities were almost as important in accounting for their international knowledge as their in-class activities, underscoring the necessity to go beyond internationalization of the curriculum (Hembroff, Knott and Keefe 1990). Too often internationalization of an institution is limited to a discussion of formal course work, possibly augmented by internships and overseas study programs. However, the results of international knowledge tests empirically document that the numbers of co-curricular events (foreign plays, lectures, films, etc.) that students attend and the amount of their exposure to media with international content, also significantly contribute to their knowledge of international affairs. Accordingly, internationalization strategies need to pay attention to the internationalization of student life and culture. The available

strategies are multiple and their adoption needs to be related to institutional resources and mission. Among the most obvious such strategies are:

- Taking full advantage of the opportunities afforded by residence hall life and central locations (e.g., student unions) for co-curricular programming like plays, musical events, or alternative sports events.
- Increasing the use of foreign students as a resource, after one has assessed their level of interest and expertise. For example, foreign students can: (a) be useful participants on on-campus radio and television stations as commentators on current events in their countries; (b) conduct foreign language conversations in dining halls, teach culture, etc.; (c) work with students going on overseas study programs, or potential peace corps volunteers; or (d) work with faculty in developing modules for inclusion in their courses.
- Expanding the use of C-Span and foreign films for educative purposes, with faculty-led discussions afterward to insure that students have gotten the most possible out of the viewings.

LESSON THREE: WORK COOPERATIVELY ACROSS THE INSTITUTION AND WITH OTHER INSTITUTIONS

A team effort that involves other institutions and is intercollegiate within one's own institution, is an invaluable approach. At times this will mean adopting the leadership role, but more often it means overcoming institutional and disciplinary rivalries and jealousies. Such an approach is exemplified by recent research on the role of public enterprises in Nigeria, conducted by two MSU faculty—one from James Madison College (a social science college) and the other from the Department of Marketing in the College of Business. Not only have these two professors begun to write together, but their respective political economy and marketing courses have changed as well.

LESSON FOUR: ADMIT MISTAKES AND SHARE THEM WITH OTHERS

From our experience as researchers, we all know that the learning curve is much different if we can profit from the mistakes of others who are plowing the same path. That lesson needs to be carried over into the area of institutional reform as well.

LESSON FIVE: EXPLOIT TECHNOLOGY IN INTERNATIONALIZING
CAMPUSES

The use of electronic bulletin boards, on campus and across campuses, needs to be enhanced, especially for the purpose of sharing information about campus visitors. As the field of business depends increasingly on allied fields for its intellectual growth and as more and more fields need to learn from those in the various business disciplines, such sharing *must* grow. At MSU, the Western European Studies program was the first to use an electronic bulletin board for these purposes.

LESSON SIX: USE ALTERNATIVE AND COMPLEMENTARY APPROACHES TO
INTERNATIONALIZE THE CURRICULUM AND THE CAMPUS

Infusion

The concept of infusion is quite simple: to introduce comparative, international, and cross-cultural dimensions into preexisting courses throughout the curriculum (see Chapter Two by Jeffrey Arpan). The goal is to get students to think comparatively in all of their intellectual inquiries.

In order for infusion to be successful, the focus needs to be on required courses—those in the core curriculum including general education offerings when they are a part of every undergraduate's curriculum, and introductory courses for majors (Atlantic Council of the United States 1989). For example, MSU's new "integrative studies" curriculum, which replaced its general education courses in 1992, has significant new international dimensions. Thus the infusion strategy requires that examples used in an introductory marketing or advertising course, for example, include those drawn from other countries and not simply from the United States. Moreover, faculty need to explain the cultural reasons for variations in marketing or advertising techniques in different places in the world, and not simply describe those differences.

Adopting an infusion strategy for introductory and required courses provides a foundation on which other courses can build. It also inspires students to bring international examples into disciplinary courses, and might even get them to demand comparative perspectives in their more advanced and specialized work. To an institution, it offers a number of advantages, most notably in terms of the numbers of students influenced. Equally important, however, such a strategy affects students across economic, racial, geographic, gender, and skill categories. And not of least importance, it is a relatively inexpensive strategy; it does not require hiring large numbers of new faculty and supporting them with money for field research. It also avoids "ghettoization" of international phenomena, as would result, for example, from requiring all students to take a single "third world" culture course. The latter can have the unfortunate and unintended consequence of allowing students to think that international and comparative phenomena are things to be gotten over with and are not essential to one's major. Therefore, the infusion model seems apt for institutions, such as two-year community and four-year liberal arts colleges, which are often short on resources for internationalization, but which have a number of key required courses for majors, as well as others across the institution.

At the same time, however, the infusion model has a number of disadvantages as an internationalization strategy. It is a strategy maximizes breadth at the expense of depth. Courses are taught by nonspecialists, who can be inaccurate at times, and who lack the passion and commitment of field-trained specialists. They are likely to skip the international, comparative and cross-cultural materials if they find themselves running short on time in the classroom since they usually lack confidence in teaching them anyway.

Addition of Specialized International, Comparative,
and Cross-Cultural Courses

In many ways, adding new courses to the curriculum appears to be the least creative internationalization strategy. But it need not be, for example, if one conceives of such courses in innovative ways, as exemplified by interdisciplinary, general education courses in which business history, culture, ideology, and politics are all blended.

Not surprisingly, the advantages and disadvantages of this strategy parallel those of the infusion model. Adding specialized courses, taught by knowledgeable experts with passionate commitment, and taken by interested and committed students (who, in turn, add to the faculty members' excitement, knowledge, and commitment) is a comparatively expensive strategy. It requires a serious financial commitment on the part of the institution, one which must be continuous in terms of research support and money for faculty replacements. Moreover, such courses frequently tend to be enrolled in by those least needing them—students already sensitive to international phenomena and already possessing some of the skills needed for the world in which all of our graduates will live. Obviously then, such a strategy is appropriate for institutions with greater resources available to them and who see one of their goals as provision of the leadership class for the next generation.

International Business Majors and Minors

Here the strategy aims to bring together a number of disciplinarily disparate courses. The attempt, therefore, is to make students' academic programs more cohesive than they might otherwise be. Such a strategy offers students an exciting field of study. Students studying substantively exciting materials more readily develop skills. Simultaneously, the existence of such programs allow faculty, who might not otherwise do so, to meet and work together in devising, teaching, monitoring, and revising such programs. As a consequence of such interaction, they might also develop joint research and/or outreach activities.

On the other hand, development of such minors and majors might take pressure off those responsible for general education, and other more traditional majors, to internationalize their courses. Thus this strategy offers the potential of depth of exposure at the cost of breadth, especially in terms of the numbers of students whose academic programs are affected.

Foreign Language Instruction

It does not seem necessary, nor perhaps even relevant to review debates connected with foreign language entrance and graduation requirements. Rather it seems useful to underscore the point that for foreign language courses to serve as part of an effective internationalization strategy, they must teach more than simply grammar and literature. They also need to teach culture, geography, politics, history and economics; that is, substantive knowledge about the countries in which the languages being studied are spoken. Therefore, in order for this strategy to have a significant impact on students, their study of foreign language *must be reinforced in their non-foreign language courses*, for example, by having faculty in those other courses recommend foreign language sources be used by those having foreign language skills. Such recommendations should, wherever possible, appear on course syllabi. The reasoning behind this, of course, is the same rationale as that for the so-called "writing across the curriculum," i.e., to make sure students know that the study of a foreign language is deemed critical in all disciplines and is a highly treasured research skill.

As with the infusion strategy, this strategy involves risk taking: having faculty teaching outside their fields of expertise and passion.

Overseas Studies

There may be no single set of experiences of greater long-term benefit to a student, in terms of expanding her or his international and cross-cultural perspective, than to participate in an overseas study program, especially one that is in a cultural setting significantly different from the one with which she or he is most familiar. In developing and expanding overseas study options, attention must be directed toward their integration into the curriculum as well as the variety of locations at which they are offered. Predeparture orientations and post-return debriefing sessions are critical to ensure that students maximize their off-campus learning experiences.

One of the limitations of this internationalization strategy is that, even under the best of circumstances, it will never involve large percentages of the student body. To some extent, however, this defect can be compensated for by developing specialized programs to attract students who do not ordinarily enroll in such programs. The pattern for overseas study programs has traditionally been that of junior year abroad programs, often focusing on the liberal arts (history, language, culture). Our data suggest that such programs are most often enrolled in by upper middle-class Caucasian females majoring in the liberal arts. Without discounting the value of such approaches at all, other programs need to be developed for students with limited financial means and rigid curricular demands, i.e., few elective courses.

To the extent that any one campus lacks the infrastructure to offer the variety of programs inherent in such an internationalization strategy, students should be made aware of consortia opportunities as well as offerings at other institutions, perhaps through electronic bulletin boards.

International Internships and Jobs

International internships and jobs offer many of the advantages of overseas study programs, with the possibility of overcoming some of the financial obstacles that often accompany the more traditional overseas experiences. To implement this strategy, institutions need to have the wherewithal to establish centralized offices where students can obtain the necessary information for enrolling in such programs. Given the likelihood that demand may way exceed supply, and that many students without the necessary skills may be interested in applying for such opportunities, such offices will be well served if they develop *written* materials describing the sorts of skills and knowledge that students need to have for such activities as well as visa requirements and restrictions. Moreover, right from the outset, institutions need to differentiate academic internships from work experiences, differentiating in terms of skills needed, credit to be awarded, and outcomes to be achieved.

LESSON SEVEN: A SINGLE STRATEGY CAN SERVE MULTIPLE PURPOSES

Not surprisingly, different strategies often require different means for implementation. But not always. For example, each of the above-mentioned strategies calls for faculty and staff effort beyond what they have traditionally expended. Accordingly, successful internationalization strategies may require a modification of an institution's reward system to accentuate the importance of participation in the institution's internationalization efforts. Achievement of such a bold, yet almost cost-free step, requires that the institution ensure that its major decision-makers have a commitment to internationalization efforts.

Likewise, an across-the-institution competitive grant procedure can be developed for faculty wishing to gain the expertise to infuse international dimensions or to add specialized international course offerings. In the former competition, emphasis should be placed on faculty not traditionally involved in teaching such courses, whereas in the latter competition, those with international expertise would be expected to be prominent among the awardees. In both instances, however, emphasis should be on student impact rather than on the means by which the faculty will gain the necessary wherewithal to have that impact. In both instances, as well, faculty members' academic units should be expected to contribute to the grant, ensuring that the unit has a vested interest in the faculty member's successful implementation of her or his proposal and that it is part of the academic unit's overall internationalization efforts. Efficiency in resource allocation will also be enhanced if institutions develop workshops for faculty with similar interests and needs. Such workshops can be run by area study centers where they exist, or augmented by external lecturers, as faculty prefer learning from those off-campus even in those instances where those off-campus may not have more substantive knowledge than on-campus resources!

OVERCOMING THE "TWO CULTURE" PROBLEM: BUILDING BRIDGES ACROSS CAMPUS AND ACROSS DISCIPLINES

Oversimplifying a bit, the rationales for internationalizing an institution can be placed under several rubrics:

1. *pragmatic* reasons—commercial advantages, the need for students to be prepared for the 21st century, and the need for an institution to be competitive with its peers;
2. *liberal and liberating rationales*—the fact that exposure to international phenomena and cross-cultural issues opens students' minds to an entirely different world and the fact that international education is inherently interdisciplinary, thus providing at least one means for overcoming the fragmentation of students' learning habits; and,
3. *civic education*—providing our students with the tools necessary for making educated and ethical decisions about the principles of goverance.

Business faculty members' reaction to the above may be that (1) this is nothing new or revolutionary, (2) if they had to articulate the reasons, they might have framed it a bit differently, or perhaps, (3) they would keep it simple and omit the second and third rubrics.

But that's the key point. Faculty in the arts and humanities, upon whom business faculty must depend for providing a major part of international education to their students, are offended by such direct language. They don't want to hear that there are pragmatic reasons for studying foreign languages and cultures. They do not want to hear that business faculty have altered their introductory marketing course to add an international dimension to it so as to make their graduates more marketable or even that it provides them an internationalized education. And until business faculty learn to alter their language, they will always find only a token of arts and humanities folks willing to work with them, and those less so during eras of economic prosperity when enrollments in their own programs are doing quite well.

Let me provide one example of how business faculty might engage arts and humanities folks across the campus in a way that will ultimately show the arts folks that the business faculty are made of the same stuff that they are and that everyone needs to work together.

What I have in mind is a serious intellectual dialogue about the merits of melding the teaching and researching of multiculturalism and internationalism (i.e., the focus on national diversities—differences in terms of race, ethnicity, gender, geography, sexual preference, age—with the focus on things foreign). Faculty throughout the United States are being barraged with demands that they alter their curricula to take into account both of these phenomena, but few think of their obvious connections and common tensions.

However, faculty of international advertising, management, marketing, and so on, have always recognized the challenges of segmentation, be they minority populations within a country or outside the country. Here the issues of cross-cultural sensitivity—whether within a single country's boundaries or across them—are issues with which business faculty have grappled for a long time and for which they have a handle on how to cope.

That's the sort of dialogue that business faculty must initiate in order to build bridges across the two clashing cultures.

CONCLUSION

Each college or school of business owes its students an international education, and not merely because the AACSB mandates it. As educators, all of us are responsible for ensuring that our graduates have the requisite skills and knowledge to be effective citizens, leaders, employees, and employers. And considering life in the 21st century, that means graduating students whose lives in college have been infused with a substantial international dimension. The means for achieving this end are multiple. The choices that a college, school, department, and individual faculty member make will depend on the institution's mission, traditions, and resources. But the chosen method must be effective and efficient. To ensure effectiveness, evaluative mechanisms must be put in place. To achieve maximum efficiency, bridges need to be built across campuses and across disciplines.

REFERENCES

The Atlantic Council of the United States. 1989. *Post World War II International Relations as a Component of General Education in American Colleges and Universities*. Washington, D.C.: The Atlantic Council of the United States.

Hembroff, L., J. Knott, and M. Keefe. 1990. Survey of Michigan State University Students' Knowledge of International Affairs. East Lansing: Center for Survey Research, Michigan State University.

Schechter, M. 1990a. "A Challenge to Undergraduate Educators: The Wingspread Conference on International Education." *Political Science* 23: 461–63.

_____. 1990b. "Internationalizing the Undergraduate Curriculum." *International Education Forum* 10: 14-20.

_____. 1990c. "The Role of Area Studies at a Land Grant and AAU University: The MSU Model." Dynamic Transformation: Korea, NICS and

Beyond, ed. Gill–Chin Lim and Wook Chan. Urbana: Consortium on Development Studies: 437–50.

Schechter, M. N.d. "Internationalizing the Undergraduate Curriculum on Historically African–American Campuses." Greensboro, NC: University of North Carolina.

The University of Southern California Approach

JACK G. LEWIS

INTRODUCTION

I would like to share with you the approach to internationalization adopted by the School of Business Administration at the University of Southern California (USC) over the past fifteen years. The USC International Business Education and Research Program (IBEAR) approach may not, in its specifics, have great utility to others. Yet, in that it has very explicit answers as to how to conceptualize and how to organize the process of internationalization, its areas of success or areas for further improvement may be of interest to some. Among those questions USC has developed its own answers to, are:

1. How do forces favoring internationalization gain influence in a business school?
2. How do you initiate the process of internationalization?
3. How do you organize effectively?
4. If the business school in question is a large one, with many students and programs, where does one start?
5. How long does the process take?

SCHOOL CONTEXT

The task of internationalization at USC is a formidable one, in part, because the school has many students, faculty, programs, and units. USC's School of Business Administration enrolls 3,850 students, including 2,750 junior- and senior-level undergraduates, and 1,100 graduate students. Enrolled in four types of MBA programs— a full-time two-year program, an evening program, an Executive MBA Program, and the IBEAR MBA Program—are 1,025 students.

141

There are also 75 Ph.D. candidates. These programs are served by 170 full-time faculty.

The school subscribes to the matrix organization form; it consists of five functional departments, eleven academic programs (like the IBEAR MBA Program, the Food Industry Management Program, and the Entrepreneur Program), and six research centers (including the Center for Effective Organizations, and the Center for Telecommunications Management). Each of these academic programs and research centers has its own staff, priorities, and interests; each therefore has to compete for the attention of our faculty. In this context, the task of internationalizing the business school involves considerable effort and resolve.

The IBEAR Program: Origins And Objectives

Planning for the school's International Business Education and Research Program began in 1976 under the leadership of former dean, Jack Steele, and former associate dean, Roy Herberger, 1992 president of the American Graduate School of International Management (Thunderbird). Steele, who served as dean for twelve years until late 1987, believed that he could improve the school's quality and national stature by adding specialized programs and research units, under the leadership of well-known faculty often attracted from other institutions, to the conventional functional departments. Steele and Herberger also believed in internationalization and felt that USC's internationalization efforts would benefit by taking advantage of its location and therefore emphasized the Pacific Rim. Herberger, a marketing faculty member, aggressively promoted this new international business unit. It is surprising to note, even after fifteen years, how close the activities of the IBEAR Program are to the original vision of the mid1970s. The strategic purpose of the IBEAR Program still is faculty development—to attract international business faculty to USC and to prompt existing faculty to become more interested in, and knowledgeable about, the international dimensions of their disciplines.

The solution to accomplishing this was innovative. The core activity of the IBEAR Program was to be a one-year, mid-career, international MBA program that emphasized, in particular, Pacific Rim business. Participants were to be from all over the world, but needed to share a substantive interest in doing business between Asia and the rest of the world. Faculty from the functional departments would be rotated through the program, each for a minimum of two or three years. The intensive contact with an experienced, mid-career class from several countries would enhance their interest and understanding. Funds generated by the program would be used to finance international research and travel by these faculty. Since 1978, sixty-one USC faculty have taught in this program and undergone this "socialization" experience.

In addition to the IBEAR MBA Program, the original plans in 1976 foresaw that this new international business unit would engage in internationally focused executive education, promote international business research in the school, and provide support to the dean in the school's broader efforts at internationalization.

In August 1978, the first IBEAR MBA Program class was launched. It took more than ten years and two generations of IBEAR administrators to begin to fulfill the original vision for the unit. From 1978 to 1985, IBEAR was predominately occupied with establishing and administering the new IBEAR MBA Program and, to some extent, supporting the research of its faculty. Because the program concept was so distinctive in focus and length, substantial efforts were required to attract participants and their sponsoring firms.

The time period of 1986 through 1989 saw the program experiencing a second stage of development wherein the IBEAR MBA Program grew from fifteen (1978) to its target size of forty-eight; simultaneously participant maturity and diversity were significantly enhanced. Thanks in large part to a substantial federal grant, Pacific Rim-focused education programs for American executives were introduced concurrently, and Pacific Rim-oriented research and research conferences expanded significantly.

A third stage in IBEAR development began in October 1990 with the announcement that USC had been selected by the U.S. Department of Education as one of sixteen national centers for international business education. The three-year, thirty-project effort is seen as an opportunity to more aggressively expand internationalization throughout the school in cooperation with other units throughout the University.

In 1992, fifteen years after the initial planning, IBEAR is active in all of the areas foreseen by its founders.

IBEAR MBA PROGRAM

The IBEAR MBA Program remains the core of the unit, a new class of 48 beginning in early August each year. The outgoing class, having completed a three-week academic orientation program and

19 MBA courses (56 units), graduates in the last week of July each year.

The IBEAR MBA class of 1992 consists of 48 participants from 16 countries, and averages 33 years of age and 10 years of work experience, as compared to 30 years of age at IMD and 28 at INSEAD. The average age has remained at 33 since 1987. Two-thirds of all participants are corporate sponsored. Slightly more than half the class is from Asia, with the remainder from the United States, Canada, Chile, and Europe. The increased American participation in the program began in the mid-1980s with matching scholarships provided by a U.S. DOE Title VIb grant. Whereas in 1984, almost all participants came from Asia, soon one-half of the class will come from Asia, one-quarter will come from the United States, and the remainder will come from Canada, Mexico, Europe, Latin America, and elsewhere. As tuition and special program fees are similar to two years in a private university, the program is self-supporting and generates resources to support the school's internationalizing effort.

IBEAR INTERNATIONAL EXECUTIVE PROGRAMS

IBEAR's executive programs unit manages a series entitled Pacific Rim Management Programs in June each year, the Asia/Pacific Business Outlook conference each March, and administers customized programs to firms, associations, and foreign universities.

The Pacific Rim Management Programs are the only series of Asia country-specific executive education programs in the United States. Since their inception in 1985 with the support of a U.S. DOE Title VIb grant, thirty-three programs have been presented serving more than 300 firms from throughout the United States. Programs on Japan, Korea, China, Taiwan, Southeast Asia, and Mexico were scheduled for June 1993.

The Asia/Pacific Business Outlook conferences, cooperative ventures between IBEAR and the U.S. & Foreign Commercial Service of the U.S. Department of Commerce, take place in March each year. At these conferences, the Senior Commercial Officer (SC)) from fifteen American embassies in Asia, Canada, and Mexico and an American executive in Asia—selected by the SCO—come to USC to provide current information about changing opportunities and risks for American firms in the Pacific Rim marketplace. Totally, seventy-five academics, executives, and SCOs provide over 160 seminars and workshops during the three-day conferences.

Since their inception in 1988, nearly 1500 American managers from 900 firms have attended the Asia/Pacific Business Outlook conferences. These programs attract participants from throughout the nation (only one-third come from California) from small, medium, and large firms. In accordance with the cooperative agreement with the U.S. Department of Commerce, funds generated by this conference are used to provide scholarships to U.S. citizens in the IBEAR MBA Program.

IBEAR RESEARCH PROGRAM

IBEAR supports international business research by school faculty and USC social science faculty by providing research grants, supporting numerous international conference travel grants (requiring the delivery of a refereed paper), and by organizing five research conferences. A significant amount of the financial support for this effort was obtained by joint proposals with USC's East Asian Studies Center. Between 1983 and 1986, over $450,000 in grants was awarded to this EASC/SBA partnership by the U.S. Department of Education's International Business Education Program (Title VIb). In addition to numerous scholarly articles that have resulted from IBEAR's research support, eight books have been published by Oxford, Lexington, Ballinger, Wiley & Sons, and Prentice Hall presses.

CIBEAR

IBEAR also assists the school and the university in its internationalization. As part of this effort, on behalf of the University and in cooperation with the School of Letters, Arts and Sciences, IBEAR successfully applied to the U.S. Department of Education for designation as one of sixteen national Centers for International Business Education in 1990. Thirty curriculum development and research projects over the initial three-year period beginning in October 1990 all helped to extend internationalization to many additional programs and faculty in the school and university. In addition, more recently the Department of Education awarded two additional $100,000 grants to CIBEAR, as part of Secretary Baker's Southeast Asia Initiative (USC's national center is called CIBEAR and is housed as a unit of IBEAR).

Many of CIBEAR's projects are aimed directly at expanding the international opportunities of undergraduate and MBA business students. For example, the school and the College of Letters, Arts & Sciences are working together to develop new international business minors for business undergraduates and graduates. Another team is designing a joint undergraduate major in Business and East Asian studies. A summer business internship program for MBA students in Asia has begun and a second program for Europe is planned. Another project provides support for a spring MBA seminar and field trip to Japan. Twenty MBA students participated in the first CIBEAR-sponsored trip in 1991 and twenty-four participated in 1992. Twenty-four other MBA students traveled to Europe to study its telecommunication industry. Other project teams are developing an elective, a Doing Business with Asia seminar for MBA students, and studying how to implement admission preferences for "internationalized" American applicants to the MBA program.

The University curriculum committee approved in 1992 a proposal designed by the school's International Business Task Force, chaired by Professor Larry Greiner, for a two-and-one-half year international MBA track for full-time MBA students, which includes language study and an internship abroad. This innovation will allow the school to serve a larger number of two-year MBA students who want more robust international business education.

Other CIBEAR curriculum projects are designed to provide new opportunities to nonbusiness majors and to the business community. For example, CIBEAR funds ensured that intensive summer language courses in Japanese, Chinese, and Korean at the beginning and intermediate levels are available, even if enrollments are limited. A year-long international business course for nonbusiness advanced degree candidates, staff, and faculty has been developed by business school faculty, and a multidisciplinary seminar on East Asia for graduate students has been developed by Asian studies faculty from various disciplines.

Other CIBEAR projects enhance IBEAR's ability to deliver executive education programs to the business community (e.g., a new program on Mexico) or faculty development. A host of research conferences and research projects are scheduled. Finally, the two projects funded under Secretary Baker's Southeast Asia Initiative allow IBEAR to establish linkages with two Indonesian educational institutions while contributing to faculty research and development related to Indonesian business.

IBEAR ORGANIZATION

In USC terms, IBEAR is a program, not an academic department. School faculty are housed in five functional departments—

Accounting, Decision Systems, Finance and Business Economics, Management and Organization, and Marketing. Faculty who teach in the IBEAR MBA Program or who take part in IBEAR-sponsored research do not have joint appointments in IBEAR.

IBEAR is directed by two academics whose appointments are as full-time administrators. Both are Ph.D.s and have adjunct faculty titles. Their primary responsibility is to manage and market IBEAR programs. Both teach one course per year in the IBEAR MBA Program and in executive programs. Much of their time is spent in "outreach" activities with the business and government communities.

IBEAR's director since 1982 (Richard L. Drobnick) and associate director are supported by two assistant directors—one responsible for IBEAR MBA admission and staff oversight, the second in charge of CIBEAR and IBEAR Executive Programs; two program managers, one for the IBEAR MBA Program day-to-day management and the other to support the assistant director for CIBEAR and IBEAR Executive Programs; a secretary/receptionist, a part-time publications consultant, and work-study students. In addition, IBEAR employs a senior research associate and hosts several visiting scholars. Funds generated by the IBEAR MBA Program, IBEAR executive programs, grants, and gifts allow it to operate on a self-supporting basis.

USC's Approach To Business School Issues

Approaches to business school internationalization are many and varied. USC's approach over the past fifteen years clearly has its strengths and weaknesses. Painted with a broad brush, the most important components of this approach are discussed below. My emphasis here is, however, different from other descriptions of business school internationalization, most of which emphasize content or substance issues—what types of courses should be taught in which degree programs. The implication is that the design of the program is the most important factor in explaining successful internationalization.

My own opinion is that organization, resources, and marketing should be given more attention in the process of internationalization. For example, can we better explain the University of South Carolina's rapid increase in stature in international business by the design or content of the MIBS program, or by the nature of the faculty and administrators that were hired and the way they were organized? I suspect that leadership, organization, motivation, and commitment explain South Carolina's success better than program design.

LEADERSHIP SUPPORT FROM ADMINISTRATION

IBEAR was established as a result of the initiative of the dean and associate dean of the school in the mid-1970s. The initial director was the associate dean. From the beginning, IBEAR enjoyed the benefits of support from the senior leaders in the school.

Furthermore, the tenure of the dean who established IBEAR continued through the program's first ten years. He selected the two individuals who have served as IBEAR directors during these fifteen years and was also involved in selection of the three associate directors. These factors assured that IBEAR consistently received strong support and attention from the school during its formative years.

ADMINISTRATIVE CONTINUITY
AND PROFESSIONAL MANAGEMENT

IBEAR has been led by only two directors and three associate directors since planning for the unit began fifteen years ago. The present director, associate director, and one assistant director have served for 10, 8, and 12 years, respectively.

Assuming that the leaders will remain motivated and energetic, this level of continuity can provide significant benefits to an organization. There have been no major changes in the mission of IBEAR or the philosophy underlying the IBEAR MBA Program throughout their history. This stability has permitted the original strategy to unroll in a rather smooth, continuous manner over the past fifteen years. In addition, one or more of our present staff members is personally familiar with almost all of our IBEAR MBA Program graduates. Personal relationships and our determination to keep track of the location and position of all of our graduates have facilitated IBEAR MBA recruiting. Nearly 50 percent of new IBEAR participants first learn of the program from our graduates or from past sponsor firms.

In addition, the IBEAR director and associate director are hired as full-time administrators, charged exclusively with managing and marketing IBEAR programs. They have no formal responsibility to teach in the school. By their own choice, both teach one course each year in the IBEAR MBA Program. This allows them sufficient time and fixes responsibility of planning, administration, outreach, and program promotion.

STRONG REVENUE BASE

The IBEAR MBA Program generates revenue each year equivalent to that generated by 90 two-year, full-time USC MBA students. This is adequate to cover staff, faculty, overhead, and operating expenses for IBEAR. Over and above this, it also generates sufficient funds to support faculty research. IBEAR's executive education programs have also been self-supporting on a full-costing basis. Two large U.S. Department of Education grants in the mid-1980s and early-1990s have further stabilized its position in the school. This revenue base allows IBEAR to promote internationalization within the USC business school more effectively than would otherwise be possible.

MARKET-DRIVEN, MARKETING-ORIENTED

Two IBEAR senior administrators spend more than one-half of their time promoting IBEAR programs and developing relationships with the corporate and government communities in the United States and abroad.

The relative youth and unique one-year, mid-career design of the IBEAR MBA Program and IBEAR's emphasis on non-degree international executive education shape the culture of the unit and the demands on these administrators time. Both require more promotion than two-year MBA programs or general management executive education programs. In both cases, the potential audience is relatively small.

Earlier, I mentioned the growth of the IBEAR MBA Program from an initial class of 15 in 1978-79 to a full class of 48 for each of the last four years. This growth reflects the extensive marketing efforts of IBEAR since 1985. Two IBEAR administrators travel to Asia and Europe regularly. The typical three-week trip entails as many as 90 meetings with past and potential sponsor firms, alumni, academics, American executives in the local chapter of the American Chamber of Commerce, and potential participants.

This personal contacting is supported by an aggressive direct mail and advertising campaign during the year. At present, 15,000 program booklets and 13,000 smaller brochures are printed for program promotion. Three thousand booklets are mailed each fall to potential sponsor firms. Nearly 20,000 pieces of direct mail are sent during the year using GMAT Search Service mailing labels. We also keep in contact with IBEAR supporters by mailing 3,000-5,000 copies of the IBEAR quarterly newsletter.

This direct-mail effort is supported by a print ad campaign in magazines such as *The Economist, Far Eastern Economics Review,* the *Asian Wall Street Journal Weekly,* the *Asian Wall Street Journal* and others.

Finally, a network of IBEAR alumni serve as admission advisors to potential applicants. After 14 years, nearly one-half of our participants come to us though alumni referrals or repeat sponsorship by past corporate sponsors.

NICHE-ORIENTED

Many years ago, the USC business school decided that IBEAR would emphasize the Pacific Rim. It has remained true to that commitment. While some faculty members are involved in research, consulting, and executive teaching in Europe and other regions (and, of course, use many international cases in their teaching), we have decided that we cannot effectively emphasize all regions equally well.

Further, students with a strong interest in Latin America or Europe will soon be able to apply for internships in those regions through CIBEAR. However, those with exclusive interest in a region other than the Pacific Rim may find better support for that interest at other institutions.

This niche approach has allowed USC to benefit significantly from the incredible growth of trade between the United States and Asia and from the fact that other universities do not provide similar Pacific Rim focused programs. For example, over 60 percent of the participants in our Asia country-focused executive programs come from the Midwest and East Coast.

TOP-DOWN, TRICKLE-DOWN INTERNATIONALIZATION

In its first twelve years, IBEAR emphasized its mid-career degree program and executive education. IBEAR's internationalizing impact was stronger on the executive MBA Program and on executive programs than on the two-year MBA or undergraduate programs. Its main impact came indirectly through faculty who came to USC, in part because of IBEAR's existence, or who became more international in orientation because of their teaching experience in the IBEAR MBA Program. As explained earlier, the recent CIBEAR grant has allowed IBEAR and the school to engage in a much broader range of curriculum development projects.

"WE DO IT WITH MIRRORS"

Few business schools have enough resources to internationalize in great depth using only their own faculty. For a variety of reasons, including the backgrounds of its senior staff and the incentives of the U.S. Department of Education grants, IBEAR uses faculty resources from wherever they are available. It has developed a significant partnership with USC's Asian area studies and language faculty. It uses academic faculty from throughout the United States in its executive education programs. Many executives serve as guest faculty in its programs.

These are the major components of the USC IBEAR approach to internationalization. While much remains to be done, this relatively distinctive approach has served us reasonably well to date.

Internationalization as Strategic Change at The Western Business School (Canada)

PAUL W. BEAMISH

INTRODUCTION

As all business schools have discovered, internationalization is not easy. It legitimately means different things to different people; it is constantly evolving; expensive in time and money; multifaceted; and to those of us who are among the committed minority, absolutely essential for institutional relevance. The purpose of this paper is to share the recent experiences of the Western Business School, Ontario, Canada, in its attempts to further internationalize its faculty, curriculum, and programs. It is not intended as a general guideline or blueprint for what other business schools should or should not do because internationalization in its operationalization is situation specific: greatly dependent on the prevailing institutional culture, history, resources, and attitudes.

The basic premise of this chapter is that internationalization is an exercise in strategic change. A change framework we have found useful provides a structure for the discussion. The first part of the chapter provides an overview of the school and its major international programs and emphasis. This context is essential to understanding the current stage of the school's internationalization activities, as described in the second section. It looks at the school's activities in relation to a framework on "Achieving Readiness for Strategic Change." Here the change targets are the development of awareness, capability, and commitment. The second part concludes with a review of some of the school's yet-to-be resolved questions.

Internationalization is defined as the evolving awareness and acknowledgement by the manager/organization/country of the impact of nondomestic forces on its economic future, and the translation of the latter into new attitudes and behaviors regarding the establishment and conduct of transactions with those in, and from, other countries. In the context of a business school, it is the evolving awareness and acknowledgement by the faculty—and ultimately the students—of that impact.

Internationalization is not a goal unto itself, but a means to an end. This point is important if an institution is not to lose sight of why it is internationalizing. The desired end is to increase the competency possessed by the managers we train. Numerous studies, including those conducted in Canada by the National Centre for Management Research and Development, and The Corporate Higher Education Forum, have consistently pointed toward the necessity of increasing the international competency of Canadian managers. The issue is not whether to internationalize, but how to do so.

HISTORICAL OVERVIEW OF THE WESTERN BUSINESS SCHOOL

The Western Business School is a professional school within The University of Western Ontario, one of the oldest of Canada's sixty-five universities. Founded in 1878, Western is now an academic community of seventeen faculties and professional schools, serving more than 26,000 students with over 4,000 faculty and staff.

Located in London, Ontario, a city of 300,000 people in the most densely populated area of Canada, it is halfway between Toronto and Detroit and 100 kilometers from the United States border at Port Huron. It is within a morning's drive of thirteen Canadian universities, sixteen community colleges, and several U.S. campuses.

Historically, the school has been a leader in management development. A partial list of achievements follows. They illustrate the proactive nature of change at Western, and provide the context for the school's internationalization efforts.

- In 1922 the first undergraduate business department in Canada was established;
- In 1932 the school began to publish its own journal. Known initially as the *Commerce Journal* it changed its name in 1950 to *Business Quarterly* and has been published regularly ever since. It reaches out to both academic and management audiences and in 1991, enjoyed a circulation of 10,000 in twenty-five countries;
- In 1948, establishment of Canada's first executive development program (from the beginning, faculty members were

required, as part of their responsibilities, to produce case material for the new programs being designed);
- In 1948, establishment of the School of Business Administration and the first MBA program in Canada;
- In 1961, Canada's first Ph.D. program in business was introduced;
- In 1974, official designation by the Government of Canada as Canada's first Centre for International Business Studies (CIBS). Financial support for this Centre was provided by the Federal Department of External Affairs. In 1991 the role of CIBS is catalyst and coordinator for the school's international activities. The staff involves a director (quarter time), a full-time executive assistant, and associates hired on a per-project basis. CIBS receives annual federal government funding of $90,000. The CIBS Director enjoys a great deal of discretion regarding funds allocation;
- In 1975, opened its own case and publications office. This office holds an inventory of 2500 Canadian cases and is the Canadian clearing house for 5000 Harvard cases;
- In 1978, commencement of its first international student exchange program with the London Business School, England;
- In 1984, the school took a leading role in establishing the National Centre for Management Research and Development with support from the Canadian Federal Government;
- In 1986, the Hall Report assessed Western as the leading school in Canada according to all of the groups questioned—managers, government, academics;
- In 1987, the case clearing house at Cranfield in the UK began to distribute Western cases in Europe. In 1991, Western cases were being distributed to over 100 teaching institutions and 100 corporations in over 20 countries; Western is the second largest producer of management case studies in the world, with over 1,000,000 copies studied each year by people outside the university;
- In 1992, Western was selected to be home for the next five years to the world's most prestigious academic journal on international business, *Journal of International Business Studies*.

As of 1992, the school had 65 full-time faculty who taught 500 MBA, 300 undergraduate and 50 Ph.D. students, plus executives in a wide range of programs. Its broad objective is to be widely recognized as one of the top 10 business schools in the world on the basis of its outstanding teaching programs, with a creditable research record in selected areas.

Internationally, the school has regularly been involved with major offshore projects, and currently is involved in China and five republics in the former Soviet Union.

PREVIOUS OFFSHORE PROJECTS

CAMBRIDGE

From 1965 to 1985, a team of Western Business School faculty was the core resource at the International Marketing Programme held at Cambridge, England. This was a four-week program attended by functional executives from Western European companies. In 1986 the program transferred to Ashridge Management College in England.

THE UNIVERSITY OF THE WEST INDIES

In 1971, a five-year contract was signed with CIDA (Canadian International Development Agency) to assist the University of the West Indies in developing the business program on its Jamaica and Trinidad campuses. The scope of this project included assistance in developing faculty in Canada and in the Caribbean, preparing teaching materials, designing and delivering degree and executive programs, and designing and building new physical facilities.

BRAZIL

From 1976 through 1981, a consortium of major corporations operating in Brazil sponsored a series of annual executive development programs offered by the school in Brazil. This initiative laid the foundation for a Brazilian-based executive development organization, which continues to operate very successfully.

KENYA

The Canada-Kenya Executive Management Program was an annual two-week, residential, senior general management course taught in Kenya, which ran from 1983 to 1987. The program was sponsored locally by Kenyan corporations with some financial assistance provided by CIDA. As part of this program, the Western faculty produced over twenty case studies on African companies.

PAKISTAN

In 1985, a group of major corporations and businessmen in Pakistan established the first, privately financed university-level management education institution in Lahore. Western's Business School has established an informal relationship with the new Lahore University of Management Sciences. Western's dean was a member of the school's Visiting Committee along with academics from such schools as Harvard, IMD, and the London Business School. In 1988-89, a Western faculty member served as dean in Lahore.

CURRENT OFFSHORE PROJECTS

PEOPLE'S REPUBLIC OF CHINA

Since 1984, Western has been linked with Tsinghua University in Beijing (and more recently also Dalian University of Technology, and Southeast University in Nanjing) to assist in the development of Chinese institutional capacity for management education. This has involved visiting scholars to Western, short-term instruction in the PRC, and the development of teaching materials. In 1992-93, eleven books will be published in Chinese coauthored by Western faculty, five are new international casebook compilations and six are translations). Also, the design, development, and delivery of a pilot program to train the trainers took place in the PRC in 1992.

COMMONWEALTH OF INDEPENDENT STATES (EX-USSR)

In May 1991, a new initiative saw twenty-seven Western students/ recent graduates, in Moscow and St. Petersburg, either teaching Introductory Business or writing case studies on Soviet-foreign enterprises. This program has been organized through the efforts of CIBS and the student International Business Club. This internship experience was repeated in 1992, this time with fifty-five students, and funding from External Affairs and International Trade, Canada.

OTHER MAJOR INTERNATIONAL ACTIVITIES

THE STUDENT EXCHANGE PROGRAM

Western's international student exchange program is one of the most extensive in the world. Introduced in 1978, over forty Western MBA and undergraduate students and forty foreign students

EXHIBIT 1

Achieving Readiness for and Implanting Strategic Change

Change Target Development	Potential Obstacles	Common Management Tactics
Awareness understanding: Establishing a general appreciation of the need for, and direction of, change	Ambiguous change requirements	Informal contact, lobbying
Building a greater depth of knowledge of the situation, its consequences, and potential remedies	Inertial resistance Information bnecks Limited capacity to understandstand	Loosening up exercises-target exposure, involvement Short-term task forces
Capabilities: Developing capacity to perform new tasks	Personnel bottlenecks—inadequate training and experience Support systems bottlenecks Behavioral resistance	Training programs Support systems development Personnel changes Direct coaching
Commitment: Developing genuine agreement about and support for the required changes	Displacement of the problem Behavioral resistance Inaentive systems Weak position of power and incentive systems Weak position of power	Involvement activities Partial solutions and demonstrations Negotiations Coalition building Coercion Personnel changes
Adoption: Achieving change in behavior, effective performance	Tangible risk Lagging resistance, support factors Poor readiness	Close monitoring Intensification and recycling of readiness efforts Mop-up action
Reinforcement: Sustaining effort and diligence in performance of new tasks	Loss of commitment Resource and organizational inconsistencies	Rewards for new behavior Adjustment of resource and organizational factors
Recycling: Defining and implementing improvements and new directions	Problems in linking a series of changes Complacency	Training and structuring for flexibility Continuous challenges for improvement

now participate in it each year. The students selected to take part spend one term of their second year at a high-quality business school overseas, while a similar number of exchange students come to Western. Foreign language fluency is necessary at some exchange locations. In mid-1992, formal relationships existed with fourteen institutions. Plans are underway to increase the number of linkages.

INTERNATIONAL PROFESSORSHIPS

In 1990, the Management Board of the National Centre for Management Research and Development announced two new international professorships. The Royal Bank Professorship in International Business is for a research program entitled "Managing for Global Effectiveness." The Donald F. Hunter Professorship in International Business (A Maclean Hunter Endowment) is for a program on "Doing Business in the United States". In 1991, the William G. Davis Chair—which alternates between the Departments of Economics and Business Administration—began a four-year term in the business school and focuses on international business.

MBA AND UNDERGRADUATE INTERNATIONAL COURSES

The HBA (Honors Business Administration)/MBA international elective courses offered during 1990–91 were: International Business, International Management Behavior, International Finance, Global Operations Management, Multinational Management, and Independent Study. In 1991–92, a multisection Multinational Marketing course was also offered. Enrollment in an international elective averaged over one per student, from a total requirement of eight electives. In 1992, the required second-year two-term Strategic Management course became, for all intents and purposes, an International Strategy Management course.

EXECUTIVE PROGRAMS

The school offered a three-week executive International Management Course (IMC) from 1977 to 1990. The course attracted participants from around the world, and was the only comprehensive international executive program annually available in Canada. With the increased internationalization of the other schools' executive programs, IMC was discontinued. An example of the increasing international content in the other programs is the visit of the Executive MBA class to the PRC in 1993 to fulfill one of its course requirements.

INTERNATIONAL PUBLICATIONS

A prominent area of research is in international joint ventures and alliances. The Western Business School is the leading school, worldwide, for research on international joint ventures and alliances. Books and articles for leading journals have been written, and on-going research—in part through doctoral studies—is under-taken/conducted.

The quality of the school's international research is reflected by the prominent position occupied by its published articles in the world's leading international business journal, *Journal of International Business Studies*. Western ranked second in the world among contributing institutions in articles published over the 1987-1991 period, and first since 1989. The international research output of the faculty is escalating.

INTERNATIONALIZATION AS STRATEGIC CHANGE

Exhibit 1 provides a general framework to achieve readiness for and implant strategic change. A similar approach has been used in Chapter Two. In this section, the first half of this framework has been applied to the issue of business school internationalization. The CIBS director or the school's administrators have implicitly or explicitly used this framework to guide activities for achieving change. Achieving readiness for change is only half the process, as the appended exhibit would suggest. In our experience however, it is the place where the greatest effort is required. The international-ization examples provided are intended as illustrations of the variety of initiatives used at Western.

STAGE 1—AWARENESS UNDERSTANDING

The first stage in achieving readiness for strategic change is Awareness Understanding—establishing a general appreciation of the need for, and direction of change; and building a greater depth of knowledge of the situation, its consequences, and potential remedies. This is an oft-overlooked stage, with many potential obstacles. One obstacle is a limited capacity to understand the importance of the change. As Chapter Three notes, over three-quar-ters of the faculty members at North American business schools (including Western) never took an international business course as graduate students. Theoretically, however, it should be easier to internationalize a Canadian business school than an American one. Due in part to the 1989 Canada-U.S. Free Trade Agreement, which received far more public discussion in Canada, most Canadians are well aware of Canada's dependence on trade in order to maintain its high standard of living.

A second obstacle is inertia. For some, the attitude seems to be: "I have achieved a successful career at a leading business school without personally adopting an international orientation, so why should I change now?"

A third obstacle is ambiguous change requirements. Some faculty members acknowledge that they hear the oft-repeated mantra—to "globalize." However, they quickly conclude that it is so complex and fuzzy that they do not know where to start—and hence don't.

These and other obstacles can be overcome by utilizing various tactics. One tactic initiated by a recent dean at Western was the use of short-term task forces. In a comprehensive review during 1989-90 of potential international activities that the school could engage in, a total of eighteen faculty/senior staff were divided into task forces to investigate particular issues. Many of these individuals were intentionally included because they did not have a particular international background. However, every task force had at least one member who was internationally experienced.

A second tactic for overcoming a lack of awareness understanding is to target certain individuals for particular attention. One of the internationalization changes that the CIBS director ultimately hoped to see in place was the creation of a required course in international business at the doctoral level. However, such a change was not originally on the Ph.D. program chairman's agenda. In order to help him develop a greater depth of knowledge of the need for such a change, numerous meetings were held, and relevant articles provided to him. In a relatively short period of time he became a strong supporter of the proposed change. He recognized that the internationalization dimension in his jurisdiction involved ensuring that all future faculty (i.e., Ph.D. candidates) received the relevant training; International Management Theory and Research became a required course in 1992.

Another way of involving faculty is to keep the issue of internationalization on the agenda at faculty meetings. In virtually all of the recent annual two-day faculty retreats, the dean has ensured that internationalization was a focal issue for discussion.

STAGE 2—CAPABILITY

The second stage in achieving readiness for strategic change is to develop the capability for change. While individuals may appreciate the need for, and direction of, change, without the capacity to perform new tasks, the process stops. One of the common obstacles to change is inadequate training and experience among existing personnel. Although faculty may not have had Ph.D.-level training in international business, there certainly exist postdoctoral methods of acquiring a similar perspective. However, are they in place? A second obstacle to developing capability is bottlenecks in the support systems. An example of this would be a faculty member who would like to do research/casewriting in another country, but is unable to obtain funding due to lack of an international track record. A third obstacle preventing faculty from developing the capacity to perform new tasks is their own behavior. They may acknowledge the importance of changing, but continue to resist change by not allocating the time to develop the capability.

In order to overcome capability obstacles, several strategies can be employed. The first of those used at Western are internal training programs. With financial assistance from a corporate sponsor, eight faculty visited England for a two-week study tour during the summer of 1990. A separate initiative involved having the faculty who teach international business conduct a two-day seminar on what they teach, for noninternational business faculty.

A second, more frequently used tactic for developing capability, is direct coaching. For example, to assist a faculty member visiting a country for the first time, this could involve one-on-one discussions regarding such things as teaching through interpreters, suggested background readings, names of contacts, briefings on cultural differences likely to be observed, and so forth.

A third capability-building tactic is support system development. The school's Director of Research and Publications has assisted here by building a bias toward international research into the financial support provided to school-funded projects.

STAGE 3—COMMITMENT

The third and final stage for achieving readiness for strategic change is commitment. Here we see the development of genuine agreement about, and support for, the required change. A variety of potential obstacles inhibit the development of commitment. One of these is displacement of the problem. Here, for example, one may hear the argument that while internationalization is important, it is no more important (or less important) than such things as ethics, women in management, entrepreneurship, or other topics of the day. A second obstacle is behavioral resistance. Since we are now approaching the actual adoption of the change, it is here that we sometimes observe individuals backing away from their tentative commitments. Examples would include canceling meetings or trips. A third obstacle to the development of commitment can be inadequate or inconsistent support or incentive systems. For example, a faculty member newly oriented toward international business may find that previously promised support from existing International Business faculty to be too brief. The final, and perhaps most obvious, obstacle to the development of commitment to internationalization is a weak position of power. Without the ability to ensure the allocation of the necessary resources—whether financial or human—the speed and effectiveness of internationalization are impeded.

The first tactic available for overcoming obstacles to the development of commitment to internationalization is involvement activities. We have observed numerous examples that have led to such a commitment. These range from inclusion of noninternational business oriented faculty on international consulting project teams or training programs, to requests from the school's senior administrators to these same faculty that they perform a task on the school's behalf. Such activities range from representing the school at an international meeting or conference to making a pre-arranged presentation on the school's international activities, to collecting data on the international activities of other schools.

A second tactic for developing commitment is to aim for at least a partial solution or demonstration so as to show progress. Examples we have used are offering new international course electives or negotiating new student exchange programs on a two-year trial basis.

Building coalitions or alliances is a third useful tactic for achieving commitment. We have often observed individual faculty with an attitude that they would be ready to commit if one key limitation could be overcome. This limitation might relate to a foreign language deficiency or discomfort at arriving in a strange country without knowing anyone. Through previously established coalitions, we are often able to reduce anxiety by arranging for an interpreter or guide—and typically also permit the host contacts to play some additional role of interest to them.

When the desired commitment is not forthcoming, personnel changes are sometimes required. These are obviously not personnel changes of the toe-the-line-or-be-fired variety. Rather, they more frequently relate to careful selection of people for key committees affecting internationalization, or changing the desired criteria for new faculty recruitment.

Certainly a way of looking at the whole question of achieving readiness for change, which was not explicitly addressed in the framework, is to tie the entire internationalization question back to personal incentives. We have observed that many faculty ultimately buy into internationalization, only after they have concluded that to do so will bring personal advantages. Potential personal advantages that can trigger a faculty member's willingness to change are many. These include:

1. recognizing that the environment of business has changed and that there is a professional responsibility to keep pace;
2. financial incentives either through consulting, executive training, or research funding;
3. a desire for new experiences, which may lead, for example, to a desire to visit for some time at a foreign institution.

To facilitate internationalization, a key task is to identify faculty's source of motivation.

CONCLUSION

The faculty at Western has made solid progress on some dimensions of internationalization. Yet, we acknowledge that the school is still grappling with a number of basic questions. Fundamentally, these relate to knowing when to say NO to requests.

1. *Geographic Focus*—Should there be a school research/case writing program focused on certain countries/regions? If yes, which should they be? The current responses range from (a) faculty should focus on wherever they want to; (b) they should focus on Canada's major trading partners (present and projected); (c) they should focus on an America's trading bloc, and so forth.
2. *Area-Group Emphasis*—In order to reduce the probability of the development of divided camps of committed versus uncommitted faculty, should attempts be made to have faculty internationalization proceed at a pace that is roughly uniform across all area groups? Western operates with a functional area group structure wherein internationally oriented faculty are distributed among seven area groups. Enormous variability exists among area groups and their international business capability and orientation. For example, in March 1991, the most internationally oriented area group—the Business Policy group—decided to eliminate their high enrollment, multisection International Business elective and roll all of its key international content into the

three terms of required courses that they teach. This, to them, was the most significant step they could take regarding curriculum internationalization since they believed that "business is international business." In contrast, some of the other area groups have minimal international content in either the required or elective courses that they teach—and no obvious plans to change. Thus, in terms of area group emphasis, should each area group be encouraged/ permitted to do as they see fit, or should there be a certain desired range?

3. *Scale of Involvement*—How do we know (if ever) that we have enough international course content, experience, and so forth? Although we have a broad consensus on reasonable targets for the numbers of visiting foreign faculty, students participating on international exchange etc., in other areas there is less certainty. At the urging of Dean Adrian Ryans, in 1991, data were collected on the international activities of other major business schools in Europe and the United States that Western considers to be within its reference group. It nonetheless remains an open question: "How much internationalization is enough?"

4. *Target Audiences*—There are a range of constituencies with varying, sometimes conflicting, interests in internationalization. These include faculty, clients (students), and customers (employers). Recognizing that what is good for one group may not be good for another, where should the relevant emphasis be placed?

5. *Profile of International Activity*—Some business schools primarily engage in international activities that have a high profile. This is done in order to maximize external publicity (and/or fund-raising potential), to provide a symbolic rallying point, or for reasons of focus. There is no necessary correlation between the profile and the internal value of international activities. Western has grappled, without resolution, with the question of whether to engage in a high profile activity such as the establishment of an offshore campus. As the attached exhibit indicates, a great deal of variability exists regarding the profile of the international activities that business schools can engage in.

6. *Who Decides*—Relating to all five of these basic questions facing Western is the issue of determining a process for resolving these questions. Do we wait for a complete faculty consensus to develop? Does the dean decide? Does the CIBS director attempt to champion a particular approach?

EXHIBIT 2

**The International Activities Business Schools Can Engage In
and Their Profile With Various Constituencies**

	Student	*Corporate Employers and Donors*	*Faculty*
Low Profile	Provide International Electives	Solicit funds for, and advice on, faculty research	−Most research/case writing −Participate in study tours by Faculty −Provide Ph.D.-level course in international business
Medium Profile	Provide International Student Exchange Programs	Solicit funds for international research chairs	−Provide specialized out-of-country training assistance programs
High Profile	Provide Specialized International MBA Program	Seek participation in a specialized ongoing executive program in international business	−Become publicly recognized as a/the leading authority on a high-interest international business topic −Obtain editorial responsibility for a lead international business journal.

Unresolved internationalization questions remain. As with international business in general, this should not surprise anyone. Due to the constantly evolving environment of international business, business school internationalization will never be a steady-state phenomena. Nonetheless, to a point, it can be managed.

Perspectives On Curriculum: Indiana University

JOHN D. DANIELS

INTRODUCTION

I was asked to discuss perspectives on internationalization based on the experience of Indiana University's School of Business, hereafter referred to as IUSOB. Given the long history of extensive efforts to internationalize at IUSOB, I am tempted to extol or justify what has been done to date. But given this volume's objectives, my comments will center on those items that serve as lessons for business schools as they attempt to internationalize.

IUSOB, like most other schools, has both teaching and research missions, and it serves different publics—students (both degree and nondegree), employers, other academic institutions, and society at large. These publics are interrelated. For example, pertinent international business research may influence public policy and company practices, be injected into classroom assignments at IUSOB and elsewhere, and help train students for relevant employment within firms, other universities, and elsewhere. My primary emphasis will be on the *direct classroom internationalization* process; however, it is inevitable that I will make some secondary forays into related areas of internationalization. I shall assume that the need for an international perspective is a "given," rather than rehash evidence on growing global interdependence and the weakened U.S. competitive position. (The need for internationalizing is well covered in the chapters by Claude B. Cellich, Ben L. Kedia and Robert E. Scott.)

First, I will examine IUSOB's curriculum within the framework of its three degree programs and then I will discuss some of the indirect methods IUSOB has used to infuse more international components into its programs. The views expressed throughout these discussions are my own, inasmuch as I have made no attempt to gather a collective or representative opinion.

UNDERGRADUATE CURRICULUM

I shall first discuss the undergraduate curriculum because it is:

1. IUSOB's largest, with about 1300 graduates per year as compared with 300 for the MBA and 25 for the Ph.D.;
2. the only program with an already instituted international dimension; and
3. where some recent and unexpected data have been collected on the first students to graduate under the international dimension requirement.

At the undergraduate level, there is no international major or minor; however, there are two international business designated courses, and nine other courses with a significant international or foreign content within functional business areas or Economics. Students may fulfill their international dimension requirement by taking any two of these courses, by participating in an overseas study program, or by taking two advanced courses in either a foreign language or in one of seven area studies programs. A brief description of these courses is included in the appendix. IUSOB's approach is *to build a level of awareness or understanding*, rather than competency, for all undergraduate students through specialized courses, rather than infusion. (See the Chapter Two by Jeffrey S. Arpan for explanation of distinctions.)

A proposal for a concentration in international studies for business majors has recently been approved. This concentration will require that students complete an additional nine credit hours from among those courses acceptable under the international dimension. These need not be from the same category of courses, e.g., not all need be within a particular area studies program; however, students are required to demonstrate linkages among the courses they select. The purpose of recognizing this concentration is to encourage students to use their electives to internationalize themselves further, and perhaps move from an awareness to an understanding level, but not necessarily to a competence level. The concentration is institutionally significant inasmuch as IUSOB does not recognize minors, and this is the only sub-concentration permitted to be designated on transcripts. Both the requirement of an international dimension and the concept of an international concentration are largely the result of a proactive push by the director of undergraduate business studies. My suspicion is that faculty support would not have been as forthcoming had the proposals originated and been pushed by international business faculty, who might have been perceived as personally benefitting from the changes.

I was not a faculty member at Indiana University (IU) when the international dimension requirement was enacted. I must speculate somewhat since faculty who were at IU at the time of enactment now have very different perceptions and memories about the requirement's origin, rationale, and composition. However, because the class of 1991 was the first to graduate under this requirement, I have been present throughout the implementation and feel confident of the correctness of my surmise. There was evidently no study conducted on the extent to which students had heretofore been exposed internationally. Nevertheless, there was a general belief that most students had minimal international exposure and a general agreement that they needed more. (See Chapter Five by Ben Kedia.)

The decision to allow different means of fulfilling the international dimension requirement was based largely on resource availability, although there are pedagogical issues to which I shall return in my discussion. The expectation was that most students would prefer to take business and economics courses, particularly a redesigned two semester international business sequence (those with a D prefix in the appendix). However, the number of students who could be accommodated therein was quite limited for three reasons. First, there was no foreseeable faculty line addition. Second, a concomitant down-scaling of the Ph.D. program meant fewer doctoral students to staff undergraduate IB classes. Third, physical plant limitations hampered moves to larger classrooms. Therefore, foreign language and area studies programs, for which there was usually excess capacity, were seen as receptacles for overflow demand.

Data were collected in spring of 1991 on all the seniors who had applied to graduate in May 1991. These data include a substantial portion of the first group of students who needed the international dimension to graduate. There were two major surprises:

1. that fewer than class-capacity had opted to take business and economics courses for fulfillment, and
2. that so many had taken foreign languages to fulfill the requirement.

EXHIBIT 1

Fulfillment of International Dimension Options
Spring 1991 Seniors*

Option	Percentage
Language	52
Area Studies	25
International Business & Economics	12
Overseas Studies	11
Total	100

*Data are on 851 Indiana University School of Business students who had completed the requirement and applied to graduate in May 1991.

Exhibit 1 shows the percentage using each option for the 851 seniors who applied to graduate *and* who also completed the requirement. Excluded from these figures are three groups: foreign students who are exempt from the requirement (about 10), seniors who did not apply to graduate (about 386), and seniors who applied to graduate but had not yet fulfilled the requirement (about 139).

Only 12 percent took two or more of the eleven eligible business and economics courses to fulfill their international requirements. This surprised us, especially in the case of the two international business courses; however, there is evidence from recent registration figures that this is unrepresentative of future demand. One possible explanation is that the restructuring of the two international business courses, including course numbers and prerequisites, impacted on the 1991 senior class in their junior year. The change caused that class some confusion and made some students ineligible to take the courses. There were atypical problems in offering sufficient sections of international business courses that led not only to an inability to accommodate demand in sufficient popular time slots, but also to some likely decreased demand because students were skeptical that there would be sufficient course offerings for them to complete an international business sequence once they started one. This atypical situation was caused by a simultaneous leave of absence and an administratively reduced teaching load by two international business faculty members at the same time that the new course sequence was implemented. Further, IUSOB lacks some of the undergraduate international courses that are popular at other institutions, such as international marketing and international accounting. Area studies and language faculty also have indicated a likely future difficulty in accommodating many business students because of changes in liberal arts curricula.

That over half of the students opted for foreign language study surprised us, especially since freshman-level language courses did not qualify. The number is much higher than one would expect from figures by the Presidential Commission on Foreign Language Studies for U.S. students in general, or by the Dunhill Personnel System for U.S. managers. In retrospect, the most plausible explanation seems to lie in the relationship between the characteristics of the IUSOB student population and a loophole in the international dimension requirement. Business majors at IU are ordinarily admitted only after completion of their sophomore year, and entry has been the most competitive of any undergraduate college on campus in terms of SAT scores and GPAs. This group is more likely than the student population as a whole to have had high school language training, often for three or four years. Students can get credit for freshman or even advanced courses by taking language proficiency exams. This testing option also has GPA advantages, which are especially useful for gaining entry into the business school. To the extent that students gain advanced credit in foreign languages through proficiency exams, the international dimension is not likely to increase international exposure above what students had on entering the university. This testing-out of the international requirement may lessen in the future if entry into the business school becomes less competitive. The number of fall 1991 applications was down from prior years. Nevertheless, the loophole probably needs to be closed, which will then put more stress on the capacity of existing courses.

IU offers over 60 different foreign languages, purportedly a greater variety of foreign languages than any other university in the world; we therefore examined what languages were chosen by the 851 seniors who had fulfilled their international dimension requirement. The results are shown in Exhibit 2. These students received credit for 923 courses at the 200 level or above. Not surprisingly, 92 percent of these were in the traditional "big three," 46 percent in Spanish, 32 percent in French, and 14 percent in German. These are also the languages most frequently offered in high school, but they differ somewhat from a 1989 poll of U.S. firms on

EXHIBIT 2

Selection of Advanced Foreign Language Courses
Spring 1991 Seniors*

	Number	Percent
Chinese	17	2
French	291	32
German	126	14
Japanese	27	3
Italian	14	1
Latin	14	1
Spanish	424	46
Other	10	1
Total	923	100

*Data are on 851 Indiana University School of Business students who had completed their international dimension requirement and applied to graduate in May 1991.

the most important foreign language for the 1990-2010 period. This poll placed Spanish clearly ahead with 44 percent, followed by Japanese with 33 percent. The only other languages receiving at least a one percent response were French (8 percent), Chinese (6 percent), German (5 percent) and Russian (1 percent). A possible conclusion from these data is that few business students are apt to take advanced courses in other than the "big three" foreign languages because introductory courses are not available in their high schools. This signifies a continued deficiency of business school graduates who study those languages that are growing in importance, such as Japanese, Chinese, and Russian. It may therefore be advisable to experiment with incentives to take the non-traditional languages at the university level. For example, IUSOB could allow freshman courses in Japanese, Chinese, and Russian to fulfill the international dimension requirement.

That 25 percent of students took area studies courses to fulfill their international dimension requirement was about what had been expected; however, the choice among area programs is inconsistent with that of language studies. For example, East Asia accounted for 52 percent of the area studies courses, although Chinese and Japanese comprised only five percent of the language

EXHIBIT 3

Selection of Advanced Area Studies Courses
Spring 1991 Seniors*

	Number	Percent
Russian and East European	77	12
Uralic and Altaic	27	4
Near Eastern	6	1
African	26	4
West European	111	17
East Asian	328	52
Latin American and Caribbean	63	10
Total	638	100

*Data are on 851 Indiana University School of Business students who had completed their international business requirement and applied to graduate in May 1991.

courses taken. Latin American and Caribbean studies accounted for only 10 percent of area studies courses, although Spanish comprised 46 percent of the language courses taken. An implication is that *we may be graduating students who know the foreign language but not the history, geography, culture and politics where the language is spoken, or vice versa.* The proposed concentration in international studies may mitigate this situation somewhat.

Overseas studies programs in the Netherlands, Singapore, Yugoslavia (now Slovenia), and Germany accounted for 11 percent of the international dimension fulfillment. Although we have additional overseas programs in both a start-up and planning stage in France, Chile, and Australia, this option is not apt to play much greater future importance. Realistically, in a state-supported institution, most students can probably not avail themselves of foreign study opportunities.

The first senior class to be required to take the international dimension took an average of two and a half of the qualifying international courses, although only two were required. Unfortunately, we do not know whether a few or a large number of students account for most of the extra courses taken, how the average number of courses taken now compares with the average taken before the international requirement went into effect, or whether some courses serve as catalysts for further international course work.

MBA Curriculum

Students may select international business as a major or minor within the MBA program, and we encourage, but do not require, students to select a second major along with one in international business. Study abroad programs exist in the Netherlands, France, Finland, and Switzerland, and internship programs in France and Germany. No mandated international dimension for all students has been instituted; however, this will change. A new MBA structure has been approved to become operative with the incoming MBA class for fall 1992.

The first year of the new program is lock-step, and a substantive international dimension component is mandated for inclusion in each functional core course therein. Basically this is an infusion model, and this type of model has heretofore generally resulted only in very superficial (awareness level) treatment of international components as faculty are either unprepared or find there is no time to add the international course components. (Chapter Two by Jeffrey S. Arpan addresses this issue.) The challenges of the IUSOB infusion model within the MBA program are (1) to assure implementation beyond a shallow level and (2) to coordinate and complement that content, with coverage in specialized international business courses, which will continue to be offered. Between the first and second year of the program, all students must spend the summer in noncredit professional development work. This may take one of several forms, such as community involvement or an approved internship. One of the possible options is to participate in a concentrated language and area studies program to be offered by liberal arts faculty, essentially paralleling parts of the York University program described in Chapter Fifteen. In year two, students will have the option of taking functional or cross-functional majors and minors (the international business major will continue and be cross-functional), but all major sequences are supposed to include a substantive international dimension component. Students may take an international strategic management course to fulfill their strategic management requirement. Again, there is the challenge of implementing this component adequately.

A survey was administered to the entering MBA 1989 class prior to incorporating international content into the proposed MBA curriculum. This survey involved self-administered perceptional ratings on the degree of international proficiency based on guidelines that included foreign language training, foreign work and living experience, attendance in international business related courses, and international responsibilities within the workplace. The results showed that 53 percent had no international experience beyond a year or two of high school foreign language study. Another 17 percent were characterized as having minimum experience and barely usable skills. The remaining 30 percent had considerable international experience and skills. This latter group comprised 57 percent U.S. citizens and 43 percent foreign students. Further estimates showed that only about 35 percent of MBA students have been taking a specialized international business course before graduation, and about a quarter of these are made up of the group that already possesses high international skills. The implication from these data is *that the majority of the clientele to be served under the proposed MBA program would otherwise graduate with no more than a minimum of international exposure and some would otherwise graduate without even a level of awareness.*

DOCTORAL PROGRAM

IUSOB doctoral students may major or minor in international business (IB). This is a small program that has recently averaged only one student admission as a major and about three as minors per year. Because numbers are so low, it is difficult to speak with certainty about trends; however, my observation is that international business is increasingly perceived to be associated with the field of management at IU, rather than with other fields such as finance, marketing, business economics, and accounting. This may be partly because the international business program is now located within the management department and partly because other departments are requiring even more narrow specializations by permitting fewer choices of minors. The result is that nearly all the more recent majors and minors are studying IB in conjunction with strategy, which is also within the management department. It would be a helpful exercise to research whether international business is similarly associated with a single area at other schools. For example, if it is an appendage of the marketing department, does it take on a marketing focus? Such information would be useful in the long-standing and ongoing debate of whether IB should be a separate department/institute or part of a traditional department.

I have been quite vocal in recent years about my belief that business schools will never internationalize all their courses until all doctoral students are required to study and become proficient in the international nuances of their own areas, such as having all finance majors study the global integration of capital markets. (Chapter Three includes data on the overall internationalization of Ph.D. programs and indicates that only 17 percent of doctoral business graduates in the United States have taken one or more international courses.) If this were done, at least in the larger Ph.D. programs, we would begin to have a larger cadre of faculty over time who feel comfortable and compelled to include international dimensions in their own courses. They would more likely discuss international implications within their research. They might even integrate internationalism within their text books, which so far tend to put "international" into a separate chapter, if it is included at all. In the meantime, schools try to retool existing (usually senior) faculty, which may be expensive, too late, and not effective in solving the new-supply problem. (Chapter Twelve addresses the issues of retraining, inertia, and ambiguity of older faculty. See Chapter Five for an alternative viewpoint.) Unfortunately, IUSOB's doctoral program is akin to almost all other doctoral programs in business, in that it does not mandate an international dimension. The proposed changes within the IUSOB MBA program, if more than superficially implemented, may help to alleviate this problem inasmuch as doctoral students generally take many masters level courses, either during or in preparation for a doctoral program. Furthermore, after MBA changes are implemented, IUSOB may be able to focus on the doctoral program since it is the only remaining one without a mandated international component.

FOREIGN OUTREACH ACTIVITIES

IUSOB, like many other large business schools, has a long history of contractual arrangements abroad, including study abroad programs, executive development teaching, and management contracts to help start business programs. A major purpose of these arrangements is to create foreign opportunities for faculty to build an international commitment among participants. There is ample anecdotal evidence that returning faculty members are enthusiastic about their international experiences, but as far as I can determine, no one has systematically studied this experience at IU or elsewhere. My impression is that there are now more than enough international opportunities for faculty, but that there is a problem in getting the right faculty to take advantage of them. Further, more information would seem to be useful in formulating policy to implement international objectives, particularly since these outreach programs tend to be of high cost in terms of an institutional time commitment. For example, are faculty participants already more enthusiastic about internationalism than other faculty before they even go abroad? What is the before and after international content within their courses? Does the experience lead to an ongoing change in research focus to include more international perspectives? What percentage of faculty have participated once, and on multiple occasions? Until we have this information, we must make decisions based on intuitive assumptions that may or may not be correct.

IUSOB and other large, experienced business schools have long had in place most of the components often assumed to lead to student-internationalization. For example, IUSOB seems to have no shortage of foreign students (at least at the graduate level), foreign-born faculty, and foreign short- and long-term visitors. But once again, what has been the impact of these components?

INDIANA GLOBAL BUSINESS CENTER

Through private funding, IUSOB established the Indiana Global Business Center (IGBC), which was initially directed by a committee made up almost entirely of people teaching general or functional courses in international business. This committee believed that international business should eventually permeate every relevant course, rather than remain compartmentalized forever. IGBC suffered from the predictable problems of trying to operate by committee, especially since committee members received no perks for the responsibility. The committee members' objective of pushing international business throughout IUSOB also led to credibility problems inasmuch as that objective seemed too associated with the members' own personal and programmatic interests. The committee recommended that a director be appointed for the IGBC who would not be thus associated, and such a director was appointed half time in 1989. The internal advisory board is similarly now made up primarily of faculty outside the international business area. Effectively, the faculty constituency to foster international development has thus been greatly expanded, and when that constituency makes recommendations, they are less perceived as fostering the interests of the international business group than before. The downside of this approach is that there has thus been a great deal of "wheel reinventing," rather than a direct transfer of information from international business specialists to nonspecialists.

Probably the most notable impact of the ICGB so far has been on the proposed MBA program. None of the international initiatives that I have discussed were within the initial document prepared by the faculty committee that studied, drew up, and recommended program changes after several years of meetings. The ICGB advisory board then met with the committee and convinced it of the need for the international dimension aspects. The ICGB also established faculty grants to aid implementation of the changes, which greatly helped in gaining support. These grants can be used for faculty to add international dimensions to existing core functional courses that they teach by such means as workshop attendance or hiring of consultants to provide materials. Grants may also be given for developing and offering of the international noncredit summer work, such as for foreign travel/study tours, or workshops on specialized topics such as cultural awareness, European unification, business with historically planned economies, a Western Hemisphere free trade agreement, etc.

Two other types of grants have already been implemented by the ICGB. However, neither has yet achieved the primary objectives for which they were intended. In time, they may. The first is the granting of summer international research grants in addition to those offered already under IUSOB's extensive competitive summer program. ICGB decided to set its stipends at higher than those offered by the regular summer research program in order to encourage faculty to add an international dimension to their projects. In the first year, ICGB funded nine projects; however, in at least eight cases, the projects are by faculty who regularly do international business/economics research anyway. In all probability, there was little, if any, shift by the faculty as a whole to more international orientation in their research. (Chapter Four discusses the situation of promotion and tenure within narrowing functional specialties and the problem it creates in getting faculty to add international dimensions to their research.)

The second type of grants are for developing new international courses or adding a significant international dimension to an existing course. In the first year, an undergraduate international course was added in business law; however, the faculty member in question was not aware of the grant possibilities until after the course was developed and approved. This situation undoubtedly points out how difficult it has become to get faculty to even notice new initiatives, given the amount of memos and paperwork that deluge their offices.

STUDENT INITIATIVES

Of the most important recent impetuses for adding international dimensions to IUSOB, two came completely from student initiatives. A marketing club organized a two-day international conference attended by high-level individuals and teams from fifteen large international companies. Most made presentations in two classes. In addition, there were panel discussions and other meetings. These were very well attended and attracted high international visibility throughout IUSOB, which has helped gain support for other international initiatives.

The second initiative came from an international business club. Its members felt that neither international business students nor foreign students were being served adequately by the IUSOB placement office. Against considerable initial opposition, the club organized a two-day international and foreign career program. Five large firms sent speakers and interviewers, and over 100 students attended the conference. This program is now an annual affair, with more corporate participation and full cooperation from the placement office, which is now much more supportive of international business and foreign students in its overall placement activities.

CURRICULUM-PERFORMANCE RELATIONSHIP

In conclusion, I would like to put forward a plea for research relating types of international training to performance. Most of us are progressing on the basis of assumptions, which may or may not be accurate. Unless studies are undertaken, we may provide educational options that are suboptimum or require options that are inappropriate to particular career needs. Basically, the two major approaches to international training are content and process, each of which may be subdivided into other categories. For example, the content approach may focus on the examination of issues, problems, descriptions, and theories that are specific to the international arena. The specific content may be broken down further by function, region, or institution, usually by emphasizing factual nuances that may necessitate adjustments in operations. The process approach emphasizes tools to aid managers in perceiving, accepting, or adjusting to differences, although they may not anticipate what those differences are ahead of time. For example, sensitivity training may aid in gaining empathy with other values, and foreign languages may aid in learning about other areas more easily and in gaining acceptance from people therein.

But do all students need all of these approaches? Do all students need the same level of awareness, understanding, and competency? Probably not. Differences may exist along a number of dimensions, such as between students who will work as international business specialists, those who will have indirect international responsibilities within a multinational firm, and those who simply need to understand the effects of international competition within their own countries. Certainly, expatriates may have different needs than domestically based managers, even though both may have similar levels of international responsibilities. Needs may also differ for managers working for a U.S.-based multinational enterprise (MNE) and managers working in the United States for a foreign-based MNE. Of course, both content and process needs may differ, depending on where and in what function one works.

It would seem that there is now enough experience within firms and within business training programs that we can begin making assessments. Many of these assessments may have to be qualitative, rather than directly measurable. Once the assessments are complete, we may all begin to alter our curricula as needed to fit the specific needs of our own students, thereby leading to the improvement of international performance.

APPENDIX

INTERNATIONAL DIMENSION REQUIREMENT (BLOOMINGTON)

The international dimension requirement of the School of Business Undergraduate Program can be fulfilled in any one of the following four ways:

I. Language
Six hours of above 100-level courses in a foreign language.

II. International Business and Economics
Two courses selected from the following list:

BUS	D301	The International Business Environment
BUS	D302	International Business: Operations of International Enterprises
BUS	F494	International Financial Management
BUS	G494	Public Policy and the International Economy
BUS	L410	International Law
ECON	E306	Undergraduate Seminar in Economics*
ECON	E311	Modern Asian Economic History
ECON	E333	International Economics
ECON	E433	International Monetary Economics
ECON	E483	Population Change and Development
ECON	E497	Soviet-type Economics

III. Participation in Approved Overseas Study Programs
Participation in any approved overseas program of Indiana University will fulfill this requirement.

IV. Area Studies
Selection of two courses from one of the following area studies programs at Indiana University.
A. West European Studies

WEUR	W301	Contemporary West European Politics and Society
WEUR	W302	Contemporary Western Europe
WEUR	W405	Special Topics in West European Studies*
WEUR	W406	West European Integration

---

* This is a variable topics course. Credit is applied toward the international dimension requirement depending upon the topic. Students must obtain prior approval from the Business School Counseling Office.

POLS	Y331/	
	W405	British Politics
HIST	B357/	
	W405	Modern France
HIST	B361	Europe in the 20th Century
HIST	B372	English Constitutional History
HIST	B378	History of Germany Since 1848 II
GEOG	G428	Geography of Western Europe
SOC	S302	Bureaucracies

B. **East Asian Studies**

EALC	E100	East Asia: An Introduction
EALC	E256	Land and Society in East Asia
EALC	E271	Twentieth-Century Japanese Culture
EALC	E350/	
	E351	Studies in East Asian Civilization*
EALC	E302	Geographic Patterns in China
EALC	E394	Business and Public Policy in Japan
EALC	E457	Nationalism in Japan and China
ECON	E311	Modern Asian Economic History
GEOG	G340	Geography of South East Asia
HIST	H207	Modern East Asian Civilization
HIST	H208	American-East Asian Relations
HIST	G462	Modern China
HIST	G468	Modern Japan
HIST	G469	Miracle in Asia: Japan since 1945
POLS	Y362	Chinese Politics
POLS	Y334	Japanese Politics

C. **Latin American and Caribbean Studies**

LTAM	L300	The Latin American Experience
LTAM	L301	Contemporary Problems in Latin America
LTAM	L400	Contemporary Mexico
LTAM	L401	Seminar on Contemporary Latin America
LTAM	L402	Contemporary Brazil
LTAM	L406	Contemporary Peru and Chile
LTAM	L426	Special Topics in Latin American Studies*
POLS	Y337	Latin American Politics
ANTH	E321	Peoples of Mexico
ANTH	E322	Peoples of Brazil

D. **Russian and East European Studies**

ECON	E497	Soviet-type Economies
GEOG	G423	Geography of Eastern Europe
GEOG	G427	Geography of the Soviet Union
HIST	D302	Contemporary Soviet Society

HIST	T425	Soviet-American Relations Since 1945*
POLS	Y332	Soviet Politics
POLS	Y340	East European Politics
POLS	Y348	Comparative Communist Systems
HIST	D410	Russian Revolution and Soviet Regime
HIST	D418	Russian and Soviet Foreign Policy in the Twentieth Century
HIST	D428	Eastern Europe: 1914 to the Present

E. **Uralic and Altaic Studies**

URAL	U190	Introduction to Inner Asia
URAL	U251	Modern Turkey: Development and Culture
URAL	U370	Uralic Peoples
URAL	U394	Islam in the Soviet Union
URAL	U423	Hungary in the Twentieth Century
URAL	U469	Mongols of the 20th Century
URAL	U497	Inner Asian Peoples and the Nationality Policy in the People's Republic of China

F. **Near Eastern Studies**

NELL	N231	Peoples and Cultures of the Middle East II
NELL	N241	Contemporary Israeli Culture I
NELL	N242	Contemporary Israeli Culture II
POLS	Y339	Middle East Politics
REL	R356	The Religion of Islam
HIST	C392	History of the Modern Near East

G. **African Studies**

AFRI	L232	Africa in the Twentieth Century
ANTH	E310	Introduction to the Cultures of Africa
ANTH	E311	The Ethnography of Eastern Africa
GEOG	G425	Africa: Contemporary Geography Problems
HIST	E432	History of Africa II
HIST	E433	Conflict in Southern Africa
POLS	Y338	African Politics
POLS	Y342	Topics in the Regional Politics of Africa

---

* This is a variable topics courses. Credit is applied toward the international dimension requirement depending upon the topic. Students must obtain prior approval from the Business School Counseling Office.

Foreign students enrolled in the School of Business will be considered to have fulfilled the international dimension requirement.

Students entering Indiana University in Fall 1987 and afterwards, are subject to this requirement.

Language and International Trade at Eastern Michigan University[1]

RAY SCHAUB

INTRODUCTION

In 1978 Eastern Michigan University (EMU) initiated an undergraduate and graduate interdisciplinary degree program in language and business studies, to which it gave the name Language and International Trade (L&IT). In the years that have intervened, the program has had quite an interesting history. At the undergraduate level, L&IT has attracted the attention of a number of other institutions—foremost among them Clemson University, Southern Illinois University, and the University of Tennessee at Knoxville—who have emulated our initiative by developing similar programs modeled after ours. According to J. David Edwards, executive director of the National Council for Languages and International Studies, the undergraduate program in L&IT also served as a key model program for the federal legislation in 1988 that provided funding for the new International Business Centers through Title VI of the Higher Education Act. In 1989 and 1990, the *North American International Business* magazine gave us national recognition by ranking EMU's Master's degree in L&IT among the top twenty international business programs in the country, and by spotlighting our International Cooperative Education Exchange as one of the best known international co-op programs in the United States. And to round things out, in 1991 our own Board of Regents issued a special resolution in which it commended the faculty and staff of the Foreign Language Department, the College of Business, and the World College for all the fine accomplishments of L&IT.

185

This chapter describes salient aspects of the background, development, and impact of L&IT at EMU, and provides information on our experiences and perspectives that might be of value for other institutions now considering the development or refinement of their own international business programs.

ORIGIN IN CRISIS

L&IT was born in crisis. During the early 1970s, foreign language enrollments in U.S. colleges and universities underwent a major downturn. At EMU the decline was catastrophic. In the space of just a few years, the Foreign Language Department suffered a staggering loss of roughly 90 percent of its declared student majors. The primary reason for this was absolutely clear to those of us in the department who had been most actively involved in student advising. For a number of years, the great majority of our students—most of whom had studied foreign language in order to become foreign language teachers in the public schools—could not find teaching jobs. In those years, Michigan schools were severely affected demographically by declining populations of school-age children, and were hard hit financially by declining state tax revenues due to cutbacks in the automotive industry which were caused by the OPEC oil boycott. The result for the Foreign Language Department was inevitable. Most of those students, who in previous years would have majored in foreign languages, voted with their feet by entering other disciplines.

Our predicament worsened when the governor of Michigan appointed a special commission on higher education to review academic programs at state-supported colleges and universities. Among other things, the commission recommended to the governor that EMU's Foreign Language Department—which had fallen on demonstrably bad times—be abolished. While in time it became apparent that no one in Lansing or in our own administration intended to heed this advice—the recommendation looked like a flagrantly cheap shot because the commission had not even conducted an on-site inspection in our department but had instead obviously selected an easy mark for budget-cutting—the fact remained that the commission's report had received a lot of attention in the major newspapers in southeastern Michigan, and the plight of the beleaguered Foreign Language Department at EMU stood spotlighted for all the world to see. Coping with our department's problems and trying to come up with solutions had been difficult enough among ourselves, and our sudden notoriety in the press merely added insult to injury.

Although stunned by the crisis and the accompanying bad press, some of us in the Foreign Language Department felt challenged by all this adversity to do something about the situation we were in. Most of all, we felt challenged in a totally new way to defend the viability of our discipline and to demonstrate the value of foreign language study for a career field outside of foreign language teaching. And in responding to our predicament in this way, we were able to turn the crisis into an opportunity for positive change. We began to focus our thinking on the need to develop a new program of study to augment the traditional curriculum, a new program that would be more attractive to a greater number and a different population of students.

For several key reasons, the basic question of changing the curriculum never became the object of political dispute in the department. Because no one could deny the severity of the disaster that had befallen us, the crisis itself tended both to promote consensus among the more proactive members of the department and to silence those colleagues who, if times had been better, would have defended the status quo. Looking back, the crisis was in this sense an advantage. An equally important reason was that the faculty members who brought a high level of commitment to reforming the department were equally committed to and capable of working together as a team, thus also minimizing dissension. But perhaps the single most important factor that helped to preserve departmental unity in those troubled times was that the university administration—and first and foremost the dean of the College of Arts and Sciences—gave us full assurance from the outset that our teaching, research, and service in support of a new departmental curriculum would be rewarded on the same basis as professional activities in more traditional areas. It was only on the basis of this coincidence of internal consensus and support from the administration that the Foreign Language Department was able to focus its energies and find a solution to its problems.

EVOLUTION OF THE PROGRAM

During these years, the new challenge that foreign competition was posing to worldwide American business interests, and especially to Michigan's automotive industry, was assuming increasing importance. A few of us therefore began experimenting in the early

1970s with the idea of developing a new interdisciplinary program in language and business studies for students interested in careers in international business. By 1975 our internal discussions had progressed far enough to allow us to draw up a proposal for such a program, which would be housed in the College of Business and co-sponsored by the Foreign Language Department. In a meeting at which we presented the proposal to the dean of the College of Business, the dean gave us and the proposal very short shrift. In turning us down, he stated his opinion that (1) because English was already established as the language of international trade, it was unnecessary for Americans engaged in its conduct to speak a foreign language, and (2) international business was not that important for the economy of the United States anyway. While this unexpectedly blunt rejection stymied us temporarily, it actually served to strengthen our resolve to go forward with the proposal, because it convinced us that we were right and the dean of business was wrong. In time, we came to realize that this confrontation helped us more than it hurt us, because, in capsulizing so clearly the problem of American insensitivity toward our country's needs and its dangerous predicament in world trade, it helped us to focus better on the problem. It also showed us that, if anything was going to be done in the matter, the Foreign Language Department would have to play the central role in getting it done. With this realization, we went to work to design the basic framework of what we considered would be a credible and workable interdisciplinary program in international business.

In order to present a complete account of our working relationship with the College of Business in the years that have intervened since 1975, it is important to point out that every successor to the dean who at one point turned a deaf ear to us has now been fully supportive of our efforts to develop interdisciplinary international business programs. This cooperative relationship is now so well established—especially since the American Assembly of Collegiate Schools of Business began to mandate instruction in international business—that the Foreign Language Department and the College of Business see themselves as full partners and co-owners of these initiatives. In all fairness to the dean of business in 1975, it also should be said that at that time it was much easier for the Foreign Language Department to see the need for curricular reform, given its disastrously declining enrollments, than it was for the College of Business, which for many years had been and would continue to be inundated with students. In terms of this basic strategic difference, it was only right and proper for the Foreign Language Department to have the obligation to initiate the new program and to persuade the College of Business to support it.

It took three years—from 1975 to 1978—to put the L&IT program in place. Paradoxically, the key to success was another rejection. In 1976, the Foreign Language Department submitted to the Title VI, A grant program of the U.S. Department of Education a grant proposal that was not funded. The written remarks of the outside readers made it clear that our proposal of an interdisciplinary program in language and business studies needed to have much stronger commitment from the College of Business. After reviewing this official feedback from the Department of Education with the Foreign Language Department, the university administration took action to put the proposal back on track. In a display of the crucial support mentioned above, the administration intervened by instructing the College of Business to collaborate with us on the resubmission of a revised and improved grant proposal. This was one of the key turning points in the evolution of L&IT that sustained and safeguarded the momentum to develop a new program. If the administration had not intervened in this assertive manner at this critical juncture, it is quite possible that our efforts to innovate would have come to nothing.

A second grant proposal, written with the full participation of several faculty members in the College of Business who had already established their own interests and credentials in teaching and research in international business, was submitted to Title VI, A the following year. As a result, funding was provided in 1978 to EMU for the creation of a bachelor of arts degree and a master of arts degree in Language and International Trade. This funding, which came to us at a time when EMU had virtually no internal resources available for new program development, allowed us to initiate the program and to assemble the components of what has now become one of the most often replicated curricula in its field. The B.A. curriculum consists of primary concentrations in language, business language, and business administration, with additional requirements in economics, political science, history, geography, and practical training. The graduate program is made up of concentrations in language, business language, business administration, and economics with a practical training assignment also required for graduation.

While over the years, new internationally focused courses have been developed in all of the participating departments, the most basic initial innovation in L&IT occurred with the development of business language curricula in the Foreign Language Department. In all our foreign languages—French, German, Japanese, and Spanish—new sets of advanced-level undergraduate and graduate business language courses have been introduced, which are focused on the economic geography, recent and current economic and business developments, social and cultural aspects of the business environment, and the technical business language of the foreign country. All instruction is given in the foreign language, with primary methodological emphasis on the acquisition of active, functional language skills. We chose to locate these courses at the advanced level of instruction in order to allow students to reach professional competence in the language. And because they are at the advanced level, the courses in French, German, and Spanish also prepare students for the very difficult and internationally respected business language competency examinations now administered worldwide in these languages. The examinations are sponsored for German by the Goethe Institute, the Carl Duisberg Centers, and the Association of German Chambers of Commerce and Industry; for French by the Paris Chamber of Commerce and Industry; and for Spanish by the Madrid Chamber of Commerce and Industry.

In addition to diversifying and enriching the curriculum of the Foreign Language Department, these business language courses have produced ancillary effects that have contributed significantly to the success of L&IT. For example, because of their interdisciplinary character, the courses—which focus primarily on language acquisition and secondarily on business concepts, and therefore do not threaten the academic turf of the College of Business—have stimulated the development of various kinds of collaboration in the form of joint activities and mutual assistance between foreign language and business colleagues. This has strengthened the sense of coownership of the program in both academic areas. In another way, the courses have helped to create new kinds of liaison with external, nonacademic communities. This has resulted from a variety of activities, including arranging student internships and job placements, organizing guest speaker presentations by government and corporate officials, and conducting program-related research and surveys. These and other activities have helped to break down the isolation that traditionally characterizes the relationship between the foreign language teacher and professional communities outside the university. Through such externally focused networking activities new kinds of alliances and partnerships have been developed with the public and private sectors in support of the program.

L&IT was inaugurated in the fall of 1978 and produced after only a few years astounding enrollments and a complete reversal of the crisis faced by the Foreign Language Department in the early 1970s. By the early 1980s we had far more majors (several hundred per year) in L&IT than we had ever had in our best post-Sputnik years. The main factor to which we attribute our success in this regard was that in the first few years of planning and development, we placed heavy emphasis on recruiting high school and community college students for the program. They responded with great interest and enthusiasm by entering the program in large numbers that have, over the years, continued unabated. More than anything else, this student response to L&IT convinced the Foreign Language Department and the College of Business that the program was on the right track. And just as importantly, it reassured the university administration that its active support of our efforts to reform the traditional curriculum had been fully justified.

Universities with programs similar to ours have experienced the same kind of initial and sustained high student demand for admission to the program that we have seen at EMU. On the basis of our experience and that of these institutions, we have concluded that there is a substantial population of American high school and college students who are interested in careers in international business and are highly motivated to prepare themselves for their careers by majoring in interdisciplinary liberal and practical arts programs like L&IT.

From the perspective of the Foreign Language Department at EMU and its curricular reform strategy, it is also very important to point out that all L&IT majors are considered language majors, because the program was created on the initiative of the Foreign Language Department and is therefore housed there. For the last few years, annual enrollments in L&IT have been stabilized at approximately 250-300 majors, and have not been allowed to increase because of limitations on the number of faculty positions allocated to the Foreign Language Department.

The scope and impact of L&IT were greatly enhanced in 1979 with the addition of an international practical training component in the form of the International Cooperative Education Exchange (ICEE) program. As noted above, both the undergraduate and graduate programs in L&IT require practical training for completion of the degree. The practical training assignments, which at EMU are called cooperative education, or co-op, assignments, are sponsored and evaluated by faculty members for academic credit, and must be business administrative in content. They may be completed in the United States or abroad. While the services of the EMU Office of Cooperative Education were available in 1978 for the coordination of domestic assignments, there was no organizational mechanism for international co-op until ICEE was initiated the following year. Once in place, ICEE became one of the most attractive components of L&IT for students, and was one of the key reasons for the initially very rapid enrollment growth of the program.

Like L&IT, ICEE was planned and developed almost exclusively with external grant funding. This outside support included what was, as far as we have been able to determine, the first federal funding for international cooperative education from the Fund for the Improvement of Post-Secondary Education (FIPSE) of the U.S. Department of Education from 1981 to 1984. Earlier funding for ICEE had come from the government of West Germany, and after FIPSE additional grants were received from the Exxon Education Foundation and the Ford Motor Company. Most of this outside assistance was used to provide large amounts of faculty release time staffing and operating expenses. Without it, it is very unlikely that ICEE could have been developed.

ICEE has become the primary framework through which cooperative linkages have been developed with foreign partner institutions in support of L&IT. It is an exchange of advanced-level intern students and is based on full reciprocity with respect to student placement, supervision, and evaluation. During their assignments, students work full time in companies for periods of three to twelve months, under the direct sponsorship of the foreign school. Since 1979 we have exchanged approximately 300 interns with business and polytechnic schools in Germany, France and Spain. In the last few years, our most active partners have been the Export Academy of Baden-Wüerttemberg and the Karlsruhe Polytechnic in Germany; the Graduate School of International Trade (ESIDEC) in France; and the Graduate School of Business Administration and Management (ESADE), and the Graduate School of Management and Marketing (ESIC) in Spain.

The companies that have employed ICEE interns have included, among many others, General Motors, Ford, Bechtel, and Siemens in the United States; Ford, Daimler Benz, Siemens and Bosch in Germany; Renault, General Motors, ELF, and Kiwi in France; and SEAT, Pepsico, and the Foreign Trade Bank in Spain. In these and other companies, our students have worked in a great variety of organizational and functional areas, including accounting, finance, data processing, computer programming, internal and external auditing, marketing, import-export, personnel, production planning and analysis, administrative services, business planning, and sales.

As international exchange programs go, ICEE is very affordable. While our students are responsible for paying all travel costs and an exchange program fee to EMU, their co-op assignments are salaried. We stipulate that the company provide an income at least adequate to pay normal living expenses for the duration of the internship. And so far, most ICEE employers have provided somewhat more than this minimum level of support.

Participation in ICEE is very selective. In order to qualify for placement, students must (1) have reached the advanced level of competence in the foreign language and business language, (2) be at the advanced level of business studies, (3) show by GPA a consistently high academic performance, (4) have substantial previous employment in a business setting, and (5) demonstrate a high level of personal responsibility and maturity. Applicants to the program are also required to pass a formal interview in the foreign language before a faculty selection committee. We have found it important to require advanced levels of performance, especially in language skills, for participation in ICEE, because foreign training assignments are uniquely demanding experiences that often involve some degree of stress and culture shock. In order to minimize the risk of failure, students must be selected on the basis of their ability to meet these challenges.

Over the last thirteen years, the results of the ICEE program have been very positive and confirm in our view the appropriateness of a careful and rigorous selection process. Almost all students who have participated in the program have reported that the total immersion in the language, culture, and professional business environment of the foreign country provided one of the most intensive and sustained learning experiences of their lives.

In 1985 another key event occurred in the development of L&IT when the State of Michigan provided permanent, additional line-item state funding for the non-instructional, administrative function of the program. In so doing, the State relieved us of the necessity of continually replenishing our administrative operating funds from external grant sources, and directly acknowledged its own vested interests in the maintenance and continued growth of the program.

RIPPLE EFFECTS

As noted at the beginning of this chapter, L&IT has served as a model for similar curricular innovation at other institutions and for the federal legislation that has funded the development of the new International Business Centers. In addition to these external developments, L&IT has produced a number of other important ripple effects that have contributed to a broader internationalization of our own institution. For example, the program created the environment and provided the administrative expertise and financial resources for the annual EMU Conference on Languages and Communication for World Business and the Professions. With its eleventh meeting recently concluded, the conference is regularly attended by some 200 to 300 participants from the United States and numerous foreign countries, is a forum for the presentation of over 100 papers and workshop sessions each year, and is widely recognized as the leading annual meeting in the field of interdisciplinary language, business, and professional studies in the country. The framework of the conference is also now being expanded to include international relations in other fields.

To return to the College of Business at EMU: The success of L&IT has led to the creation of a new, federally funded degree program, the BBA/BA in Language and World Business (L&WB), which is housed in both the College of Business and the Foreign Language Department. L&WB contains all of the language, business language, economics, political science, history, geography, and practical training requirements of the BA in L&IT, plus a complete major in business administration, including a new set of restricted electives in international business. The seven international business courses now offered to undergraduates in the College of Business are International Transportation and Logistics, International Marketing, Managing World Business Communications, International Management, International Finance, Production/Operations Management—A World View, and International Accounting. To satisfy the AACSB standard in international business, all eleven business core courses now have international components.

L&WB is a five-year, double-degree program, which requires at least 156 semester credit hours for graduation. It does not replace L&IT, but complements it as a stronger business degree program. All L&WB majors are considered to be both business and foreign language majors. Now in its fourth year, the program has attracted over 100 majors, some of whom have already completed their degrees. An important indicator of the much-improved working relationship—in comparison to that in 1975—between the Foreign Language Department and the College of Business is that "Language" is the first word in the title of the degree at the request of our business colleagues.

Another spin-off development of L&IT is the currently pending proposal to create a new undergraduate degree, to be called Language and International Relations (L&IR). Similar to L&IT as a group concentration major, L&IR consists of two main concentrations in language and political science, with additional requirements in history, sociology, and practical training. The new degree was approved and implemented in 1993.

In institutional terms, the most significant outgrowth of L&IT is the World College at EMU. The World College evolved out of the administrative function of L&IT and reports to the provost and vice president for Academic Affairs and to the executive vice president. Created by action of the Board of Regents in December 1987, the World College is one of the newest offices on campus. Its administrative staff consists of a director and associate director on annualized faculty release time assignments who were previously director and assistant director, respectively, of L&IT in the Foreign Language Department. Its budget was assembled from already existing internal resources, the largest part of which was the noninstructional, administrative budget of L&IT.

The World College is not a college in the traditional sense of the word, designating an academic unit in which faculty teach students in academic programs. Instead, the World College was created to be a new kind of administrative unit, the purpose of which is to promote the internationalization of EMU in as many areas as possible. During several decades prior to 1987, a substantial number of international programs and projects were developed at EMU, involving a great variety of activities and working contacts with some fifty foreign countries. But while it was clear that EMU could claim a track record of some significance in the international arena, it was also clear that there had been little or no focused facilitation or coordination of these activities across programmatic lines. There had been no larger plan to make EMU more international. Organized on the basis of the proven administrative expertise and resources of L&IT, the World College was established to provide this internationally focused facilitation and coordination function on a campuswide scale, in cooperation with as many other university offices as possible.

The main functions of the World College are to:

- Serve as a clearinghouse of information and referrals regarding internationally focused projects, programs, events, and activities.
- Provide faculty release time for international projects
- Fund faculty and staff travel to international conferences and other professional meetings
- Develop and maintain international initiatives with other academic institutions, government agencies, and business organizations, both in the United States and abroad
- Obtain new external funding for the development of international curricula and programs
- Administer the International Cooperative Education Exchange program and extend it to new disciplinary fields
- Coordinate the annual EMU Conference on Languages and Communication for World Business and the Professions, and sponsor other international meetings
- Host visits to campus by international guests
- Provide support for other internationally focused projects and activities

Created to be an agent for change, the World College represents a dramatic extension of the basic cooperative strategy that underlies L&IT—to develop new kinds of cooperation across institutional boundary lines and to provide new resources for the accomplishment of these collaborative initiatives.

CONCLUSION

L&IT has been a truly remarkable success at EMU. It has had a broad impact on program development and administrative realignment at the university, and has provided a model for innovation at other institutions. On the basis of our experience with L&IT, we strongly advocate that other universities comparable in structure and mission to ours consider taking similar interdisciplinary approaches to the development of international business programs.

NOTE

1. Portions of this chapter first appeared in the following publications and are included here with the permission of the publishers:

Proceedings of the DAAD Conference on German Studies in the USA: A Critique of "Germanistik"? 1989. Tempe: Arizona State University.

Proceedings of the Clemson Conference on Language and International Trade. 1989. Clemson, SC: Clemson University.

The International MBA at York University

CHARLES S. MAYER

Chapter One in this volume, "Internationalization of Business Education: Defining the Challenge," as well as some of the other chapters, spell out well the rationale and major issues involved in setting up an international business program. Viewed from the Canadian perspective the problems associated with internationalization are similar. There are, however, two aspects that make the need for formal international education in Canada even more urgent. First, as a percentage of gross domestic product, a greater proportion of Canada's output is aimed at export markets. Second, Canadians are even less well prepared for international business than their U.S. counterparts, as opportunities for mid-level expatriate training usually occur in the United States, rather than abroad.

There are basically two approaches to the internationalization process:

- International considerations are so important that they must be taught as a separate discipline by internationalists
- International considerations are too important to be confined to the internationalists. They must pervade the entire core curriculum.

Both of these approaches have much to commend them. Also, in my opinion, they are not diametrically opposed. In this chapter, I shall attempt to show how we at York University, Toronto, Canada, are attempting to incorporate both approaches, or to be more specific, to trace the current thought process in launching our new International MBA program.

HISTORICAL PERSPECTIVE

PRECONDITIONS

In order to launch a distinct and comprehensive international program, a number of facilitating conditions have to already exist. These are a "mission statement" that clearly recognizes the importance of "going global," and a faculty willing to give it a high priority among its alternative objectives; a "champion," or better still, an ad hoc committee, dedicated to making it happen; a dean who is strongly supportive of the effort; a foundation that includes internationally trained and experienced faculty with access to international academic networks; and a group of international functional courses already in existence that can be expanded and built upon to provide the required core for the program. If the program can be delivered in a school that is part of a major university (i.e. that can draw on the strengths of established departments in political science, sociology, history, and languages), and if that university is located in a major international metropolitan center, that will certainly help. The final, and probably most stringent, requirement is the ability to attract the significant financing that such a program requires. By 1985, all of these conditions had been met at York.

THE INITIAL PROPOSAL

In 1985, responding to a growing awareness of the incomplete training of MBA's in the field of international business, York University's Faculty of Administrative Studies proposed to the Ministry of Industry, Trade and Technology (MITT)—a provincial body— that funding be made available for the creation of a Centre of Excellence in International Trade in Ontario. This Centre would conduct research, develop a training program for both students and business people, and in general improve the international business performance of Ontario-based firms. Needless to say, all of this was to be housed at York University.

The proposal met with strong positive support at MITT, and a grant was about to be made to York, when the Ministry of Colleges and Universities (MCU) heard about it, and insisted that such a grant be funded through MCU, and should be based on a competition among Ontario universities. The York proposal, in fact, became the background document on which the request for proposals, sent to all universities, was based.

A STRATEGIC ALLIANCE

At this stage it was decided that a joint-venture proposal between the University of Toronto and York University—both major players on the Ontario business scene, and both located in Toronto, the heartland of Canada's business—would have the strength of a virtual take-out bid. Both universities also had strong law faculties, and these would participate in developing a program on Trade Law.

The alliance of two rivals was deemed desirable on two grounds. First, it ensured that the venture had the international strength that would be attractive to the province. Second, many of the other bidders were forming alliances as well, so as to reach a critical mass. This joint-venture strategy proved to be correct, as it generated the winning contract, with the proviso that Wilfrid Laurier University be added to the joint venture. The Laurier proposal to set up a Trade Support Centre to small and medium-sized businesses was so different from what the other bidders were proposing, and so appealing to the government, that Laurier was added as a partner.

This led to the creation and funding, in May 1987, of the Ontario Centre for International Business (OCIB), a joint-venture partnership among three universities and five faculties, the three business programs of the partners, and the two law schools.

THE NEW PROGRAM

Once it came to the division of the spoils, it became clear that various tasks had to be allocated to different units. In particular, the new degree—so far called the "enhanced MBA"—had to be administered at one university, since the degree had to be granted by that university. The responsibility for developing this program fell to the Faculty of Administrative Studies at York. Input from other programs, and help in the design of the curriculum, was a task in which all of the partners were involved, through the administrative structure (Management Committee) and Advisory Committees of the OCIB.

The other members of OCIB continue to be a source of support and strength. For example, the research program generates materials for classroom use; some of the research papers can be reformatted as cases too. The data base generated for trade development is accessible and useful for the students. And, the legal materials and research papers are a specialized pool of information for students needing that type of input. Visiting lecturers to any of the partners are available to the other partners, as are individual faculty members of the partner institutions. In this way the program benefits from many synergies.

DESIGNING THE PROGRAM

The designers of the new program obtained information about many international programs through their published literature, the exchange of letters, telephone calls, and personal campus visits. Also, an advisory committee of business leaders was established to gain pragmatic input from that community.

A number of issues became clear. First, there were few truly international programs in existence around the world. Of those, each offered something a bit different. As a newcomer, the York program could borrow the best from them all.

Second, and seemingly at a much lower level of significance, each program offered a different degree—essentially an undifferentiated MBA, MIBS (Master of International Business), MIM (Master of International Management) or something similar. Our research showed that students wanted to still receive an MBA, but also wanted to have it clearly differentiated. This resulted in the creation of a new degree—the International Master of Business Administration (International MBA) degree, which was a new degree. Overcoming various objections, such as that a master's degree has to start with an "M," the International MBA designation was eventually accepted.

In Ontario, all education is under provincial jurisdiction. Prior to being able to grant a degree, the granting institution required a number of approvals. This is a long, time-consuming process, which first starts within the Faculty, then moves to Graduate Faculty, then to a committee of the university's Senate, then to the Senate, followed by a screening committee formed by all universities, the Ontario Council of Graduate Studies (OCGS), and finally to a Council of University Affairs (OCUA) before receiving ministerial consent and, most importantly, public funding.

All of these requirements have now been met by York's International MBA. The whole process took slightly longer than two years, which is probably a record time for a new program approval. Rather than get involved in the iterations needed to evolve the present program, it might be more useful to discuss the components of the present program in some detail. Of course, more specifics are available, to the point of detailed outlines for each course. We would be glad to share these with any interested party. In a way, it would serve to repay our debt to the many institutions that helped us in developing our program.

It is also noteworthy that we graduated our first batch of International MBA students in August, 1991. After completing their internships abroad, they returned to Toronto in August to participate in a four-week capstone course, followed by graduation. Currently, they are spread around the globe, with all of them holding worthwhile, and highly visible jobs. But, let us return to the details of the program.

THE INTERNATIONAL MBA PROGRAM

Before describing some of the details of the program, it is important to note that the International MBA is not strictly delivered by business school professors, but relies heavily on other faculties and institutions within the university. For example, the Joint Centre for Asia/Pacific Studies (JCAPS) is staffed by scholars from both the University of Toronto and York, and assists us in delivering regional- and country-specific courses for that area. The individual actually delivering the courses is a member of York's Political Science Department (1992). Similarly, the different language courses are taught by interested members of the various language departments. Thus, our kind of program could be delivered only in a large, multi-faceted university.

It also draws heavily from such diverse domains outside the university as the business and government communities, visiting scholars and dignitaries, and opportunities presented by such activities as the 1990 AIB Conference, which was held in Toronto. Thus, it would be impossible to deliver our kind of program in an environment isolated from the center of international activities in a country. Fortunately, Toronto is the ideal Canadian location for such a program.

The program, by its very nature, has to be highly interdisciplinary. In fact, the concept, "interdisciplinary," is probably the key to operationalizing an international business program.

PROGRAM SIZE

The International MBA is designed for no more than fifty students per year. This size has some fundamental implications. First, the program will never be very cost efficient. However, with the individual attention that is required for students in a program of this nature, we believe that size constraints are necessary. Moreover, it is not clear that the Canadian business community, or the global business community for that matter, will be ready to absorb at this time a large number of such specially trained students, technically competent to implement international transactions, and to survive and function effectively in foreign environments. We see the demand as limited for two reasons. First, it is unlikely that many of our students will find their entry-level jobs with companies outside of Canada. International postings are reserved for people who have already proven themselves domestically. And, the Canadian demand for internationally trained people, at this time, is limited by what firms perceive their future needs will be. While we hope that this will grow in the future, at present the demand is low.

This limited demand, coupled with our firm belief that similar programs will be appearing in many schools during the next few years, leads us to limit the size of our program. We are adopting a clear "niche" strategy. By being the first (in Canada) in our "niche," by establishing ourselves firmly in a sector with high entry costs, and by attempting to deliver a high quality program, we feel that we will dominate our specific market position.

Program Highlights

The program is built on the same base of core functional courses as the regular MBA (i.e., accounting, economics, finance, marketing, organizational behavior, policy, quantitative methods, etc.). This feature facilitated development immensely, as we did not have to design a totally new set of courses for the whole twenty-four months of our new program. However, as will be shown later, even these core courses are influenced by the fact that they are intended for the International MBA students.

An important aspect of the common core is that students who for some reason cannot complete the requirements of the International MBA, can still qualify for the regular MBA without too much loss of time. This "soft landing" feature has both benefits and disadvantages, but on the whole it protects the investment that the students make.

There is a sequence of specific core courses developed for the International MBA, which are required. These include the following:

- courses dealing with specific issues concerning the environment and practice of international business;

- regional and country specific courses that focus on the culture, history, political background and methods of doing business in a selected area of the world, currently concentrating on three regions—Asia/Pacific, Latin America, and Western Europe;
- language courses specifically developed for this program, which concentrate more on oral proficiency, and which cover business/cultural topics as part of their content, with the country and language courses are linked;
- electives that must be taken with an international focus;
- biweekly seminars led by business leaders;
- a required internship with a company or institution in the country/language of specialization; and
- a capstone course that integrates the International MBA experience.

In addition, students have the opportunity of spending one additional term abroad, studying at one of the universities with which we have signed exchange agreements. We have such partners currently in Brazil, China, France (three), Germany, Hong Kong (two), Italy, Japan (two), Korea, Mexico (two), Singapore, Spain, and Thailand. In 1991, more than half of our students elected to participate in these exchanges. This percentage should increase in the future, as we develop sources of financial support to subsidize these exchanges, and as our network of exchanges continues to develop. We need such a large network of exchanges for two reasons. First, since there are so many different country/language groupings in our program, we need matching exchange partners. Second, we do not believe that we should send or receive a large number of students from a specific partner institution—hence we limit the number to three.

It can be mentioned in passing that our exchange network has been most helpful in locating foreign internship sites in return for our finding internships for foreign students in Canada. Since one tends to be better connected in one's home market, it makes sense to get involved in such quid pro quo arrangements. For example, we found two interesting jobs in Toronto for one of our French partners, and they found two jobs for us in Paris, to our mutual benefit. Also, it helps to have somebody in the country of the internship who is involved in, and who can handle the day-to-day problems that tend to arise with internships.

The twenty-four-month program detail is given in Exhibit 1. More detail on all of this is available in one or more of our publications, which we will be glad to send out on request.

YORK UNIVERSITY

International Master of Business Administration

PROGRAM OF STUDY

Faculty of Administrative Studies	YEAR ONE			YEAR TWO			
	FALL Semester 1 (Sep O N D)	WINTER Semester 2 (D J F M A)	SPRING/SUM Semester 3 (A M J J)	FALL Semester 4 (Sep O N D)	WINTER Semester 5 (D J F M A)	SPRING/SUM Semester 6 (A M J J)	Sem 7 (J A)
STUDY/WORK ABROAD							CAPSTONE INTL 6070 Advanced Seminar on Business Topics
Core MBA **STUDY AT YORK**	ACTG 5010 Financial Accounting for Managers	FINE 5020 Introduction to Finance	ACTG 5020 Introduction to Management Actg.	MGTS 5020 Operations Management	(Optional) EXCHANGE[5] Study Abroad	INTL 6001 Internship Abroad	
	ECON 5010 Microeconomics for Management	MKTG 5020 Marketing for Management	ECON 5020 Macroeconomics for Management	OBIR 5020 Organizational Analysis	FRANCE GERMANY SPAIN	BELGIUM FRANCE GERMANY SPAIN SWITZERLAND	
	MGTS 5010 Introduction to Administrative Statistics	OBIR 5010 Behavioural Components of Organizations	INTL 6010 International Strategy Study	INTL 6010 International Strategy Study	HONG KONG JAPAN	CHINA HONG KONG JAPAN TAIWAN	
Core Intl MBA	INTL 5010 Environmental Framework for Intl Business	INTL 5020 Managing Intl Business	INTL 6000 Intl Strategy Formulation and Implementation	INTL 6040[3] Region Study Series	BRAZIL MEXICO	BRAZIL MEXICO	
					INTL 6050[6] Country Study Series	HUNGARY USSR	
Electives				ELECTIVE A[4] ELECTIVE B	ELECTIVE A ELECTIVE B		
Language	INTL 00*1[1] Language	INTL 00*2 Language	INTL 00*3 Language	INTL 00*4 Language	INTL 00*5 Language		
Bi-weekly Seminars	INTL ***1[2] Seminars	INTL ***2 Seminars	INTL ***3 Seminars	INTL ***4	INTL ***5		

(SUMMER BREAK between Semester 3 and Semester 4)

1. The third digit in the code refers to the language: French=2, German=3, Japanese=3, Spanish=5, Mandarin=6, Russian=7, and the fourth digit in the semester.
2. During the period of study at York, students are required to attend bi-weekly seminars on international topics.
3. Options: INTL 6041 Asia-Pacific, INTL 6042 Western Europe, INTL 6043 Latin America, INTL 6044 Europe East.
4. Provided prerequisites are met, students can take electives in any order. Two of the four electives must be international electives.
5. In semester 5, students have the option of studying abroad; the Exchange Program consists of 4 full-time courses which replace INTL 00*5, INTL 6050 and two electives.
6. Options: INTL 6052 France, INTL 6053 Germany, INTL 6054 Spain (additional countries will be added as required).

LANGUAGE REQUIREMENTS

All of our students will have reached a high level of oral proficiency in a foreign language before they graduate—in fact, it is one of the requirements for graduation. To give students some measure of security, they have up to twelve months after the completion of their formal courses to pass the language tests. Currently, the languages that students can take are French, German, Japanese, Mandarin, and Spanish. Russian, Cantonese, Korean, and Italian may be added in the near future.

In order to achieve the exit proficiency required (based on the ACTFL tests), students to date have entered the program with some prior exposure to the language. We still have to experiment with intensive language training prior to the start of the program for students who have had only limited exposure to a foreign language. Since the program is so intense, such basic preparation will have to occur during the summer before the start of the first year. However, it is one of our goals to make this program available to all highly motivated, bright students, regardless of their initial language capabilities.

CURRENT CHALLENGES

It would be great if we could state that our program is complete and stable. However, that is hardly likely with a new program. In this section, some of the key problems yet to be resolved will be discussed.

PLACEMENT

In launching this new program, York was proactive rather than reactive; in other words, we did not respond to a pressing need felt by the business community. This could be a dangerous strategy. If we are too far ahead of the perceived need of the business community, the graduating students may not find enough attractive jobs. In the first few years, this will not be a problem, as the program has enough publicity behind it to place the limited initial output. However, in the steady state, we are betting on demand growing with supply. If this does not happen, the attractiveness of the program will quickly fade.

Placement poses another special problem due to our program design. In order to send well-prepared students abroad (both in functional areas and language), the internships are set up for the spring/summer term of the second year. Furthermore, if students opt for an exchange, they will be away from Canada from January to August of their final year. Many will not have jobs by December of the previous year. Unless companies are willing to be more flexible in their hiring practices (i.e., hire in September), or if many internships do not lead to permanent jobs, placement could be made difficult by the structure/cycle of the program.

INTERNSHIPS

Closely linked to placement are sites for internships, which are a requirement for our program. Again, the school has built an adequate network to be able to place the small number of students initially. However, in the steady state, we have to be able to organize 50 positions annually. This requirement will be made that much more difficult as other schools from all parts of the world vie for the same few available places (e.g., U.S., Canadian, European, and Australian programs planning to place students in internships in Japan).

At this stage, we realize that finding internships will be a difficult job, and are allocating resources toward managing it. A person has been hired to augment our regular placement activities whose full-time responsibility will be to find and manage internship sites. If our students do well as interns, the proportions of "repeat customers" should be high.

COOPERATION FROM THE REST OF THE UNIVERSITY

Response from highly qualified members of other faculties has initially been very favorable. Business schools are always seen as rich, and initial cooperation from members of other departments was both exciting and financially rewarding. Whether scholars, say in political science, will find it in their long-term interests to continue working with us, especially when there may be pressures from their home departments to return to their own disciplines, is still a moot question. We are attempting to reduce the risks by hiring some specialists within our own faculty. For example, our new recruits include a split appointment with a business historian, and an expert in cross-cultural negotiations who holds a Ph.D. in political science.

FUNDING

Once our seed funding is exhausted, the provincial allocation per student will be insufficient to cover the costs. This is not a cost-

efficient program. Hopefully, however, it has enough attractiveness
to spearhead a private sector funding drive. The success of that
campaign will determine the future of the program. Indications for
the future are positive, but the economic climate in Canada is such
as to make too strong a statement on the future fundings of the
program unwise.

Keeping the Faculty On-side

It would be an exaggeration to claim that all faculty are fully
behind internationalization. In fact, the "silent majority" probably
feel threatened by it. Unless a conscious effort is made to involve a
growing number of faculty members in the internationalization
process, and an opportunity is given to all to internationalize, the
program will quickly be seen as drawing resources from all for the
benefit of a few, and will start to encounter resistance. Therefore, a
priority is to make available to new faculty members the many foreign assignments that are cultivated.

Competition

Internationalization of curricula implies more global competition. Regional/national "niches" are not likely to persist. The best
students will be attracted to the best schools on a global basis. So,
the best schools will get even stronger, while the others will fall
behind. Needless to say, we will strive to be the best, but so will all
the others. To be the best regionally, simply will not be good
enough.

Future Directions

At the outset of this chapter, I tried to suggest that internationalization has to occur not only in a specific program aimed at turning
out managers in tune with global realities, such as the International
MBA program, but also in the more general MBA program. Let me
summarize how we are attempting to cope with this at York.

Having the critical mass of a full section of the International
MBA students who take their core courses together, we are currently assigning our more internationally oriented teachers to
teach these sections. Both the nature of the student body, and the
direction given by the program, are permitting these instructors to

introduce more international material into the core MBA courses. In areas where we do not have the current strength to do so, we are obtaining help from our joint-venture partners in the OCIB. Moreover, our dean has clearly indicated to all areas that new hirees need to possess strong international business expertise.

Hence, the International MBA program can be viewed as the testing ground, and as the catalyst which will ensure that international content will pervade our total MBA offering. It would be disappointing if a greater part of the material that we are currently introducing into the International MBA were not part of the regular MBA of the future. At the same time, we expect that there will always be room for a program that is at the "cutting edge" of international development. Thus, there will always be new material that will be discussed initially only in the International MBA program, but will eventually, if proven useful, find its way into the regular MBA.

What is being proposed, therefore, is what marketers are familiar with as the "trickle down" theory. The first step in internationalizing a business program is the formation of a specialized unit focused on international issues, such as the International MBA. The very presence of such a unit, however, will ensure that international issues will also become more widely discussed and treated in the regular MBA program. Jeffrey Arpan, among others, discusses the concept of internationalizing through infusion (see Chapter Two). Our model could more appropriately be called diffusion as the basic international elements of the International MBA program are diffused over time through the rest of the MBA curriculum.

Should international content be taught by internationalists, or should it pervade the whole curriculum? Our answer is *both*, with specialization in the International MBA eventually being diffused to the general MBA curriculum. Arpan, in his chapter, suggests three levels of preparation: awareness, understanding, and competency. If we can create competency in our International MBA and understanding in our regular MBA, then awareness will cease to be an issue.

Building on Foreign Language Proficiency: The Brigham Young University Experience[1]

LEE H. RADEBAUGH

INTRODUCTION

In a recent interview in the *New York Times*, deans of some of the top business schools in the nation were asked about the major questions facing business educators in the coming decade. Meyer Feldberg, of the Columbia Business School, identified the major questions for him and his school: "What is the most appropriate mechanism for internationalizing our program in a very fundamental way? How do we make sure that all graduates at the end of the program, regardless of what their major was and regardless of whether they're specialists or generalists, come out with a good understanding of the nature of the global competition?"[1]

Why are Dean Feldberg and the other deans around the country focusing so intently on questions of internationalization with regard to their curricula? The answer is that American business is not as dominant a force in the world as it once was. The consolidation of the European Community, the democratization of Eastern Europe and the Soviet Union, and the strength of East Asian economies have all led American business leaders to be more cognizant of the international business environment than at perhaps any previous time in American history since the Revolutionary War.

A unique advantage for international business education in the Marriott School of Management at Brigham Young University (BYU) is the extremely high proportion of students who are fluent in foreign languages and have nearly twenty-four months of foreign residence to their credit. Partly as a result of the foreign experience of the students, a number of programs have been instituted to further internationalize the faculty and students and help prepare graduates for the challenges of a global economy.

The purpose of this chapter is to describe the international experience of the students at BYU, with the primary emphasis on building their foreign language expertise, discussing some of the major internationalization efforts underway, and identifying some key issues we face as we attempt to prepare students for jobs in the global marketplace.

FOREIGN LANGUAGE PROFICIENCY AT BYU

PROFICIENCY PROFILE

As noted in Exhibit 1, 30 percent of the students enrolled at BYU during the 1990 fall semester were bilingual. The characteristics used to determine if the students were bilingual are as follows:

1. Foreign nationals who speak a second language—a relatively small percentage of the total student body.
2. Students who served a two-year full-time mission for the Church of Jesus Christ of Latter-Day Saints, in a country where English is not the primary language—a relatively large percentage of the total. (The LDS Church is the sponsoring institution of BYU, a private school.)
3. Students who have taken more than two years of a foreign language at the university level.

Exhibit 2 illustrates that of those who are bilingual, the majority speak a European/Latin American language; only 7 percent of the student body is fluent in an Asian language (see Chapter Thirteen by John Daniels).

Exhibits 3 through 5 demonstrate that the dominant European/Latin American language is Spanish, whereas the dominant Asian language is Japanese, with nearly 1,000 students exhibiting a reasonable level of fluency (this had risen to over 1500 by 1992). These students, who have studied Japanese, have been referred to by Ezra Vogel of Harvard as "a national treasure."

The language proficiency of the students in the Marriott School of Management (MSM) is higher than that of the university at large: 43 percent of the undergraduate students are bilingual, compared with 30 percent for the university as a whole. A major reason

EXHIBIT 1: Language Profile–BYU Fall 1990

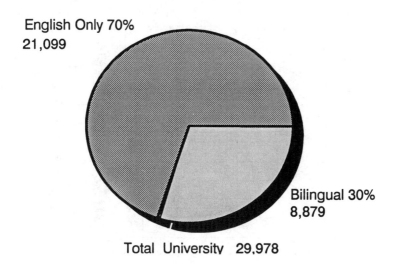

English Only 70%
21,099

Bilingual 30%
8,879

Total University 29,978

EXHIBIT 2: Language Profile–BYU Fall 1990

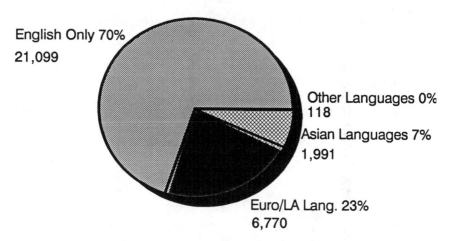

English Only 70%
21,099

Other Languages 0%
118

Asian Languages 7%
1,991

Euro/LA Lang. 23%
6,770

Total University 29,978

EXHIBIT 3: Asian Language Background 1990–BYU Fall 1990

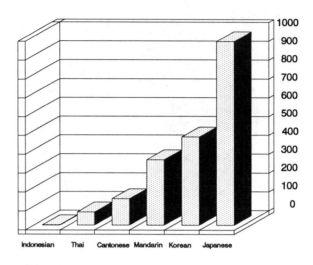

Asian Language Bilinguals = 1991

EXHIBIT 4: Euro/Latin American Languages Breakdown–BYU Fall 1990

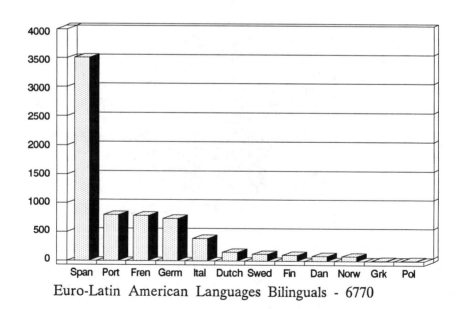

Euro-Latin American Languages Bilinguals - 6770

EXHIBIT 5: Other Languages Breakdown–BYU Fall 1990

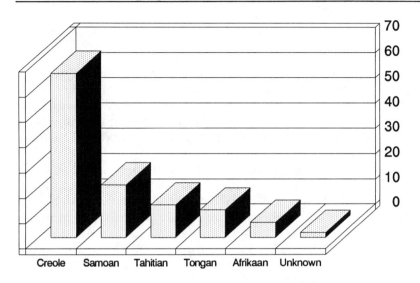

Other Language Bilinguals - 118

for this difference is that students are not admitted to the MSM until their junior year. Most students who go on a church mission will have done so before their junior year. Thus, the upperclass students tend to be more bilingual than freshmen and sophomores. While 73.3 percent of the bilingual MSM undergraduates are fluent in a European/Latin American language, 25.2 percent are fluent in an Asian language. Those numbers are 76.2 percent and 22 percent for the university as a whole.

At the graduate level, 58 percent of the MSM students are bilingual, compared with 30 percent for the university as a whole and 43 percent for the undergraduate students. However, these numbers appear to be understated, because 87 percent of the 1992 MBA class are bilingual, and since 1980, this percentage has not dipped below 71 percent. It is interesting to note that of the graduate students who are bilingual, 27.6 percent speak an Asian language, which is not much higher than 22 to 25.2 percent of the university as a whole or the undergraduates in the MSM.

There are thirty-five different language programs at BYU. Since the Church has opened missions in Eastern Europe and the Soviet Union since 1990, there will soon be a number of BYU students fluent in East European languages, leading to a demand in courses on those languages.

DEVELOPING LANGUAGE FLUENCY

Although BYU is relatively unique in terms of how its students gain foreign language expertise, especially in terms of the extensive overseas living experience, most universities graduate students with foreign language fluency. The problem is in convincing those students to also major in business at either the undergraduate or graduate level.

Students have a better opportunity to gain foreign language fluency at the undergraduate level, because they have more credits to work with. However, it is a myth to assume that a student can develop fluency with only two years of collegiate study of a foreign language. The more complex languages of Asia take significantly more study than do the European/Latin American languages, and a student almost needs a minor or major to demonstrate competency or fluency in the language.

At the graduate level, students have a more difficult time fitting foreign language courses into the curriculum. If the students do not enter the program with foreign language fluency, it is doubtful that they can obtain it, unless they enroll in intensive language courses. As a result, MBA programs need to recruit students with foreign language fluency and then provide them with opportunities to take foreign language classes as electives in the program.

Outside of traditional collegiate studies, students can enroll in intensive language programs. This would be especially helpful for graduate students with little undergraduate foreign language experience. The CIBER at the University of Michigan published an informative brochure for its business students identifying some intensive language programs available in different parts of the country. The intensive approach is excellent, because it allows the student to focus solely on language. The MIBS program at the University of South Carolina immersed its students in intensive language programs during the summer of the first year and during the summer between the first year of the program and the student's internship. This allows the student to achieve a good mastery of the language (see Chapter Thirteen by John Daniels).

In addition to academic training in a language, an international business student should utilize the language in a study abroad or an internship program. Either program would be good, but an internship would allow the student to learn `business' language and culture, something rarely taught in a language class or in a study abroad program.

UTILIZING LANGUAGE FLUENCY IN A BUSINESS PROGRAM

At BYU, we attempt to establish study groups for our first year MBA students that are based on three criteria: language expertise, undergraduate major, and work experience. In the case of language, we group students on the basis of fluency in the same language. However, it was not possible to do that with all language groups. We also try to get one foreign national in a group of U.S. students who speak that foreign language. In one group, for example, Hiro Kawamura, a student from Japan, is in a group with five U.S. students who speak Japanese. This year for the first time, we have one group with two students from the Former Soviet Union (FSU) and two U.S. students who speak Russian. We hope to attract more U.S. students with Russian undergraduate majors to combine with our FSU students in the future. Unlike the language groups, we mix undergraduate major and work-experience-basis classified students so that we have a heterogeneous group of students.

The difficulty is getting the language groups to use their language in general and professional conversation. Some of the groups take advantage of their language expertise, while others do not. The language departments are currently developing business language course proposals. At the School of Management, we have developed a program that will provide the language groups with conversational language experience. We have identified four languages for our initial focus: Korean, Japanese, Spanish, and German. Graduate student groups will meet weekly to discuss business, economic, and political issues using the foreign language. The curriculum will be developed by our language faculty in conjunction with a second-year MBA student who is a foreign national from a country of the respective languages. Based on our current experience, additional languages will be added.

The University of Utah, which has foreign language expertise similar to that of BYU, offered two of their core courses this year in a foreign language. A section of the required operations course was taught in Mandarin Chinese by a visiting professor from Nankai University of the People's Republic of China. The class was very small, but the students made good oral presentations in Chinese by the end of the term. Their business Chinese was very limited at the beginning of the term, but it improved significantly. This is an excellent way to utilize foreign scholars, since they can actually make the presentations in their native language. However, it is a very demanding experience for the students.

There are five major needs that can be addressed by the university community in terms of academic programs:

- enhancing the international component of managerial education;
- combining area expertise with managerial skills;
- integrating areas studies and business programs within a university;
- providing educational experiences overseas; and
- internationalizing the faculty.

Because of the language expertise and foreign experience of our business majors, at both the graduate and undergraduate levels, we feel that we need to combine language with each of the above five areas.

ENHANCING THE INTERNATIONAL COMPONENT OF MANAGERIAL EDUCATION

In an article describing the need for an international focus in American business programs, Arnoldo Hax suggests five steps that the United States must take in order to compete effectively. The first of these steps is to "develop internationally sophisticated, bilingual managers" (Hax 1979).

These needs are not only expressed by academics but by business people as well. One of Tom Peters' five recommendations in "Facing Up to the Need for a Management Revolution" was to push internationalism. He sees the new international competition—firms in developed, newly industrialized, and rapidly industrializing countries—as some of the major forces pushing American corporations in new directions in the 1990s. One of the more important directions that companies need to move toward is internationalization. Peters argues that public policy should support programs for foreign-language education and tax breaks for U.S. citizens working abroad in order to further this internationalization (Peters 1988).

Besides the fact that business schools around the country are revamping their academic programs to incorporate internationalism, there is other evidence that schools are unable to meet the needs of international management in their present condition. William Roth points out that most management programs in

American institutions of higher learning are too "narrow and overly quantitative" to prepare managers to cope with the increasingly complex problems inherent in "the international character of business" (Roth 1988).

In order to take advantage of the international interest of our students and to meet the objectives of an international education as described above, we have developed one course required for all undergraduate business majors and another course required for all graduate business majors. The first course is actually a three-part course: international business, ethics, and the regulatory/government environment. In the international course, we help students understand some of the key political, economic, and cultural environments, as well as some of the international functional issues in finance, marketing, organization, and human resources. Although this is mere exposure to international issues, our goal is to sensitize students to some of the key issues that they need to consider. We spend a significant portion of each class period discussing current events issues, so that the students become familiar with the current literature.

One hopes that students will develop a greater interest in international issues and opt for some elective international business courses too. BYU offers a co-concentration in international business that requires the student to take two of the international business courses and demonstrate foreign language fluency. Our belief is that students need to have a solid foundation in business rather than specializing in international business. With the solid foundation, the co-concentration can help round out the students' education. Recruiters are interested in graduates with solid technical skills, not just international skills.

At the graduate level, the required international business course for all first-year students has a different focus from the undergraduate course. It is called Business, International, Government Environment (BIGE), and it focuses on country and regional analysis from the perspective of the foreign investor. The co-concentration at the graduate level requires three international business courses rather than two.

COMBINING AREA EXPERTISE WITH MANAGERIAL SKILLS

One of the problems that business schools have in internationalizing is interpreting the mixed signals sent to them by practicing managers. "Recruiters look for people who can land running in an accounting or marketing slot, while CEOs talk loftily of the need for visionary leaders with a broad cross-functional understanding of business and its place in the universe" (*Fortune* 1989).

These mixed signals are mirrored in the experiences of executive recruiters in Japan during the decade of the 1980s. In the late 1970s and early 1980s when the need for Japanese language skills in a business organization was recognized by top management, most of the executive searches undertaken by the largest headhunter in Tokyo for U.S. firms were for "country experts." These experts were managers who had lived for a significant amount of time in Japan or had graduate educations in Japanese language or culture. Often the home office was disappointed in these newly hired executives because of their lack of basic business skills. While these country experts made good ambassadors for the company, they were not qualified as managers.

The backlash against the country experts came in the middle and late 1980s when they were replaced with individuals who had strong managerial experience. Obviously language and culture skills were still desirable, but managerial experience was imperative. Many corporations have grown to assume that post-secondary institutions of higher education are unable to produce in one person both language and business competencies.

The key is to take advantage of the students' unusually extensive previous experiences of living and working in foreign countries. Once businesses recognize that country expertise and managerial skills can be combined in a single person, the demand for graduates of this program will intensify considerably. The need for this combination of country and business expertise is important not only for the top executive who manages an overseas operation, but also for an entire echelon of lower managers in foreign countries and at the home office.

The attraction of students with significant undergraduate foreign language experience to our graduate business programs is an attempt to mix together the language and business expertise. We also strongly recommend to our undergraduate students in business that they strengthen their foreign language skills, and many of our foreign internships have actually been for undergraduate business majors with language expertise.

We are looking at the possibility of developing a specialized Japanese language/business program. One model that we are considering would involve identifying students as early as the junior year. The students could take a combination of Japanese language (including a course offered in Japanese by a former Japanese businessman) and business with a significant Japanese internship. The student could graduate with a bachelors and masters degree in five years rather than six due to the economies of scheduling courses. This approach has encountered significant resistance from some faculty members, but it is a very efficient way to structure the educational experience.

A second approach would lead to a three-year MBA consisting of more language courses and a six-month internship in Japan. The ideal student to attract to this program would be a Japanese language undergraduate major or a technical undergraduate major and Japanese language minor. The MBA program would have to be restructured to allow students to take more language courses, but this approach would be more in line with the traditional MBA experience and, thus, more politically acceptable.

A third approach that is closer to reality is to admit a section of the MBA program in June rather than September. During the summer, students would take the first semester of the core and a Japanese business language course. During the fall semester, students would take the second semester of the MBA core and an additional Japanese language course that would meet once a week and would be designed to build on the more extensive summer course. The students would go on internship from the first of January to the end of August and return for the second year of the MBA program. The students would end up with a 24-month MBA, eight of which would be an internship abroad.

INTEGRATION OF AREA STUDIES AND BUSINESS PROGRAMS WITHIN A UNIVERSITY

In order to create the combination, the university's country-expert and managerial-expert programs—which have not traditionally been combined—need to be integrated tightly. The first step toward this integration is to look at MBA/MA programs, like the one at the Darden School at the University of Virginia, in which students with no background to Asian languages or cultures are exposed to it for the first time as part of the MBA program.

A comprehensive foreign business language instruction must include more than just language instruction. Instructors must be thoroughly familiar with the cultural factors affecting the business environment of the target language in addition to grammatical considerations (Joy 1987).

At BYU, we have a small number of students in a joint MBA/Master of Arts program in International and Area Studies. The MBA degree is four semesters, and the MA degree is two semesters plus a thesis. By double counting some of the courses, we are able to cut the program to five semesters plus the thesis. This allows the international business student to take courses in political science, geography, anthropology, and history, along with the business courses. Language expertise is also required, so the program is a good complement to the language program listed above. The Japanese program that we are developing would be a combination of business, language, and international and area studies courses.

EDUCATIONAL EXPERIENCES OVERSEAS

A completely U.S.-based program could not compete with an international business program with a significant overseas component. While study abroad programs might be useful in internationalizing business students without a significant interest in foreign cultures and languages, a more significant program would be required for international specialists.

Internship experiences are necessarily labor-intensive, and adequate control is needed to ensure a successful program. For the BYU Japanese program, an internship experience is essential. Currently ten students from the university (not just the business school) are on a six-month internship experience in Japan. The sponsor of the program is interested in expanding the program to twenty students in 1992. In addition, one MBA student is on a full year internship. In order to make the program successful, we need to develop several high-quality internship experiences for our students.

Our study abroad record is not as good. All of the study abroad programs are controlled by the arts and humanities departments, and there is relatively little possibility for a business or economic experience. We need to develop institutional relationships with universities from other countries so that our business students can have an opportunity to study business abroad.

FACULTY

One of the major barriers to internationalizing efforts in U.S. business schools is the faculty themselves. A 1984 survey revealed that only 17 percent of doctoral candidates that year had enrolled in any graduate course with a significant international content

(Laidlaw Jr. 1989). (See Chapters Three and Five for more on these statistics.) This puts great pressure on university administrations to ensure that faculty will have a significant international experience as part of their internationalization effort. It would be shortsighted to internationalize the curriculum and students without internationalizing the faculty.

One approach that BYU is using to internationalize faculty is to take from two to four new faculty per year on the Executive MBA trip to Asia to expose them to different ideas. In 1991, the group visited companies in Japan, South Korea, Hong Kong, and China. In 1992, the group is considering visiting Europe. In order to maintain our contacts in Asia, we are considering sending a group of faculty to visit the companies that have hosted us in the past. The visits would involve more in-depth discussions on corporate strategy and the disciplines of the faculty members involved.

Sabbaticals and leaves abroad are also a good method of internationalizing faculty. This becomes more difficult as the children of the faculty member get a little older, and it can also be an expensive proposition. The administration needs to be willing to provide greater financial support than would be the normal case for an international leave. A Fulbright award is an excellent way to help finance a sabbatical. Although the financial support for a Fulbright is not great, the prestige to the university and the opportunities available to the faculty member are worth the extra support needed.

At BYU, we have tried to support a number of faculty members on trips to attend foreign conferences. At this point, the funding has been for faculty members who have requested the funding, but we need to make an attempt to schedule experiences for faculty members who would not ordinarily attend a foreign conference.

There are some excellent programs already existing to internationalize the faculty. Two examples are the Faculty Development in International Business (FDIB) at the University of South Carolina and a faculty internationalization program at the University of Hawaii. In the FDIB program, for example, a marketing faculty member can attend a two-week class that goes through the entire content of an international marketing course.

Rather than just send one faculty member to such a program, the faculty could invite in international experts to meet with the entire faculty. For example, the finance faculty could invite a recognized international finance professor from another university to conduct a seminar for the faculty on key international finance issues.

Another approach to internationalizing the faculty would be to have the dean announce to the faculty that he or she would like each faculty member to have a significant international experience once every five years and have the faculty member develop an idea that can be presented to the dean. Then the dean can work with the department chairs to establish timing and funding. Faculty members are inventive and can often come up with ideas that might not be considered otherwise.

CONCLUSION

The purpose of this chapter has been to show how foreign language expertise can be developed and utilized in a business school setting and how other programs need to be developed in order to complement the language component. The key is to develop a comprehensive, meaningful program. To assume that a student who has studied Spanish for two years is ready for competition in a global environment would be ludicrous. A combination of business, language, and area studies courses, with a solid study abroad or internship program, would help students be more prepared for the international marketplace. However, it is important to prepare the faculty as well.

NOTE

1. I would like to acknowledge John Beck, assistant professor of Business Strategy and International Business at Brigham Young University, for some of the background in the paper which was written as part of a grant application to the U.S. Department of Education.

REFERENCES

Fortune. 1989. "B-Schools Get a Global Vision," 17 July , 86.

Hax, A. 1979. "Building the Firm of the Future," *Sloan Management Review* 30, no.3: 75–82.

Joy, R. 1987. "Today's Business World Demands Multicultural and International Communication Skills," *Business Education Forum* 41, no. 6: 27–30.

Laidlaw Jr., W. 1989. "Newsletter: U.S. Business Schools," *Multinational Business* (UK) no. 3: 51–55.

Peters, T. 1988. "Facing Up to the Need for a Management Revolution," *California Management Review* 30, no. 2 (Winter): 7-38.

Roth, W. 1988. "Designing a New Academic Management Training Program," *Advanced Management Journal* 53, no.1: 17–22.

APPENDIX I

MBA PROGRAM
1ST-YEAR STUDY GROUPS

Group Name	Undergraduate Major	Foreign Language
Scott Cragun	Communication	French/Spanish
Derek Daniels	Business Management	French
Dylann Duncan	Electrical Engineering	French
Shyne Gbologa	Geography & Res Dev	Ewe, French
Ken Rath	Mechanical Engineering	French
Jim Butler	Japanese	Japanese
Rich Charters	Japanese/Economics	Japanese
Joe Daynes	Recreation Management	Japanese
Hiro Kawamura	Chemistry	Japanese/English
Wade Klingler	Japanese	Japanese
Bob Melanson	Electrical Engineering	Japanese
Luiz Carlos Andrade	Geology	Portuguese, Spanish
David Calderwood	International Relations	Spanish, Portuguese, French
Brent Heslop	Psychology	Spanish, Portuguese
Todd Jorgensen	Psychology	Portuguese
Chris Lythgoe	Inf Mgt/Portuguese	Portuguese
Kevin Thomas	Mechanical Engineering	Spanish

Internationalizing With Programs In Europe

GERARD E. WATZKE

INTRODUCTION

On first hearing, the theme of this Roundtable seems to be an old and familiar air. Otteson's (1968) brief bibliography traces the internationalization of U.S. business education issues to 1957, with descriptions of the needs and prescriptions for curricula appearing steadily through the 1960s. Conferences on internationalizing the core business curriculum, and considerations of faculty and institutional issues in internationalization, were vehicles driven and ridden by prominent deans and faculty with extensive proceedings reflecting serious concern and effort in addressing internationalization (see Otteson 1968; Zeff 1968). The Brookings Institution in 1975 produced a pamphlet on "The International Dimension of Management Education" in 1975 which listed a number of the issues raised in this Roundtable's prospectus. The mid-1970s also found Lee Nehrt's surveys (ACE 1977) and case studies (1981) providing data beyond the tabulations of curricula which the Academy of International Business had been supporting or undertaking since 1963 (see AIB).

With AACSB and EFMD exhorting member institutions through the 1980s to broaden the focus of their training, and with the business press (e.g., *Business Week*, *The Economist*, *Fortune*) currently popularizing internationalization, it is not surprising to find a great many actually doing what was being urged on them over the last 25 to 30 years (see Chapter Three for a definitive historical review). However, the vagueness of the AACSB mandates and the competitiveness of many U.S. business schools seems to be yielding an enormous diversity in approaches to internationalizing and no consensus on relative utility of the many types of programmatic effort. Many schools appear to be imitating others without a clue as to payoff. Hopefully, this Roundtable will be the first step in a collective effort that attempts to understand the costs and benefits of a number of different internationalization programs as experienced by the actors themselves.

This chapter, partly autobiographical, reflects on the attempts of two private U.S. business schools to use ventures in Western Europe as the cornerstone of their internationalization efforts. The assessments and conclusions presented in this personal account likely do not reflect the official views of the presidents and deans of the two schools.

VENTURE IN THE 1970S: BOSTON UNIVERSITY IN BRUSSELS

BACKGROUND AND HISTORY

As one of the larger private educational institutions in the United States, Boston University's schools and colleges have offered a number of off-campus programs for several decades. In the 1960s, its Metropolitan College offered master's level programs in international relations, education, and management to U.S. armed forces personnel, civilians, and dependents, in several European locations, through a contract with the U.S. Department of Defense.

An American expatriate entrepreneur in Brussels, who was an alumnus of one of these programs, campaigned steadily for BU to introduce an evening program in Management in Brussels for the English-speaking business community. BU sent a senior business professor, who was teaching in a program in West Germany, to investigate. He became enthused with the prospects and, as a result, the two of them planned a program for Brussels.

The proposal worked its way up to the Board of Trustees. On the day that the trustees were rejecting the proposal, the entrepreneur announced the program in the Brussels press. Faced with this sort of fait accompli, the BU administration decided to launch an MBA program under the direction of its School of Management. It had the distinction of being the first AASCB-accredited U.S. MBA program to be offered to the general population of a foreign country.

MISSION

With this unusual conception and birth, the program began classes in September 1972. BU's MBA was a sixteen-course program, with ten core and six elective courses. The Brussels program design called for the prototypical student to take two courses each semester, including summer, in order to complete the program entirely in the evening over thirty-two months.

The steady-state vision saw a mix of Europeans and Americans carrying a one- or two-course load while working their normal jobs, some less-experienced Europeans enrolled more or less full time, and some transfer students from Boston carrying whatever load they chose.

CONCEPT OF INTERNATIONALIZATION

There was no expression of an internationalization strategy as such, nor were there any models as those described by Arpan (1991) and Kujawa (1991). Students who enrolled in the program were thought to benefit from the exposure to a diverse mix of nationalities in the classroom; Americans transferring from Boston would merely have enjoyed the added learning experience of living in a major European capital. Faculty sent from Boston would be able to undertake research on-site in Europe, and would be challenged by the perspectives of Europeans working in all sorts of companies. And, of course, some administrators liked the notion of foreign ventures.

These were the benefits readily expressed when the question "why?" arose. Implementation of the program yielded day-to-day and term-to-term problems causing derived benefits to be serendipitous rather than planned consequence.

FACULTY

In addition to the resident director who taught one course each term, faculty from Boston were brought in as the program added its full complement of core and elective courses. Four full-time faculty, the resident director, and one or two adjunct faculty taught approximately twelve courses each term. The expatriate faculty enjoyed a variety of benefits so that money was not an important issue. While some suffered culture shock, most did what they had come to Brussels to do. Senior faculty taught and toured a lot; junior faculty taught, wrote, and toured less. The courses taught were the same ones taught in Boston; the European students, for the most part, liked it that way. Faculty writing, typically, was the final part of research executed in the United States. The relatively short time in Brussels—six to fifteen months—made it unlikely that any major initiative would be started, much less completed, with

Belgian- or Europe-based companies. The exceptions were two new faculty who were posted to Brussels before settling into Boston. Their contracted time in Brussels was a little longer and they had no felt need to tend to things at home.

The pool of BU faculty interested in a posting to Brussels was soon exhausted. The common reasons for disinterest were dual-career marriages, consulting, and research that required the professor to stay in the United States. Some said that the lack of adequate library and computer facilities would hinder their research potential. The School of Management successfully used the Brussels opportunity as a recruiting device, but soon the school had to rely upon visiting professors to staff the courses. The visiting faculty available, often on short notice, were content to teach and tour. On balance, in the prime years of its operation (1972-1977), the BU's Brussels MBA venture allowed a few of the regular faculty to finish their research agendas as they had to teach only two evenings each week. However, benefit gained from living and working in Brussels probably was not much more than was to be had from an assignment in one of the U.S. Department of Defense European programs administered by BU's Metropolitan College and counterparts at other universities.

STUDENTS

With no meaningful market research to support the establishment of the Brussels venture, the profile of the customers was always of keen interest. In its best years, some 130-150 persons were enrolled with an average age of around 30 years. A representative semester found this student body to comprise 40-45 percent Belgians, 25-30 percent other Europeans, and 20-25 percent Americans. It was not unusual to have as many as twenty-five nationalities in the program. Clearly, the cultural diversity in a given class was far beyond any class on the home campus, day or evening.

As in most part-time programs, large companies were heavily represented—not least because they were more likely to pay at least some of the tuition. The large companies in this case were U.S. multinationals using Brussels as European headquarters (e.g., ITT, Phillips Petroleum) or having manufacturing subsidiaries in Belgium. These companies tended to account for most of the non-Belgian Europeans, a substantial number of the Belgians, and half of the Americans. The rest of the Belgians worked in Belgian companies of all sorts and sizes. The other Americans tended to be non-working spouses, young expatriates, and an occasional transfer student. There were also a few full-time students of different nationalities who preferred to study in Brussels for all or at least part of BU's MBA program.

There were very few students enrolled in BU or elsewhere in the United States who took advantage of the Brussels operation as a study abroad opportunity. Non-systematic research revealed the reasons: a dislike of evening classes, fewer electives, lack of foreign language skills, absence of a housing program and, perhaps most telling, no awareness that the School of Management actually had such a program!

ADMINISTRATION

The School of Management administration was certainly aware of its Brussels program. Staffing the courses was a chronic problem, driven by the needs of the MBA core courses. Any other reasons for encouraging a particular professor to take an assignment, such as developing an international perspective, were of very marginal consideration. There was no interest in building institutional ties with Belgian or other European schools and their faculties because too many of the paying customers made it clear that they wanted American instructors and style of instruction. One of the resident directors added very high quality European adjuncts who had been trained in the better U.S. schools (e.g., MIT, Yale), but this was viewed by many—students in Brussels—faculty and administration in Boston as somewhat subversive because it was believed that the financial viability of the program depended on its successfully positioning itself as the only AACSB accredited MBA available in Europe, with most of the stress on the first "A."

For the rest of the administrative challenges, any textbook treatment of a company's first foreign venture would catalog the issues. The resident director, armed with a two-page delegation of authority from the BU President, had to manage all of the functions found on a campus, except room and board. The resident director had to make the School of Management's academic system work for older foreign students with only minor compromises. Happily, the school's administrators did not want to know the messy detail of day-to-day operations in Brussels. They did want copies of the auditor's reports, but these remained mysterious because the Belgian auditors had no experience with a private university operation and the accounting system imposed did not fit very well.

The resident director learned a lot about U.S. bilateral tax treaties, the vagaries of foreign exchange, European banking practices, import regulations, expatriate benefit packages, Belgian wage and benefit administration, local custom on leases and the tricks of indexation, and social custom—from protocol for the local nobility, to petty bribes for the postmen and trash collectors. Brussels lost almost all benefit of this cumulative learning experience when the resident director resigned from BU and left Belgium. The professor left with a wealth of experience and the school with the residual problems.

LESSONS IN LOST OPPORTUNITIES

The BU Brussels program enjoyed no initial great enthusiasm or support in Boston. The School of Management was preoccupied with installing a new dean and getting curriculum options in health care and in public administration up and running. There were a few courses with an international title but no programs in international business. One professor was busy recruiting and coordinating faculty placement for the Department of Defense programs administered by another BU college. The Brussels MBA program was a classic case of "out of sight, out of mind."

A faculty posting to Brussels was not part of a strategy to internationalize faculty or curriculum. Some individuals benefitted professionally and most found the experience of foreign residency to be positive in personal terms. The school made no programmatic effort to build on the faculty experience, nor did the school try to use the Brussels program as a valuable vehicle to enhance student exposure to international business. It was simply there for anyone who wanted to pursue it in the face of bureaucratic inertia.

Constant financial difficulties with the Brussels program caused the School of Management to merge its wholly-owned and operated venture into a joint program with the Flemish Free University in Brussels. The BU AACSB-accredited MBA is no longer offered. It was a program far ahead of its time and too far ahead of its home base. (Even Harvard opened and closed a venture in Switzerland in the mid-1970s.) Over a hundred MBA graduates benefitted from the Brussels program; unfortunately, BU's lack of a plan to use the venture as part of an effort to internationalize the home institution's faculty and students resulted in little positive impact on BU's School of Management.

VENTURE IN THE LATE 1980S:
TULANE UNIVERSITY IN FRANCE

BACKGROUND AND HISTORY

Founded in 1834, Tulane University is a private, nonsectarian institution located in New Orleans. Although its student population is only about 40 percent of the size of BU, the university has eleven schools and colleges and is ranked among the top thirty research universities in the United States. Its A.B. Freeman School of Business dates to 1914 and is one of the founders of the AACSB. Tulane's liberal arts component has conducted a Junior Year Abroad program with a base in Paris for over forty years.

Although Tulane's business school has had a goodly number of faculty with expatriate experience and interest in international subject matter, it made no programmatic effort to internationalize anything until 1988. Rigid curriculum requirements had discouraged study abroad with other institutions and had permitted foreign transfer students to study for less than the full degree program, on only an experimental basis. The foreign graduate student population has fluctuated from 10 to 20 percent, but these were full-time students in New Orleans for the entire curriculum. The curriculum had a number of international electives and in 1988 the faculty voted that an MBA student must take one international course of his choice to fulfill degree requirements.

In late 1987, an acting dean supported the move of the Academy of International Business Secretariat to the school in the hope of stimulating further faculty interest in internationally oriented research and course design, and of using AIB as an information center in broadening the school's international outlook. At the same time, the director of Executive Education was encouraged to pursue involvement with the newly forming International Management Center in Budapest.

MISSION

In mid-1988, a new dean arrived on campus with internationalization as one of his stated goals. More specifically, he wanted to provide study abroad programs for Tulane students. His desire for speed, coupled with the faculty's desire to meticulously screen courses offered abroad by other institutions, resulted in the straightforward approach—to establish the school's own venture, to be staffed by Tulane faculty offering existing courses.

The director of Executive Education was appointed associate dean for Continuing Education and International Programs. He understood his mission was to be to locate a cost-effective site for offering summer courses in Europe, and he concluded that the best bet was a small school in Holland unknown to any of the faculty. On learning this, the international faculty—a self-defined group—met a few times and voiced its concern about the quality of institutional association and the lack of plans for developing faculty-to-faculty relationships.

The dean apparently accepted the faculty's concern about quality of association and arranged dormitory and classroom space at HEC's Jouy-en-Josas campus. In 1990, the program offered the school's existing courses in international marketing and international strategy to nineteen MBA and five BSM students. An approach to the curriculum committee on developing new courses for the summer program was rebuffed. The package was enhanced with the offer of internships of four to six weeks in Italy, West Germany, Austria, and Hungary. With positive feedback from the participants, Tulane was encouraged to offer a program for undergraduates in Cambridge (with no affiliation with the British university) and another for MBA students in Taipei in 1991. Neither was repeated in 1992; courses were offered in Hungary and France with internships only for MBA students in a number of countries. The administration retains some ties with HEC and the IMC in Budapest but, after four years, the AIB Secretariat moved on to Wayne State as Tulane's support was systematically reduced.

FACULTY

The Tulane faculty supports the concept of broadening student exposure and experience to international subject matter and environments. The internationally oriented faculty have been excluded from program building and usually get information on the administration's plans for international activities from interested students. Those who have taught the courses in France have received the normal pay for teaching on campus plus a supplement for expenses abroad; they have concluded that the financial incentive was a bit less than break even.

Other incentives are self-generated. The design of the program finds most of the time abroad spent in class or in preparation.

There is little time during the program duration to go into Paris from HEC for corporate or other research contacts. No relations have been established by Tulane faculty with HEC faculty. Basically, if one wants to stay and do research in July and August, one does it on one's own time and expense. A junior faculty member who taught in the program and also had a prior commitment for research funding, was later denied the committed research support because he was paid to teach the courses. With faculty thus finding the summer abroad program not especially attractive, the administration has compressed the calendar time for the courses and is experimenting with adjunct and visiting professors to bolster the programs. The internships have spread to France, the United Kingdom, Spain, West Germany, Austria, Czechoslovakia, Hungary, Poland, former USSR, Taiwan, P.R.C., Indonesia, and Japan.

STUDENTS

The growth in interest in Tulane's summer abroad programs has been substantial, from 23 students in France in 1989, to 37 MBA and 22 BSM students studying in Jouy-en-Josas, Cambridge, and Taipei in 1991. Initially the deal was seen by some as too good to be true because the students could drop to part-time status for one semester after the summer courses and save tuition to offset the cost of the summer. The numbers made the internships become attractive even in a financial sense. While this opportunity has been eliminated by changing the price structure, the favorable experiences of the students returning from Europe are likely to keep demand high; the 1991 participation is about 25 percent and 15 percent of the MBA and BSM classes, respectively.

ADMINISTRATION

The dean wanted to create study and work abroad opportunities for students and the school has done so. The administration drives the system with a foreign early retiree from Exxon Chemicals lining up internships and handling the necessary public relations work with visiting foreigners and supporting the IB student club. The study abroad component has been extended to the Executive MBA program with a seven- to ten-day European visit added to the end of the program.

All of these activities are consistent with the university's vague but stated desire for an enhanced global emphasis in education.

There was little concern in the administration for developing the international interests of the faculty. The dean refused to support tenure for an internationally oriented associate professor in spite of a favorable faculty vote; the dean has given some indication that he prefers to have the traditional discipline faculty hire for the discipline first and for international orientation secondarily, rather than hire those whose primary focus is international.

TULANE'S APPROACH VS. CURRENT WISDOM

Tulane has demonstrated that focused resources can generate strong student interest in international business activities. The emphasis however is clearly on the summer internships. No resources were allocated to developing a better international business curriculum or to take advantage of the foreign sites or the internship experiences; junior faculty have been warned that teaching abroad will in no way offset any shortcoming in publication rate; and senior faculty find the financial incentive wanting.

This observer believes that Tulane's efforts and results thus far are typical of a school jumping onto the internationalization bandwagon. There is no leadership and focus as described by several contributors to this volume (see Arpan, Kujawa). Current talk of "infusing" the curriculum is being driven by the concern to keep up with the well-publicized programs of major private institutions, not by any internal assessment. The issues of internationalizing the faculty (see Chapter Four by Brian Toyne) go unaddressed. Indeed, Tulane's own doctoral program is an example of the classic doctoral training deficiency (see Chapter Three). Some aspects of Tulane's overseas linkages are consistent with the advice of Green and Gerber (see Chapter Nineteen), but the school is woefully deficient on its critical factor of centrality of the faculty in ensuring that the linkages endure. This issue of faculty noninvolvement has a very strong parallel with BU's experience of nearly two decades ago, and promises much the same consequence.

CONCLUSION

This chapter has outlined the major features of two very different types of programs conducted in Europe. One program is successfully exposing the students to a far wider international experience than would be had on the home campus. Neither approach, however, has had any notable impact on the internationalization of curricula or faculty. Any faculty enhancement has been more idiosyncratic than programmatic. Tulane today, as was BU fifteen years ago, is committed to keeping its promises to its students; this is seen as virtually a contractual obligation. In both institutions this type of commitment yielded a contractual model for faculty involvement in the European ventures: a package of salary and overseas benefits in exchange for the teaching of certain courses, frequently negotiated at the eleventh hour. Internationalization of courses, research, and any particular prescription for individual faculty development, were rarely even discussed in the rush to staff courses before registration day. The ongoing research question thus is whether an internationalization effort can be successfully institutionalized by administrators in the absence of active faculty involvement in developing program mission and strategy. The ancillary question, of course, is whether faculty can be induced to support administration-driven internationalization efforts in the absence of a coherent strategy.

REFERENCES

American Council on Education (ACE). 1977. *Business and International Education*. Washington, D.C.: International Education Project, American Council on Education.

Academy of International Business (AIB). 1986. *Global Survey of International Business Curriculum*. Cleveland. Earlier versions were published in 1963, 1969, 1974, 1976, and 1980.

The Brookings Institution. 1975. *The International Dimension of Management Education*. Washington, D.C.: Brookings.

Business Week. 1990. "The Best Business Schools," 29 October.

_____. 1991. "Wharton Rewrites the Book On Business Schools," 13 May.

The Economist. 1991. "Management Section: Passport to Prosperity," 2 March.

Fortune. 1989. "Business Schools Get A Global Vision," 17 July.

Nehrt, L. C. 1981. *Case Studies of Internationalization of the Business School Curriculum*. St. Louis: AACSB.

Otteson, S., ed. 1968. *Internationalizing the Traditional Business Curriculum*. Bloomington: Bureau of Business Research, Graduate School of Business, Indiana University.

Zeff, S., ed. 1968. *Business Schools and the Challenge of International Business*. New Orleans: Graduate School of Business Administration, Tulane University.

Tactical Approaches To Achieving Long-Term Internationalization: The University of Miami

DUANE KUJAWA

INTRODUCTION

Internationalizing business schools and faculty is a complex subject to say the least. Much of any business school's internationalization strategy must be situation-specific—reflecting institutional strengths and weaknesses, faculty desires and competencies, etc. This book seeks to examine alternative approaches, models, and procedural guidelines. I feel I can best contribute to these objectives by relating an experience with which I am very familiar—the University of Miami's recent internationalization activities.

In the summer of 1990, the University of Miami's (UM) School of Business Administration embarked upon a new direction—to become an *international* school of business administration. Several events contributed to this decision, including the appointment of a new dean in the spring of 1990, a person with international executive experience and a strong interest in international business. Further, the award of a U.S. Department of Education CIBER grant, announced in the summer of 1990, was seen as "energizing" various units within the business school, the university, and the local community, in terms of cooperation and business school internationalization.

In the summer of 1990, this author conducted an "international business base line study" which factually presented the school's international involvement and capabilities at the time. Some committees, relating to graduate programs, undergraduate programs, and faculty development, were then constituted. The graduate programs subcommittee was charged with the responsibility for developing the proposed curriculum for the (eventually designated) dual-degree program in international business (i.e., the Master of Business Administration/Master of Science in International Business, or MBA/MSIB Program). This mandate was accomplished in February 1991 and the proposed program received overwhelming approval by the School of Business Administration faculty. The program was approved by the Graduate School of the University of Miami in May 1991. We enrolled the first class in August 1992.

THE UNIVERSITY OF MIAMI STRATEGY

The School of Business currently finds itself in a position of having to establish a distinctive identity among local, regional, and national competitors. This need can be traced to the fact that (a) the traditional-age U.S. college population is shrinking (and its overall quality declining) and, (b) increased competition among universities and colleges is inevitable, especially for the more highly qualified student. Our premium price position, relative to local and regional competitors, further underscores the need to develop a distinct product and identity.

A strategy of distinctiveness through internationalization offers several advantages. First there is a real demand for an internationalized business education at all student levels. Employers are demanding business school graduates well versed in the concepts of global competition and comfortable in a multicultural, multilingual environment. Executive-level students want to prepare for the internationalization of their companies and industries; MBAs and undergraduates want training that will differentiate them from others in the job market. Some well-known U.S. business schools are already responding in this way (e.g., Wharton and Georgetown). Second, the school enjoys a number of natural and organizational advantages in providing an internationalized business education. These include location, culture, climate, international image, diversity of student body, diversity of faculty, level of faculty/administration interest, and a local international business community. More than most schools, we are endowed with factors that give us a distinct opening advantage in this area.

THE INTERNATIONALIZATION CONCEPT

Internationalization is distinct from the idea of an international business program. It is a more pervasive concept in the sense that it penetrates the school, not as the topic and responsibility of a specific faculty department, but as the overall orientation of the institution. The difference between these concepts reflects the changed nature of business itself: the principles of accounting, finance, marketing etc., are not necessarily different; their application, however, is more complicated in the more complex environment of global competition. In this model, the school's objective is not simply to offer more IB courses and process more IB majors, but to give all our students, regardless of specialization, a high-quality business education in an internationalized environment.

Organizationally, internationalization would function as an umbrella concept under which the school's current structure of centers, departments, and majors operates. (A redefined and strengthened IB specialization would simply be one of many concentrations offered by the school.) The programmatic elements of the internationalization strategy (e.g., on-campus and foreign teaching, research, faculty exchange, etc.) would be administered through the office of the associate dean for International Programs, consisting of the dean and an advisory council of interested faculty. The office would carry out its functions through a matrix structure, calling on faculty and administrative departments to staff and support its activities.

Regarding the faculty's role in internationalization, we envision three possible (and cumulative) levels of response. As a minimum response, faculty would be expected to establish, through their regulation methodologies, an international context for the subject material they already teach. This might be accomplished through selection of lecture examples, cases, assigned readings, term paper topics, invited speakers, or any other mechanism of choice. This would not necessarily entail changing the content of a course, but would alter the context in which it is presented. At the second level of response, faculty would add, where appropriate, specific international modules to their regular course content. At the third level of response, interested faculty would develop and offer new courses on the international dimensions of their specialty. It should be noted, however, that not all faculty will likely have interests in expanding their international teaching and research competencies at any of these three levels. For those who choose to pursue the international dimension, the intent is to provide the necessary support and incentives.

Internationalization is also achieved through the environment and culture the school is able to create for its members. In this regard, we envision a greater number of foreign executives, executives from local MNCs and, possibly, ministers of trade and commerce as guest speakers. Recruiting and marketing efforts would be focused on attracting greater numbers of qualified foreign students at all levels. This in turn would require increased support of, and involvement with, international professional and student groups. The objective is to create an intellectually stimulating, culturally diverse, yet cohesive business school community, with a strong network of international alumni.

ACHIEVING THE DISTINCTIVENESS GOAL

A significant number of business schools around the country will attempt to achieve greater international focus. The key competitors are those schools that already have a significant IB component— they are prepared to have in place the personnel, experience, and contacts in this area. Most schools will choose one of two strategies:

1. *Increased IB specialization.* Schools in this category will move in the direction of greater academic specialization within IB programs and majors. They will be responding to a primarily domestic demand for IB specialists or for people with functional-plus-IB specialization. Their main objective will be to train U.S. students and managers for a more global marketplace. They will remain U.S. business schools, but with greater competency in the international business area.
2. *Greater international market scope.* A second group of schools will establish linkages with overseas institutions and programs as a way of increasing the scope of their markets and thereby defending revenues and spreading risks. The major emphasis here is on taking existing faculty skills and applying them in other market environments.

We propose a goal of becoming an international school of business administration. Such a school would move along both of the above dimensions (i.e., greater IB specialization applied to a wider set of markets). Ultimately, it would share many of the features of institutions such as INSEAD, IMD, IESE, The London Business School, INCAE and other such institutions that cater to a global market, participate in programs with corporations and institutions around the world, and address issues that may relate to any one of a number of countries, to one or more regions, and on occasion to the worldwide business community. In order to accomplish this,

EXHIBIT I

Sequential Internationalization of the Business School

	U.S. School of Business	*IB -Focused U.S. Business School*	*International School of Business*
Structure	Departmental	Departmental plus IB	Department plus off-campus sites
Perspective	U.S.	International Business Increasing Global Focus	Global Focus
Student Mix	U.S. Latin America	U.S./Global Focus World	50%+, including foreign sites
Faculty Mix	U.S. trained	U.S. trained	Overseas rotation visitor exchange; 1/3 foreign born faculty
Curriculum Development	Departmental	IB Programs– Global contexts added to core courses	Global and IB permeate core and functional specialties
IB-Focused Faculty Development	IBBI funding, if available	Tied to new income from degree and non-degree programs	Tied to off-campus sites
Types Of Support	n.a.	Curriculum development Joint research with visitors Research while in overseas assignments	Off-campus site programs Programmatic research Research on issues of relevance to off-campus sites

EXHIBIT 2

Comparison Of Leading Programs With IB Emphasis

Institution	Degree/ Duration	IB Specialization	Language Requirements	International Internship	International Placement	Two-Year Out-of-State Tuition	Other Remarks
Northwestern	MBA six quarters	4-course option	None; Non-credit courses available	Available. None promised; Student exchange with Thai and 7 European schools	Major career resource center; Hosts int'l career conference	$33,100	Top 5 school; rapidly becoming more international
Wharton/ Lauder Institute	MBA/MA in area studies; 21 months	Regular functional majors plus area studies	Required for entry, additional for-credit course work	Required in summer of 1st year; required area-focused research	Extensive facility	$49,000	top 5 school; blue chip advisory board
NYU	MBA 2 acad. yrs.	IB may be combined with functional major, IB Department	None	None	Extensive list of MNCs recruit	$30,840	Ranked #1 in IB by AIB. 24 IB facult:. also offers MBA/French studies joint degree
Michigan	MBA 2 acad. yrs.	IB major possible. IB Dept. offers courses in MKT, FIN, MGMT, policy	None	Student exchange with seven major European schools	None	$31,400	Joint degrees in international studies on Japan; Near East, North Africa, Asia, East European; top 25 school

(cont.)

Indiana	MBA 21 months	5-course major. Int'l electives are offered in IB Department and other departments	None	None. Domestic internship program (Summer)	None. Extensive list of firms recruit.	$17,000	Top-25 school. Long-standing IB Department has decayed.
Stanford	MBA 2 acad. years	MBA allows 14 electives; may choose from 17 IB electives	None	Student exchange in Japan	Career center recruited by 250 firms	$33,150	CBK has been internationalized. 60% of faculty has researched, taught, or developed teaching materials overseas
George Washington	MBA 2 acad. years	4-5 "field of instruction" electives plus some breadth courses	None	None	Extensive list of companies recruit	$16,600	Heavily internationalized university and setting
Thunderbird	MIM Up to 24 months or more	12 hrs. in international studies	15 credits	Full-time overseas available	Career center 100% int'l	$26,000 5,000 language fee	Not AACSB accredited; large alumni network; generalist degree

EXHIBIT 3

Visualizing Contents of IB Degree Programs

Core	Core courses with Global Context with IB Modules where Relevant
Specialty	Functional Specialization in 1-2 Business Areas
IB	IB Specialty Courses in Environment Strategy and Area Topics
Acculturation	Intensive Language Training
	Overseas Study and/or Work Program or Exchange Program
	Participation in Lectures, Seminars, and Other IB- Focused Activities

the UM School of Business and its faculty would have to agree on a number of important changes in structure, culture, faculty, and student make-up.

As already stated elsewhere in this document, this does not mean that faculty would be expected to become specialists in the international dimensions of their chosen functional areas, although some might elect to add such a specialization. It does mean understanding and dealing with a global context in the classroom and becoming more exposed to other cultures and clientele. It also means the school would commit sufficient resources to develop and reward its faculty with concrete international interests in expanding their global perspectives.

IMPLEMENTATION

The ultimate goal is ambitious and will take time to achieve. Getting there is a serious challenge. In order to successfully carry out this strategy, we will need to make significant changes in our organizational structure and culture. Structurally, we envision the establishment of a high-level product champion (e.g., an associate dean for International Programs) who will advocate necessary changes, coordinate resources, and focus efforts for implementation. Moreover, we will need a bridge strategy that will make the ultimate goal attainable.

1. Transitional Stage: Globally Focused U.S. School

During the transition stage, the most logical step is to build on existing strengths and to broaden the global business capabilities of the faculty. This means:

- Starting high-visibility degree programs in the IB area, such as an MIBS program and an enhanced EMBA/IB degree program (These programs become a banner for globalization of the business school. Exhibit 3 shows the generic features of such IB degree programs as they are envisioned for the school.)
- Joint-venture overseas programs that will afford an opportunity for a broad cross-section of the faculty to come into contact with academic colleagues business people, students and issues overseas
- Recognizing that there will be start-up costs, there would be a commitment to investing marginal profits from additional tuition and program revenues in faculty development efforts: research support, faculty exchanges and language training
- Expanding opportunities for students to learn and work in foreign environments; attracting exchange students

The end results would be:

- All departments engaging in faculty exchange and/or overseas visiting assignments on a continuing basis
- Regular courses, particularly core courses, becoming more reflective of the global environment.
- Resources being made available for increasing globalization of existing courses and/or IB-course development
- Resources being made available for overseas and/or IB research opportunities
- An increase in the number of students pursuing IB programs
- An increase in the percentage of students from overseas, building on our existing strengths with Latin America, but expanding further into other parts of the world
- IB programs requiring international experience, language training, and more integration across disciplines

To accomplish this, we propose a matrix type of organization in which an International Business (IB) focal area is represented at the associate dean level. While departments will preserve their autonomy, it is envisioned that this area will exercise leadership support for internationalization of the School of Business. This IB position will champion the internationalization of the business school in several dimensions:

- Coordinating efforts to recruit a more diverse student body
- Facilitating exchange programs with foreign institutions
- Coordinating curriculum development along two dimensions:
- Use of examples, contexts, cases, and other materials in regular core courses that emphasize a global business context, and
- Strengthening the quality and depth of functional courses in the IB area.
- Working with faculty in the development of a MIBS program and strengthening the regular MBA's and BBA's IB specialization; strengthening the IFM program and extending its concept to other functional areas; expanding and strengthening the current International Business Executive MBA program.
- Acting as a profit center whose additional revenues from MIBS and other programs will fund several areas of faculty development:
- Grants for curriculum development tied to faculty participating in overseas and other special programs
- Grants for research projects with foreign scholars and institutions that may not necessarily be on IB topics but will enhance the multicultural exposure of the faculty
- Grants for intensive language learning, possibly tied to overseas special program assignments
- Administration of foreign internship and foreign study assignments for academically qualified students
- Developing off-campus sites for regular academic and specialized executive education programs

2. Ultimate Stage: Internationalized School of Business

Eventually we envision the school becoming a multicultural center where students from anywhere could come and work with faculty who have a degree of familiarity with foreign environments. The school would operate on a joint-venture basis with permanent (degree and nondegree) programs in all significant areas of the world, including Western Europe, Eastern Europe, Latin America, and Asia. These programs would be ongoing and would become profit centers funding a number of teaching and research activities of the faculty. The institution at this point would not be unlike educational institutes such as INSEAD, IMD, INCAE, or IESE, which operate multiple campus sites to serve the needs of students, corporations, and executives in several countries, or, like Wharton and Georgetown, which are in the process of internationalizing.

The school would be a focal point of interest for a group of corporations and international agencies, who would channel middle-

and upper-level executives to our programs. These organizations, situated in at least two other regions of the world, would be contributors to the school and would be employers of our graduates.

At this point, the need for an IB champion and administrative unit would diminish. Some departmental IB programs may, in fact, be curtailed, as internationalization creeps into the rest of the program offering.

While this may be a challenging concept of a business school, many of its features have been attained by other institutions, in environments as diverse as the UK (London Business School), Spain (IESE), Costa Rica (INCAE), and Switzerland (IMD). They have been successful in nurturing their faculty and strengthening their regular programs. Moreover, the institutions that have successfully pursued this strategy have distinguished themselves for the excellence of their research and teaching, as well as for their financial viability.

The faculty who are teaching the first two-year cycle (August 1992 through July 1994) of the program have participated in initial curriculum planning meetings. Our objectives at these meetings were to: (1) have each faculty person specifically identify how his/her course will contribute to the development of the student as an international business person or international manager, as identified in the program's own objective statement, and (2) have "brainstorming" sessions among the program faculty (identified as "Team One") on methods for internationalizing the business core courses and restructuring the traditional MBA.

Given the University of Miami experience thus far, what might I suggest regarding the key issues of internationalization?

Internationalizing business school faculty, curriculum, and programs is an ongoing, long-term process. It requires both short-term and long-term goals (which obviously must relate to one another). Since internationalization means redirection and adjusted allocations of resources and rewards, it also requires leadership at the top. There are three aspects to this—a dean that is committed to internationalization, a key person with leadership qualified to champion the effort, and substantial faculty support. The process of internationalization also needs to be a very open process. Faculty, administrators, students, business people, etc. should all be involved from the very beginning. This involvement helps not only in the design of the program, but also in the "selling" of the program—whether it be to faculty for program approval and implementation, to students as potential participants, or to business people as potential sponsors of student internships and employers of the program's graduates.

It is difficult to say which approach or model is best for any specific business school regarding its internationalization efforts. The larger schools and the leaders (such as the University of South Carolina and New York University) can, of course, define the "mainstream" regarding international business programs. The newer entrants must be careful to define their niches, or be willing to dedicate substantial resources over a long period of time to the task of being a "lead school" in this area. Internationalization, for them, must be a deliberate, calculated strategy. And, of course, there is always risk!

Linkages with Overseas Business Schools

ROBERT T. GREEN AND LINDA V. GERBER

INTRODUCTION

The establishment of linkages with overseas academic institutions is widely recognized as a mechanism that U.S. business schools can employ to aid their internationalization efforts. These linkages are types of strategic alliances that business schools can form in order to accomplish multiple objectives associated with internationalization, particularly the provision of overseas teaching opportunities for faculty and study opportunities for students. Business schools will find it difficult to build and staff international subsidiaries of the same size and quality as their U.S. "home offices." Linkages with foreign institutions can provide the synergies and other benefits frequently associated with international joint ventures in business. At the same time, many of the same problems, pitfalls, and cautions pertinent to strategic business alliances are equally relevant to the success of international educational linkages.

With internationalization a critical concern in most colleges of businesses today, many colleges and universities have rushed into establishing linkages with foreign schools. While many of these have proved successful, a far greater number have yielded disappointing results. Many linkages, forged with great expectations, lie dormant, surfacing only when mentioned in speeches by college administrators to document the university's international focus. Further, many of the successful linkages are limited in scope, either with regard to areas of cooperation or geographic emphasis.

The establishment of linkages figures prominently in the internationalization strategy being employed by the Center for International Business Education and Research at the University of Texas

249

at Austin (UT). The important role played by the formation of these alliances with foreign institutions has led to the development of considerable experience in this realm. The purpose of this chapter is to share this experience by presenting the factors that we have found to be critical in the development of successful linkages. We hope that others can benefit from our experience and perhaps avoid some of the mistakes and problems we have encountered along the way.

CRITICAL FACTORS

The ten "keys to success" presented below are not intended to be comprehensive. Many of the critical factors noted are a result of lessons that have been learned the hard way, and we certainly will commit more mistakes that can be codified at a later date. With the exception of the first three, the "keys" are not presented in any particular order of importance. The first three critical factors are crucial to the internationalization process in general, but the others pertain primarily to the formation of these strategic alliances between business schools.

DEAN'S SUPPORT

If you do not enjoy the strong support of your dean, you probably should not even start the process of linkage development. Support of the dean is one of those factors that is fundamental to all aspects of business school internationalization. The necessity of this support is strongly advocated during the initial development of linkages. Two of the main ways the dean's support will contribute to the formation of linkages are in the areas of mitigating faculty resistance and overcoming administrative hurdles.

There will be members of the faculty who strongly resist the formation of linkages with overseas institutions. These faculty are often respected and well-intentioned individuals who simply do not believe that establishing linkages is in the best interests of the school. Such opposition is frequently the result of the incipient ethnocentrism found in all faculty, with regard to many areas of activity. In the case of linkages with overseas business schools, this ethnocentrism takes the form of believing that, for instance, students cannot receive a better business education than that found in the United States. This belief, in turn, leads to the conclusion that students should therefore not study business abroad.

Strong support from the dean is essential to avoid the obstacles that such an attitude can place in the way of linkage development.

The dean's support is equally invaluable in helping to negotiate the bureaucratic maze that frequently hinders the development of linkages. Bureaucratic barriers exist at all universities, but they probably represent a greater obstacle in public and very large institutions. Public institutions are frequently governed at least partly by state agencies that apparently enjoy the promulgation and enforcement of "the rules"; usually there exists a labyrinth of policies and procedures that represents steep hurdles to any type of change. Large institutions tend to have correspondingly large bureaucracies, and these bureaucracies thrive on rules. Still, all universities possess some labyrinth of procedures, regardless of size or source of funding. The establishment of linkages will almost always involve the bending and breaking of institutional rules. Without the strong support of the dean, it becomes virtually impossible to initiate these rulebreaking activities.

While the dean's support is invaluable, a word of caution is in order. Often deans who are supportive of international efforts are unaware of the problems such linkages can present. While it may not be advisable to discourage support with excessive warnings, some education of a dean regarding possible difficulties is advisable. Clearly, probable costs associated with maintaining and establishing linkages should be understood by the dean. It is also critical to develop, with the dean, a blueprint of the priorities and strategy for overseas linkages in order to avoid initial associations that may not be in the longrun interest of the college and to encourage attention to those which are most desirable.

At the University of Texas, there is a high demand for MBA elective courses. Yet, we reserve a few seats in selected elective courses for exchange students who will be studying at our campus. There is the potential for this policy to cause resentment among UT students, faculty, and administrators, on the grounds that "foreign" students are occupying class seats that exempt some of our own students from classes they demand. We took pains to inform the dean that this might be an issue, and made him clearly aware of the fact that an equal number of our own students were studying abroad, thus not using the class seats in UT courses. We have also found it useful to explain to the dean that both faculty and students who travel abroad on exchanges or for research may experience unusual problems and general culture shock that could lead to the dean receiving some surprising, and often alarming, feedback from the parties involved. In these situations, it is critical to have open communication with the dean in order to provide the information necessary to correctly interpret these messages.

THE CHAMPION

It is not necessary to dwell too long on the necessity of one faculty member to play the role of champion for the establishment of the linkages. This is another general requirement for internationalization that is frequently discussed. There needs to be a faculty member of sufficient stature in the business school who will make the personal commitment to tackle the hurdles and to make the administrative arrangements. In colleges where international business is not central to the mission it, generally speaking would not be desirable for the champion to be an individual associated primarily with international business programs. While as noted, the dean's support is critical, in the long run a foundation of support for linkages and all internationalization activities must be built among the faculty. Support is easier established when the champion is an individual with a broad base of interaction throughout the school or college. It is also desirable for this individual to be a member of the faculty rather than someone who is exclusively an administrator. Administrators are prone to higher mobility than faculty member and, in the early stages, establishing linkages requires a continuity in personal associations and the development of institutional memory. Ideally, this would be a senior-level faculty member from a core area within the business school. The role of champion is certainly a demanding one, but it is frequently a thankless one—one should not expect any additions to pay raises— and those who undertake this role need to have commitment, drive, and a large tolerance for frustration.

THE PLAN

Do not enter into linkages without some sort of general strategy that includes the objectives to be achieved through the formation of linkages. A common mistake is an acceptance of affiliation with the first foreign schools to make an overture. These schools may turn out to have strengths that are unrelated to your objectives. As in any business activity, the best results are achieved when you enter into an activity with a plan that includes the strategic objectives to be accomplished. The existence of a plan also protects you from interested and/or enthusiastic faculty members who will recommend specific linkages based on their personal interests or associations. In many cases, these affiliations will be of limited value to your college and university, but you do not want to alienate the faculty member from supporting the international program. A well-defined set of objectives will provide the rationale for avoiding undesirable affiliations without severely dampening the enthusiasm of critical internal supporters.

The first three critical factors are common to all aspects of the internationalization effort. The discussion here has been focused on how they apply to the formation of linkages. However, these factors are equally essential to the general achievement of internationalization on the part of a business school. The remaining factors are more specific to the formation of linkages, and they represent both strategic and tactical aspects of the linkage process.

TwoWay Benefits

A strong linkage will develop with another school only if the benefits flow in both directions. This statement sounds so obvious that one wonders why it is included. Yet, it is violated so frequently that schools must give overt consideration to the benefits accruing to all partners in the linkage arrangement, before entering into an agreement. For example, the University of Texas had established a relationship with a university in Southeast Asia. The relationship developed chiefly because of a high-level administrator at the Asian university who had once been a member of the faculty at UT. Each year a few of the students from that university would study at UT as part of their graduate work. However, due to the language requirements and the nature of the curriculum at that school, no student from UT had ever studied at the Asian institution. Over time it became impossible to justify support of the exchange without any reciprocal benefits for the University of Texas. The relationship ultimately was terminated, but with great difficulty on both a personal and institutional level.

It is not at all uncommon to affiliate with a school just for the sake of affiliation, only to find that the partner school receives all the tangible benefits, whereas the only benefit your school receives is the somewhat dubious distinction of being affiliated. With the generally high reputation of American business schools, at least to foreign students aiming for greater career marketability, this can be a particular risk for colleges of business. Many foreign schools seek affiliation with U.S. business programs for primarily marketing reasons, with little interest in more substantive alignments. In general this will not lead to any exchange of benefits, and may in extreme cases lead to an embarrassing situation for the schools involved. Regardless of the objectives of the affiliation, if the benefits are not reciprocal on some level, it is virtually certain that the linkage will not exist in the long run.

An important consideration in the evaluation of benefits to the institutions is to recognize that the benefits need not be the same for both institutions. Linkages may take many forms. These include such commonly employed forms as exchange of faculty and students to participate in standard academic coursework. In addition, schools may pursue linkages to provide opportunities for doctoral and postdoctoral research, internship programs, special courses for students to learn about business activities in specific geographic regions, expansion and enhancement of executive development programs, or even assistance in curriculum development and design. It is not necessary that the activities be the same on both sides of the partnership. The two schools may have different objectives they want to accomplish through the linkage. As long as the partner schools receive benefits that equally contribute to the achievement of each school's objectives, successful collaboration can occur. For instance, the U.S. institution may be seeking overseas teaching opportunities for its faculty, while the foreign institution wishes to provide U.S. business study opportunities for its students. If both institutions value the benefit they are receiving from such an arrangement, the linkage can work. This determination can be made, however, only if you understand the goals and objectives of your prospective partners.

EQUALITY IN RELATIONS

The partner institution must be considered an equal, and not a "country cousin." This is another seemingly obvious rule that is violated repeatedly. Educational systems vary widely across nations. There is a strong tendency in industrialized nations for educators to believe in the sanctity of their own systems. This phenomenon is, once again, reflective of a natural universal inclination toward ethnocentricity. To overcome the tendency, a school seeking linkages must be able to accept the differences between national education systems and be willing to develop a "fit" between their own system and the system of the partner. It is of utmost importance to avoid the tendency to view the partner's system as inferior. In fact, the partner's system is often inferior in some respects and superior in others. A successful linkage will combine the strengths of each partner's system for the benefit of both institutions.

In general, partner schools are not inferior, but rather, they are different. This fact makes it even more important for a school to closely screen prospective partner institutions. The screening should focus primarily on the mission, standards, and resources of the partner institution, rather than on the particular educational idiosyncrasies that characterize the nation in which the institution exists. A rough compatibility in schools' missions, standards, and resources is essential for most successful linkages. Do not be influenced by public relations materials. Any group with some money can put together an impressive brochure. A personal visit is usually required, or at the very least, recommendations should be solicited from third parties who are familiar with both your school and the prospective foreign partner.

It must be noted that sometimes schools will develop linkages with foreign institutions that are definitely inferior in terms of standards and resources. This situation frequently arises when a school from an industrialized nation establishes a linkage with a counterpart in a less developed nation. Even in these cases, however, the partner needs to be considered an equal, if there is a desire to develop a longterm relationship. In most cases, such linkages develop because the LDC institution wishes to upgrade, and the partner institution from the industrialized country derives such benefits as overseas teaching and research opportunities for its faculty. The treatment of the LDC institution as "second class" virtually ensures that once that institution achieves its objective, it will sever the relationship.

It is particularly useful to take a broad view of the benefits of linkages of this sort. When partner institutions are judged based on limited, overt, and often ethnocentric criteria related to educational quality, the tendency to treat the partner as inferior is more likely. It is important for all parties within the institution to consider a wider range of advantages including the implicit benefits from contact with foreign environments, particularly those most different from one's own, in order to maintain interaction based on the premise of equality.

CREATIVITY

The establishment of successful linkages requires creative approaches that address the differences between institutions. The need for large doses of creativity arises out of many of the factors mentioned above, especially the existence of rules that inhibit your ability to collaborate, and the different structures of national education systems. The creative circumvention of the rules requires the complete knowledge and support of your dean, and at least the knowledge and acquiescence of higher administration officials. If either of these ingredients is missing, then you jeopardize the future of the linkage established. If they are present, then you are in a position to exercise your creative abilities—you can operate openly, and you are in a position to obtain feedback with regard to whether your creative solutions are breaking or bending the "wrong" rules.

For example, the University of Texas has established a joint-degree program with the Koblenz School of Corporate Management in Germany. Students who participate in this program must be admitted to both institutions. However, due to the differences in educational systems between the United States and Germany, at the time they apply to UT, the students from Koblenz have not completed university work that the UT admissions offices considers to be the equivalent of a U.S. undergraduate degree. This, of course, would exempt them from admission to UT's MBA program. To deal with this situation, the UT admissions office has agreed to conditionally admit the German students but stipulate that they may not receive their MBA until they have completed their work at Koblenz and earned their Koblenz graduate degree.

The differences in educational systems will sometimes impose apparently insurmountable barriers to the establishment of linkages. One common problem is the difference in academic years between U.S. and foreign institutions. Others include the differences in instructional and evaluation approaches and curriculum philosophies. Another significant problem when faculty exchanges are desired, is the disproportionate salaries between U.S. faculty and those abroad, particularly those in less developed counties.

If a linkage is desired, however, ways can usually be found to overcome these barriers. For example, we encountered a school with an academic calendar totally incompatible with that of Texas, making a onesemester exchange of MBA students a problematic endeavor. However, class attendance at the overseas school is more flexible than at Texas—students take comprehensive examinations at a time of their choice. The situation permits their students to study for a semester at Texas, but what about the Texas students? We decided that the overseas school would arrange for a summer internship, combined with an independent study supervised by professors from the partner institution. This solution—while less than optimal for both sides—nonetheless permitted the establishment of an exchange. The exchange has been enthusiastically received by students at both schools, and it appears to be encouraging the establishment of additional forms of cooperation between our schools.

Other universities with experience in dealing with these barriers have developed a range of creative solutions. Several universities, both in the United States and abroad, have begun to offer short-term courses and programs designed primarily for international exchange. Shorter programs allow both faculty and students participating in exchanges to coordinate disparate scheduling problems between universities' normal academic cycles. Coordinating executive development programs to coincide with faculty exchanges have helped bridge the gap in salary rates between universities. Various private and governmental grants are also available to deal with this problem.

INSTITUTIONS, NOT INDIVIDUALS

Linkages should be established between institutions, and not between individuals. Too often, linkages between schools rest upon personal relations between faculty members at the two schools. If a linkage is to have a chance of becoming a longterm relationship, it must rise above the personal level. Individuals come and go, but universities are more permanent. The method employed by the business school to establish linkages must be such that it will transcend personal relations between individuals.

For example, a U.S. state college had enjoyed a long association with a Caribbean university, which was based solely on a close friendship between the deans of the two college's business schools. The dean at the U.S. school personally had handled all of the exchanges and interactions between the institutions. When this dean was replaced, the new administration had no personal stake in continuing the relationship and no formal institutional ties had been established to allow the partnership to survive the dean's departure. The linkage was promptly severed.

There is a major caveat that needs to be expressed in conjunction with this critical factor: It is difficult to establish close institutional linkages unless there is a spirit of collegiality and trust between the people at each school who are closely involved in the process. All of the hurdles and differences noted above mean that collaboration will often involve considerable interaction and mutual understanding between the people charged with the establishment of the linkage. If these people do not like each other, or if one of the parties proves unreliable in important aspects of linkage implementation, then the collaboration is unlikely to succeed. For a while, therefore, the linkage may depend very much on the ability of a couple of individuals on each side to work well together. This fact does not negate the rule of "institutional, not personal" linkages, however. The people involved need to appreciate the fact that their responsibility is to establish an institutional relationship that will endure even if they are not there. In doing this, it is useful for the individuals involved in initially establishing linkages to consider ways in which the activities of the linkage can be institutionalized. Systems must be established to facilitate the exchange. These systems should, as much as possible, be integrated into established programs and systems within each institution, and involve as many noninternational constituencies as possible. The long-run health of the linkage will be jeopardized to the extent that the individuals from either school engage in empire building, whether intentional or otherwise.

As an example, at the University of Texas, study abroad programs for the MBA students, along with other international linkages, were initiated through the International Programs/Center for International Business Education and Research (CIBER) unit within the College of Business. However, as the number of student exchange programs grew, it became clear that they could be best administered through the normal graduate administrative branch, the Graduate Student Services Office. As a result, all existing student exchanges are handled through this office, while the CIBER continues to develop new exchanges and initiate new international programs. Now the student exchange programs are firmly established as a core activity within the college. The international programs unit (CIBER) functions as an incubator for international activities to be fostered until they are sufficiently established to be effectively housed in other operating units of the college. The same approach was used in developing international internship programs which are now administered by the college's Career Services office.

INCREMENTALISM

Linkages between schools should develop on an incremental basis. It is usually a mistake to enter into a comprehensive initial collaborative agreement with school that involves several dimensions of academic collaboration (e.g., student exchanges, faculty exchanges, research agreements, executive programs, joint degree programs, etc.). Such comprehensive initial agreements should be avoided; since the two institutions do not know each other very well, they don't know whether they are compatible with each other. Too often, schools will enter into such agreements and find out later that they are incompatible. Like Hollywood marriages, the signing of these agreements make wonderful press releases. However, without the appropriate courtship period, such agreements can waste the time and resources of the two schools. In other words, get to know each other slowly.

Texas generally begins a linkage with an agreement to exchange students. Student exchanges are our preferred way to begin collaborative relations with another school for two reasons. First, student exchange represents a lowrisk form of interaction: minimal resources are required, and with a little advance effort, it is almost certain that the students will benefit from the exchange. It is also relatively easy to sever a student exchange agreement if the schools prove to be incompatible. Second, student exchanges are continuous over time, whereas other types of collaboration are likely to be intermittent. If the partner school offers a reasonably good opportunity for overseas study, it will be relatively easy to find students each year who want to participate in the exchange. Thus, the flow will be constant, enabling regular interaction between the schools so that the "getting to know you" process can proceed in a natural, lowrisk manner. If, over time, the two schools wish to expand their relations, they can do so. If not, then at least benefits have been obtained on both sides.

Any general model will have deviations, even within a school. Our own pattern with some partner schools differs from that noted above. Institutional or environmental factors may make it inadvisable to send students in one direction or another. It helps to have a general model to use as a starting point, however. For example, in one of our recent linkages with Thammasat University in Bangkok, the partnership was initiated through an exchange of faculty for the purpose of developing a Bachelor of Business Administration program. However, we plan to incorporate student exchanges in the future. This caveat does not negate the principal of incrementalism, it merely reasserts the need to be creative and flexible in the development of linkages.

Be Opportunistic

Linkage opportunities with the "right" schools may be available only at one point in time. You need to be vigilant in seeking possibilities for linkage, and prepared to act quickly when they present themselves. If you do not move very fast, they are likely to disappear. Such immediate action is not necessary in all cases, but it happens frequently enough that those in charge of the establishment of collaboration must keep it in mind. The need to be opportunistic means that, on occasion, you will have to be in a position to commit your school to an agreement on very short notice—and this is where having the support and confidence of the dean is especially important. Without this support, you will not be able to take advantage of some good opportunities when they arise. The need to be opportunistic also underlies the necessity of having a plan for the development of relations with overseas institutions. If you know the types of institutions with which you are seeking collaboration and the objectives your institution wants to accomplish, you are in a better position to move quickly when opportunities present themselves.

At the University of Texas, we generally are very measured in our approach to developing new alliances, taking time to evaluate whether a potential opportunity for linkage is both practical, and consistent with our overall strategic approach to international associations. However, we recently established a new partnership during a one-hour, unscheduled meeting. A year previously, we had determined that it would be desirable to have a partnership with a specific university in a certain Scandinavian country. However, our lack of associations with anyone at that school had precluded the opportunity to establish a relationship. Recently, a high-ranking member of the target university's faculty was visiting an associate in another college at the University of Texas. A quick meeting was arranged, where it was agreed to exchange students during the next year on a trial basis. While seemingly hasty given our normal policy of careful evaluation, the rapid agreement was appropriate because the association had already been determined to be consistent with our strategic plan and we had sufficient prior knowledge of the partner institution.

CENTRALITY WITHIN THE INSTITUTION

The individual(s) and entity involved in linkage formation must occupy a central position within the institution. If the international linkages are formed and implemented by individuals and offices that exist on the periphery of the institution, then these linkages will remain peripheral to the institution's operations. The institution cannot relegate the task of linkage formation to an office that has little respect from those central to the school's mission. In the case of business schools, those most central to the mission of the institution are the faculty. If the office and those who run it do not have the respect and support of the school's faculty, foreign linkages are likely to play a minor role in the school's future.

The "centrality rule" dictates that faculty be brought into the process throughout its development. Faculty will frequently need to be consulted about the appropriateness of prospective partners. Their feedback needs to be obtained on many issues relating to the linkages, such as the performance of students from linkage schools in their classes. It is especially helpful if faculty can benefit from the linkages, such as having an opportunity to teach overseas. In any event, those involved in linkage formation must be constantly aware of the need to be central to the organization, and that centrality can be obtained only with general faculty support.

Final Thoughts

The concept of forming linkages assumes a longrange perspective. The aim of such alignments is to develop integrated activities that closely link two institutions over time. While permitting obvious benefits, such linkages are not appropriate to all institutions or in all situations. For smaller colleges and universities, long-term relationships may not be practical. For example, to support continuing faculty exchanges, there must be a sufficiently large number of individuals with interest in exchanges with a specific partner to provide program continuity. It is not at all uncommon for universities to establish a partnership with a foreign institution for faculty exchanges, only to have the venture die of neglect once the available pool of interested faculty is exhausted. Such "economy of scale" problems are not limited to smaller institutions. Even large universities may be able to manage only a limited number of longterm alliances. In such situations, there are alternatives to a longrange relationship.

Schools may intentionally develop collaborative activities of a limited duration or for a specific purpose. Such an explicitly limited relationship is preferable to a neglected longterm linkage in that misunderstandings and ambiguities which could diminish the possibility for future cooperation are avoided. Another alternative is to join consortia. Many universities in different parts of the world have developed such consortia to provide the economies of scale necessary to support international programs. In addition, organizations exist that can serve as middlemen in arranging joint activities between institutions in different parts of the world. Such programs can be a useful alternative or supplement to long-term linkages.

We hope that the explicit recognition of some of the rules that we have learned in putting together Texas' network of overseas affiliations will be helpful to others who are in the early stages of this process. A last piece of advice is just to note that involvement in this process is going to severely test your tolerance for ambiguity. The nature of this business is such that you will frequently find yourself in situations that are new, working with people you do not know and who represent systems with which you are unfamiliar, and seeking solutions to problems you have so far not encountered. The level of ambiguity inherent in such situations is tremendous. Yet, such is the case in much of international business, and a high tolerance for ambiguity is certainly necessary for success in this realm.

The International Trade Centre's Approach to Internationalizing Business Training in Developing Countries

CLAUDE B. CELLICH

INTRODUCTION

In today's dynamic international business environment of keen competition, integrated regional markets, and an accelerated pace of technological change, enterprises need competent, flexible, and career-motivated managers with global business skills.

The greater participation of countries in world trade, including the expansion of global sourcing, has accentuated the importance of economic interdependence between nations and its profound effects on the nature of international business operations. This new situation calls for the development of new global strategies, abilities to manage technology, capacities for product innovation, and skills in working with people of diverse sociocultural backgrounds. To face the challenges of the 1990s and beyond, business, academia, and government organizations concerned with trade development, need to cooperate more closely to provide future managers with the relevant knowledge, practical skills, and essential values required in a global setting.

International operations is a complex business and likely to become even more so as product cycles get shorter, markets more sophisticated and trade standards more stringent. For instance, manufacturers of products affecting consumers' health and the environment are likely to face a growing number of restrictions from importing countries. The challenges of globalization will therefore dictate the way educational institutions train executives engaged in international trade. Some schools have already revised their organizational structures, their relationship with business, and their research priorities in order to improve their relevance to business (*The Economist* 1991a).

Those training institutions considering internationalizing their business curriculum or upgrading their executive development programs in international trade must begin by assessing the real world problems facing practitioners. A thorough understanding of the realities of international trade, both at the macro and enterprise levels, would place these institutions in a strong position to meet present and future training requirements of the business sector.

WHY NEW APPROACHES?

Managers engaged in international business need to have the necessary skills and know-how to solve problems in a global environment. This calls for training institutions to develop executives capable of managing change and facing challenges throughout their professional career. A recent study (*The Economist* 1991b), estimates that only 7 percent of a manager's learning takes place in an educational setting, the balance being acquired through job experience. The continuous flux and fluidity of the global marketplace, is likely to render whatever knowledge, theory, or facts future managers learn, outdated by the time they reach positions where that knowledge can be applied. These realities point to the need for business executives to acquire skills that will allow them to continue learning throughout their career. Business training and, in particular, international executive development, should be considered a lifelong process. The curriculum therefore should include skills in learning how to learn, enabling managers to face the future challenges of international business. In these international economies where knowledge is becoming the true capital and wealth-producing resource, new and stringent demands on training institutions for educational performance and responsibility are called for (Drucker 1989).

THE ITC APPROACH—IDENTIFY THE TRAINING NEEDS

The needs of companies in any particular business sector should be classified into two groups: problems that training can help overcome; and problems requiring other types of action such as consultancy, reorganization, and so on. A clear distinction should be made between training and nontraining needs to avoid any illusions about the effects of training. Similarly, training-needs analyses must be comprehensive in nature, reflecting the environment in which international firms are operating. For instance, a manufacturer exporting a specific product to an international buyer will be working closely with a large number of trade services such as banks, insurance companies, freight forwarders, shipping companies, customs agents, inspection or testing laboratories, etc. Should any one of these firms fail to provide the required service, the transaction is likely to be delayed, or may not take place due to cancellation.

If the ultimate objective of developing the skills of managers is to improve the export capability and performance of enterprises, a more comprehensive and multidisciplinary approach is required. This means that future courses must reflect cross-disciplinary ventures. Greater cooperation with different departments within business schools, such as finance and marketing, or between the school of business and school of engineering, can contribute to the development of new multidisciplined courses. For example, courses in product development, quality control, packaging, and product standardization, can benefit greatly from such cross-disciplinary alliances. Integrating different disciplines is imperative, as international business operations pervade every part of an enterprise. Such an approach will ensure that international business skills cover the entire business curriculum as it has to in an enterprise. A number of schools are now revising their curricula to reflect this greater cross-disciplinary integration (*Business Week* 1991).

Training institutions offering courses in international business need to know the training requirements of enterprises engaged in the global marketplace. This information can be obtained only from training-needs surveys. These surveys can be carried out on a regional or national basis as well as at an industry or sectorial level. In other words, any substantial changes in course objective, content, methods of learning, training materials, and so forth, should relate to changing training needs. Analysts conducting training-needs surveys should avoid classifying business problems along traditional academic lines, i.e., export financing, quality control, manufacturing, product adaptation, etc. Such categories are well understood by academics but may not represent the real problems of practitioners.

The International Trade Centre has developed methodological guidelines to conduct training needs assessments at both the national (1985) and enterprise levels (1989). Both of these guidelines may be adapted to meet specific business/industry sectors or regional groups. On the basis of the needs analyses, human resource development (HRD) strategies are formulated, under which courses are designed, tested training materials developed, and resource persons identified. Priority needs requiring immediate attention are dealt with through short executive development programs. Other priority needs requiring a long-term solution are generally met through the design of long-term courses that are integrated into ongoing academic or professional degree programs.

A summary of the key features of the ITC approach is presented in Appendix 1. A significant aspect of the ITC courses is the fact that they are task-oriented with emphasis on problem-solving rather than subject-oriented skills. To offer such courses, appropriate training materials are developed. In addition, resource faculty having practical experience in international trade must be identified. In a number of countries, ITC has organized special training for the trainers, and programs for new faculty members and practitioners on modern methods of learning and effective delivery systems.

THE INTERNATIONAL BUSINESS CURRICULUM

The above approach has stressed the fact that the international business curriculum should reflect the priority training needs of business. Such an approach may be controversial to academics, but failure to do so will force business to look elsewhere to develop their future executives. A number of businesses have already started their own training programs or have contracted business schools to provide tailor-made programs for their staff. For example, Nokia Consumer Electronics, a Finnish company, has launched a thirty-one-month Euromanager program consisting of a four month introductory course followed by twelve months on-the-job training abroad, three months attending a business school, and ending with a one-year overseas assignment.

The new curriculum should direct more attention to the management of the international business environment by studying other countries' political, social, and economic structures. It should also stress the management of people of different cultures, and how to work with and negotiate across cultural borders. As doing business in the global marketplace is a long-term involvement, courses on strategy should give more weight to long-term relationships, and the development of such courses should incorporate a multi-disciplinary approach to optimize their relevance (*Fortune* 1991).

One of the major difficulties faced by training institutions cooperating with ITC has been the development of new courses based on actual needs. Establishing realistic training objectives, keeping the contents practical, and using participative methods of learning are some of the problems in the initial stages of course development. In several instances, trainers have developed academic, overly ambitious, and monodisciplinary courses despite having access to training needs data. Institutions planning to internationalize their programs or develop them further may wish to refer to the chart in Appendix 2 summarizing the ten key components of international business education (Luostarinen and Pulkkinen, 1991).

TRAINING MATERIALS

Assuming that the curriculum is based on needs assessment, programs will most likely require practical and relevant training materials, which may not be available. At the moment, too many text books, exercises, and cases used by business schools fail to reflect fully the international environment firms operate in. For example, insufficient emphasis is laid on the role of small and medium export-oriented enterprises and trade facilitating agencies in both text books and case studies. ITC's experience in implementing technical cooperation programs in developing countries and views expressed by government representatives and experts have indicated that small and medium firms can make a significant contribution to export development. According to the Institute for International Economics, 85 percent of American exports are accounted for by only 15 percent of U.S. firms, and half of these companies are active in only one market (Transatlantic Perspectives). In Europe, however, governments provide a wide range of export assistance services to help smaller firms become global competitors. Their ability to adapt their products rapidly to meet changes in the target markets is a strength small exporting firms can rely on particularly to meet the needs of smaller market segments. There will be a greater number of such opportunities for small exporting firms to capitalize on, which larger firms will have bypassed. Similarly, the role of government and state trading organizations in developing countries, and in centrally planned economies, is not properly reflected in most text books. Greater in-depth coverage and analysis of trade policies, import regulations, investment incentives, health standards, business ethics, etc., of other countries must be undertaken when internationalizing the business curricula. As far as cases are concerned, the majority of them deal with multinational corporations from a few industrialized countries, ignoring the experience of an increasing number of countries active in the international marketplace. In this connection, ITC has developed several casebooks on enterprises in Africa and Asia. Guidelines for writing cases in international marketing, taking into consideration the difficulties case writers have in developing countries, have also been published.

FACULTY

To be effective, international business programs need to have an international faculty. Some business schools may not be able to achieve this due to their geographical location, budgetary limitations and other restrictions. In such cases, alternative workable solutions should be considered. One such alternative is the setting up of joint ventures between training institutions in different countries. Under joint ventures, it becomes possible to exchange students, faculty members, research findings, training materials, and so on. International cooperation through academic linkages, in particular between developed and developing countries, can make a significant contribution to internationalizing business training.

To ensure successful linkages and exchanges, more rigorous planning, monitoring, and evaluating procedures are needed. It is suggested that linkages start on a modest scale enabling each participating institution to gain experience, acquire a better understanding of the benefits to be acquired, and to identify potential problems. On the basis of such experiences, cooperating institutions will be in a better position to widen, renew, refocus, or terminate the agreement.

The lack of clear strategies, including precise objectives, needs, and benefits when initiating linkages, has contributed to the termination of joint venture agreements. Moreover, the tendency to establish several linkages without specific objectives simultaneously may be counterproductive and detrimental to the participating institutions, their faculty and students (Cavusgil 1990).

The other possibility of internationalizing the faculty is through utilization of practitioners as guest speakers, adjunct instructors, or course consultants. Involving practitioners in teaching courses not only reinforces the practical aspects of the subject matter but also strengthens the linkage with business. Representatives of international banks, shipping companies, trade facilitating agencies, etc., are an excellent pool of speakers to draw from. Moreover, if business schools remove the disciplinary barriers within their programs, they can have access to additional faculty members with an international background or experience.

TRAINING METHODS AND NEW TECHNOLOGIES

Training methods need to stress problem-solving situations, related to the complexities of the international business environment. A balanced training mix should be maintained to allow participants to acquire technical knowledge, analytical skills and cultural sensitivity. Real-world project assignments, preferably in another country, and international business cases, should be part of the mix. The utilization of participative methods of training should develop a mindset of learning on a continuous basis. In other words, it is important to learn how to learn.

Promising new tools and techniques are increasingly accessible to training institutions offering international business courses. For example, in recent years, several leading business schools and open universities have developed distance learning video packages in international marketing.

In 1984, the Open University in the United Kingdom developed a distance learning course on international marketing. The course consisted of four parts: market research, international marketing management, getting paid (payment systems), and coping with cultural diversity. In 1987, Henley Management College in the United Kingdom introduced two distance learning courses in export marketing and export procedures. Each package consists of workbooks, audio and video cassettes, case studies, and tutorial support material. In 1990, the Open University introduced another new distance learning course on "Opening the Single Market." It is a self-taught program for executives interested in doing business in the European Community (EC).

Since 1987, the Allama Iqbal Open University in Islamabad, Pakistan, has offered a complete course in international business. This course consists of thirteen modules, covering topics ranging from the world of international business to export marketing research, product adaptation, channel management, cultural dimensions, international transport and physical distribution, promotion, costing and pricing, legal aspects of foreign trade, and export strategy.

Each module consists of a workbook, a local case together with the leader's guide, and video tapes. The aim of the distance learning package is to train new exporters in trading techniques, taking into account the increasing complexity and competitiveness in the international business environment.

To help trainers relate closely to business decision making and to improve their advisory capacities, ITC has adapted CORE (COmpany Readiness to Export) to developing countries' environments. CORE is a microcomputer software designed to assist businesses in the process of examining their strengths and weaknesses in exporting. It was developed by Prof. S. Tamer Cavusgil, of Michigan State University, in 1986. The ITC-CORE package will consist of a diskette, trainer's guide, and a technical manual. This computerized application (expert system) is extremely useful to small- and medium-size enterprises considering entry into (or expansion of) export markets.

In cooperation with the University College, Dublin, Ireland and the Program for Development Cooperation at the Helsinki School of Economics (PRODEC, Finland), ITC has produced SIMULEX, a computer-based simulation exercise for decision making on import procurement of newsprint. The same three organizations are currently starting the joint production of a multimedia computer-based simulation exercise on procurement of small-scale power generating equipment. Other similar advanced training tools are being envisaged.

DIPLOMA PROGRAM IN INTERNATIONAL BUSINESS

ITC's experiences in organizing needs-based courses in trade promotion for business executives and government officials from developing countries has revealed the lack of appropriate training programs in this field. On the basis of the need for such professional training, ITC is developing a diploma program in International Business which would be recognized internationally. The syllabus would contain a number of core subjects, several cross-disciplinary topics, a few courses specifically designed to reflect the realities of the national and global business environment, company-related projects and selected optional courses including language training. The diploma program could be offered either on a full-time/part-time basis, or on a modular basis. A number of institutions in developing countries offer various adaptations of diploma programs. They include the Export Institute of Singapore, Mexico's

Monterrey Institute of Technology, and Morocco's Graduate School of Business Administration (ISCAE).

An innovative diploma program example is one offered by the Export Institute of Singapore in collaboration with the Niels Brock School of International Business of Denmark. The two-and-a-half-year program consists of a combination of theoretical and practical training modules, each of two months duration. During the final six months of the program, trainees undertake company-based projects involving the preparation of a corporate export plan for their companies. A special feature of this program is that each company must send two staff members, sharing the same job, for training. Only one trainee attends the program at any one time. When one module is completed the trainee returns to his/her export-related tasks while the other trainee goes for training. This interchange takes place throughout the modular program.

A new diploma program in international trade launched in 1991 by Mexico's Monterrey Institute of Technology, consists of the following modules:

- Analysis of export capacity and market opportunities
- Analysis of international markets and cultural dynamics
- Logistics of international trade
- The marketing plan
- The production plan
- The financial plan and project feasibility
- International negotiations
- Development of consulting skills

Each module takes up forty hours of classroom contact time. In addition to the module, each trainee undertakes a project related to international marketing which, whenever possible, is company-based. The total duration of the program is ten months.

The International Association of Institutes of Export and the Latin American Association for Training in Foreign Trade (ALACCI) are also developing diploma programs in foreign trade for adoption by their members.

MASTERS PROGRAM IN INTERNATIONAL BUSINESS

At the request of several developing countries in Asia, Latin America and the Middle East, ITC has helped in the development of international business programs leading to a master's degree or the equivalent. A thirty-month master's program in international business education was launched in 1991 by the Center for International Business Education of the University of International Business Economics, China. In Latin America, Columbia's Graduate School of Business (ICESI) initiated a postgraduate degree in international business management and in 1987, the Indian Institute of Foreign Trade introduced a master's program in international business.

All these degree programs are fairly similar in subject coverage, hours of instruction, admission requirements, and methods of learning. Similar graduate programs are expected to be undertaken in other countries and executed by national training institutions.

DIPLOMA PROGRAM IN IMPORT OPERATIONS AND TECHNIQUES

In view of the need of developing countries to optimize their import operations particularly due to foreign exchange restrictions, ITC has provided workshops and seminars on import operations and techniques. A lengthier course has been developed to combine theory and practice with on-the-job training. This two-month course for purchasing managers from public and private enterprises, and purchasing organizations responsible for import operations and techniques, covers primarily: import management, import requirements, import procurement, materials management of imported supplies and import management information systems.

CONCLUSION

In view of the relevance of trade in the world economy, companies need to pay greater attention to the issues of internationalization. Business executives will be expected to possess problem-solving skills, technical know-how, a truly international outlook, and a sensitivity to different cultures and values. They will also need to acquire a long-term strategic perspective as opposed to short-term opportunities in domestic markets. To face the challenges in this decade and beyond, business schools must respond with new approaches to internationalizing their programs. Greater attention to problem-solving skills and the management of people in different economic and social environments is necessary. Traditional disciplines, such as marketing and finance, will have to be revised on the basis of business training needs. A shift from discipline-based courses to cross-discipline, issue-based courses is required if managers are to function effectively in global markets. In order to bring about these changes, business schools need to place greater emphasis on cooperation with the business sector, trade service organizations, training institutions in other countries, government trade agencies, and professional bodies. Forming these alliances with businesses and institutions engaged in international trade in a rapidly changing world environment thus constitutes the major challenge to international business education in this decade.

REFERENCES

Business Week. 1991. "Wharton Rewrites the Book on B-Schools." 13 May, 31.

Cavusgil, S. Tamer. 1990. *Advances in International Marketing* 4: 177–86.

Drucker, P. 1989. *The New Realities.* Harper & Row.

Fortune. 1991. "The Trouble with MBAs," 29 July, 119–27.

Luostarinen, R., and Pulkkinen, T. 1991. *International Business Education in European Universities in 1990.* Helsinki School of Economics and Business Administration.

The Economist. 1991a. "Management Education Survey." 2 March, 1–26.

_____. 1991b. "A New MBAge." 4 December, 70–72.

Transatlantic Perspectives. 1992. "Helping Small Firms Become Exporters: 10 Lessons from Europe." (Spring): 12–15.

APPENDIX I

Key Features in Internationalizing ITC Business Programmes

Table: Courses Content
— based on training needs (demand driven)
— cross-disciplinary
— stresses long-term implications
— takes into consideration the realities of a world setting, including interdependence among nations
— includes visits to relevant business organizations

Learning Methods
— interactive and team-based
— problem-solving orientation and use of real life projects
— round-table discussions with business representatives and government officials concerned with trade matters
— on-the-job applications
— self-development
— case method using local experience

Faculty
— exchange of faculty with other schools/departments
— greater reliance on practitioners/international consultants
— using a team-teaching approach representing cross-discipline expertise

Linkage
— setting up joint ventures with schools in other countries
— greater linkage with business, including banks, transportation, insurance, etc.
— closer links with government trade promotion organizations and chambers of commerce
— undertake joint practical research with international agencies on specific trade issues
— work together with other international bodies and professional associations

Training Materials
— train trainers in case development
— develop training materials clearing house from developing countries
— publish handbooks, games, manuals, videos and computer-based simulations on core subject areas

APPENDIX 2

Stages In The Life Cycle Of International Business Education

IB Variable	Starting	Development	Growth	Mature
1. Substance of IB Teaching or Curriculum	IB as an extension	Separate IB courses	IB program	Fully Internationalized
2. IB Research	Nonexistent or only a few isolated efforts by faculty	Isolated efforts by faculty, short-term research projects	Doctoral program in IB, research institute in IB Longstanding research	Doctoral program and all research fully internationalized
3. Organization	No specific organization	No specific organization; separate IB faculty	IB department	IB school
4. Faculty	Exchange and international faculty nonexistent or limited	Exchange and size of international faculty limited	Extensive exchange and size of international student body: 5-25%	Extensive exchange and size of international faculty: 25-80%
5. Student Body	Exchange and international student body nonexistent (or limited)	Exchange and size of international student body limited	Extensive exchange and size of international student body: 5-25%	Extensive exchange and size of international student body: 25-80%
6. Language Studies	Nonexistent or very limited	Recommended or one foreign language compulsory	Compulsory	Language studies compulsory and extensive
7. Language for Instruction	Native language	Native language, only visitors use foreign language	50/50 native and foreign language	Instruction provided in a foreign language

(continued)

Appendix 2 (continued)

IB Variable	Starting	Development	Growth	Mature
8. Orientation −research −teaching	Domestic	Mainly domestic but some international aspects identifiable	International but not yet fully	Almost global, domestic trade considered special
9. Attitudes of −administrators −other staff	Ethnocentric	Mostly ethno–partly polycentric	50/50 ethno-polycentric	Mostly poly- or geocentric
10. Culture of the school	Cultural sensitivity negligible	Cultural sensitivity recognized	Cultural sensitivity highly recognized	Cultural sensitivity essential

Internationalization of Business Education: An Australian Perspective

NIGEL J. BARRETT

INTRODUCTION

This chapter presents a framework for considering issues relevant to the internationalization of business education. The framework addresses the nature of internationalization in this context as well as the factors associated with such international involvement. This framework is then utilized to describe the internationalization of the marketing program at the University of Technology, Sydney (UTS). Implications and lessons for other educational institutions involved in internationalization activities are then drawn.

THE FRAMEWORK

Internationalization is a complex multidimensional construct, and consequently there is no single or simple means of describing it. Internationalization behavior is a response to situation-specific conditions as well as the general character of the educational institution, its members, and its environment.

It is appropriate to consider the issue of the "internationalization of business education" in the context of those factors which might be associated with this process. Exhibit 1 represents a useful framework for considering the nature and degree of the internationalization of business education, as well as the factors both influencing and influenced by such international involvement.

Internationalization may be viewed as a process concerned with increasing involvement in, and integration of, international activities. Exhibit 1 explains that the degree of involvement of the institution in internationalization activities and the nature of these

EXHIBIT 1

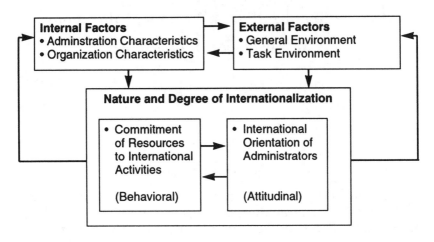

Factors Influencing an Educational Institution's Internationalization Efforts

activities are reflected in the willingness of both the senior administrators and faculty to commit resources to it (behavioral dimension), as well as by their attitudes towards it—their international orientation (attitudinal dimension). Of course, these two dimensions are interrelated—the international orientation of senior management, faculty and students both influences the commitment of resources and are influenced by it. These factors are, in turn, affected by two broad types of influence—factors associated with the internal environment of the institution and those associated with the external environment in which the institution operates.

Exhibit 2 highlights the factors associated with the behavioral and attitudinal dimensions of internationalization.

Resource commitment is reflected in the international activities undertaken by the institution such as: curriculum and teaching programs; research; consultancy; internal and external structures and links; faculty/staff and students.

International orientation reflects the attitudes toward internationalization that are held by administrators, faculty/staff, students, and key influencers (such as business executives, government officials and partners).

EXHIBIT 2

Nature and Degree of Internationalization

Resource Commitment:
* Curriculum/educational programs
* Research
* Consultancy
* Strategic planning for internationalization
* Internal structures/networks (service and administrative support; formal/informal; individual/institutional)
* External structures/networks (links, collaboration, relationships with business, government, and educational institutions; formal/informal; individual/ institutional)
* Funds
* Faculty/Staff (professional experience programs involving teaching, research, consultancy, and travel in foreign countries; incentive schemes; recruitment/ selection)
* Students (domestic and foreign); exchange programs; internships

International Orientation:
* Senior administrators
* Faculty/Staff
* Students
* Key Influencers (internal—change agents; external—business executives, government officials, consultants, faculty from other institutions)

Internal institutional factors (Exhibit 3) which, in part, shape internationalization, include aspects of both the administration and the organization—personal characteristics of senior administrators; their planning orientation and political agenda; resource availability and commitment; the organization's size, location, and history and experience; education programs; and structure, domestic and foreign links/relationships. These factors would usually be active at least at three levels in a university—the universitywide administrative level, the faculty (or school) level, and the school (department) level.

External factors (Exhibit 4) include general environmental forces, such as political, economic and sociocultural factors, as well as characteristics of the institution's task environment such as market demand—by students, industry/business and government; revenue generation potential; partners/collaborators; and competitors.

EXHIBIT 3

Internal Institutional Factors
(At three different levels: University, FacultySchool/Department)

Administration Characteristics:
* Senior administrators characteristics (age, country of birth, knowledge, experience, education, attitudes/international orientation, motives)
* Planning Orientation (mission, policies, objectives, strategies; proactive or reactive approach)
* Political agenda

Organizational Characteristics:
* International history and experience
* Domestic expansion characteristics
* Resource availability and commitment
* Location
* Size
* Educational activities (courses, research, consultancy)
* Structure (internal and external; formal and informal linkages /relationships)

This chapter is not so much concerned with measuring the degree of internationalization of an institution's business education at a particular point in time, as with the nature and process aspects of internationalization. These aspects are explored in the following discussion.

THE UNIVERSITY OF TECHNOLOGY EXPERIENCE

In the following sections the framework outlined above is applied to a description of the internationalization experience in the College of Business at the University of Technology, Sydney.

The external and institutional contexts of this behavior are described first. This is followed by a discussion of the evolution of internationalization, including details of the activities and process involved, as well as lessons to be learned.

THE CONTEXT

EXTERNAL ENVIRONMENT

Several recent reports commissioned by government and private industry underscore the vital importance of Australia's international competitiveness and international marketing and business

EXHIBIT 4

External Factors
(Domestic and Foreign)

Macro Environment:
*   Economic, political, legal, cultural

Task Environment:
*   Student demand (domestic and foreign)
*   Industry/business demand
*   Government demand
*   Revenue generation potential
*   Other educational institutions (competitors, partners/collaborators)

---

skills to its future. Boosting Australia's trade performance for its economic wellbeing is therefore an accepted imperative as is the central role that international business education must play in any such efforts. High student interest and demand for international courses also suggests an increasing awareness in the community of the need for competence in this area. There is a fundamental need to promote a international orientation among Australian universities—to move them away from their narrow, traditional domestic market focus.

The government is attempting to address the issue of international competitiveness by adopting policies designed to change the business environment, e.g., major structural reform in the transportation, waterfront, airline, communications, banking and finance sectors of the economy; reducing historically high levels of trade protection; and introducing a training levy to upgrade the industry skill base.

The export of education has also been a recent government initiative. Many Australian universities have pursued these opportunities and, in the process, have commenced the process of internationalization.

An example of government commitment to the training of international marketing professionals is the Department of Primary Industries and Energy's "Marketing Skills Program" for the period 1988–89 to 1990–91. This program was designed to facilitate the upgrading of the international marketing skills of organizations in Australia's primary industry sector by subsidizing training programs developed and conducted by various Australian universities.

Australian educational institutions, like their counterparts in private and public enterprises in many other sectors of the economy,

face a major challenge in tackling the internationalization imperative. Entirely new corporate cultures need to be developed and a
significant role must be played by the nation's international business educators in this development. It is essential that business students as well as business executives have access to the best possible
international business education facilities Australia can offer.
Indeed, this is an area where education institutions have the opportunity to lead the business community, not just follow it. Are Australian business educators ready for the challenge?

This is the environment that has emerged in the Australia of the
1980s and 1990s.

INTERNAL INSTITUTIONAL ENVIRONMENT

Consistent with the overall mission statement of the university,
the internationalization of business education at UTS aims to provide undergraduate and postgraduate education for professional
practice in the area of international business. The UTS Corporate
Plan 1989–1991 directly addresses the need to improve Australia's
international competitiveness.

The distinctive strengths of UTS include innovation in course
design, development of strong links with industry and business,
and a demonstrated commitment to further the growth of internationalization activities in higher education in Australia. The internationalization activities of the Faculty of Business build on this
base, and also address, in part, the issue of external funding for university programs.

During the last few years the university has taken a proactive
stance in its approach to the development of international linkages, and a number of faculties have established cooperative education programs and exchange programs with institutions in other
countries. By 1992 UTS had developed twenty-three exchange programs with universities in fourteen countries. In addition, approximately 500 foreign full-fee paying students from countries mainly
in the Asian region (i.e., Hong Kong, Indonesia, Malaysia, PRC, Singapore, South Korea, Taiwan) were engaged in full-time study at
UTS—50 to 60 percent of these in the College of Business. An International Programs Unit was also established in the late 1980s
within the vice-chancellor's division, to provide administrative
assistance for these students and programs. A language centre has
also been set up.

A significant aspect of these developments is that commitment
and support comes from the top—from the vice-chancellor.

Until about 1990, the internationalization of business education at UTS had occurred primarily on an ad hoc basis. The 1988 merger with another institution (Ku-ring-gai College of Advanced Education) and subsequent changes in senior faculty administrative personnel (1990–91), have resulted in internationalization being placed high on the College of Business short-term and long-term strategic agenda. Prior to this time, most innovative activities in the area were concentrated in the School of Marketing. As a result, the emphasis in the following sections is necessarily on the internationalization activities of this school.

THE EXPERIENCE

This section attempts to draw together some key factors that contribute toward an understanding of the internationalization of business education, and thereby highlight the lessons which might be learned from the experience of the School of Marketing at UTS.

The key activities, in chronological order, that have so far characterized the nature of involvement of the school in internationalization behavior, are highlighted in the discussion which follows.

AN EVOLUTIONARY PROCESS: STAGES, ACTIVITIES AND OUTCOMES

The evolution of internationalization at UTS marks a gradual incremental commitment of resources over the last seventeen years. Most of the activity, particularly in relation to curriculum development, has, however, taken place since 1985.

KEY STAGES AND ACTIVITIES HAVE BEEN:

1974–1979

Limited involvement and commitment (one course in international marketing, and some external links forged). Since 1974, International Marketing has been a core (compulsory) subject for all undergraduate marketing students. Several hundred industry-sponsored projects have been undertaken by students enrolled in this course. In the early 1970s, links were established with the Australian Institute of Export (AIEX, an industry based center for export education). This linkage has involved the provision of advice by UTS staff to the AIEX on curriculum development, and the supply of lecturers to teach subjects in its Export Diploma course and other joint UTS/AIEX industry based export seminars/courses.

1980

Strategic commitment to international business/marketing education in essentially two areas:

- Postgraduate education: An MBA, with a specialization of four subjects in international business including a compulsory subject in international marketing, was introduced. A graduate diploma program in marketing commenced. This included an elective subject in international marketing.
- Research: For one faculty member (change agent), international marketing became a major research focus. A significant study of the internationalization of Australian manufacturing firms was undertaken over a six-year period (with limited university funding). This also involved collaboration with a colleague from the University of New South Wales.

1980–1985

Consolidation and refinement of international business courses; focus on international business research; initial links established with recognized world leaders (academic) in the field through presentation of research at a major international conference; exchange program established between UTS and Oregon State University; limited resources; planning for new programs; changing economic environment and gradual recognition (internal and external) of the need for international business education.

1986

A major commitment to undergraduate education in international marketing and executive training in international business.

The Centre for International Business (a strategic alliance between the Faculty of Business at UTS and the Australian Institute of Export) was established primarily to serve the business community's management training needs in the area (e.g., the Executive Program in International Business). Projects undertaken on behalf of the participants' organizations, and involving overseas visits, have been part of the program.

The undergraduate specialization/minor in international marketing (a sequence of five subjects) was established, and has since exhibited strong growth in student demand (1986—eight students; 1990—fifty students).

A significant, and very popular, element of this specialization involves a unique overseas experience of students acting as international marketing consultants to Australian organizations. They undertake overseas market visits on their behalf, and prepare strategic marketing plans for entry and/or expansion in those markets. Each company is charged a $6,000 fee. Students engage in direct international business negotiations with foreign business people, sometimes with interpreters. This "overseas program"—International Marketing Country Study—is conducted over two semesters, involves two contrasting countries, and culminates in a major presentation "event" involving representatives from industry, government, universities and the media. Markets visited and analyzed have been: Singapore, Malaysia, Indonesia, Republic of Korea, Thailand, Hong Kong, Taiwan, Japan, and the Philippines. Since 1988, the school has collaborated with faculty and students from the University of New South Wales (UNSW) to run the program. In 1991, students from the University of Western Sydney (UWS) also got involved because of the transfer of a faculty member from UNSW to UWS. Funds raised from the government and sponsoring organizations to support this program over six years (1986–1992) are in excess of A$550,000. During this time, 177 students have completed the program and fifty-nine sponsoring organizations have been involved.

The students are closely supervised by senior faculty with extensive experience in international marketing. The standard of reports is very high, and the results have been well received by the sponsoring organizations. During the four-year period, 1989-1992, the focus has been on identifying opportunities for organizations in the Australian processed food industry. This has resulted in a substantial information resource for this industry sector.

An important element contributing to the success of the program is the collaboration with the overseas parts of the Australian Trade Commission (AUSTRADE) in the countries visited. As well as providing briefing sessions, these hosts set up the initial contacts with potential agents, contributors, retailers, wholesalers, government officials and research agencies.

A major scholarship in International Marketing ($10,000 p.a.) was endowed by a UTS graduate who has achieved national recognition as a successful business leader. The selection committee comprises chief executive officers of leading Australian international organizations, senior government officials and senior academics, and is chaired by the vice-chancellor of UTS.

1987–1989

Consolidation and refinement of programs; development of teaching resource materials (library, videos, case material, computer software); cultivation of external links for funding and sponsorship as well as institutional (academic) links in Australia and overseas (gained major government sponsor for overseas program—A\$218,000 over three years), strengthening of collaborative links with the School of Marketing, University of New South Wales (overseas program), and formation of formal research links with overseas faculty/institution; generation of external funds permitting the appointment of a part-time administrative assistant; increase in university resource commitment by way of the appointment of a new faculty member with extensive international business experience, and admission of the first doctoral student in international marketing; staff development through a professional experience program at an overseas university; participation in international conferences by staff; introduction of several government and industry-sponsored prizes for excellence in international marketing; several successful applications for government-sponsored "Key Centres"; increased awareness by the general community and government of the internationalization imperative.

1990–1991

Development of a Faculty of Business Strategic Plan with a key focus on internationalization; major strategic commitment to postgraduate education in international marketing by the introduction of a Master of Business in International Marketing with an "overseas program" component as in the undergraduate specialization; a major commitment to undergraduate education by the introduction of a major (ten subjects) in international business; the establishment of an international business exchange program between UTS and a university in the United Kingdom; the establishment of a "twinning" arrangement with Taylor's College in Malaysia whereby Malaysian undergraduate students are taught by UTS faculty in both Australia and Malaysia; a major joint research program that builds on the research of the early 1980s with funding from UTS and UNSW; strengthening of external institutional links and collaboration in research and teaching through a professional experience program at an overseas university.

An ongoing effort during the last ten years has also been the promotion of extensive media coverage of the school's international activities, particularly the overseas program and the major scholarship. This has been deliberately sought in order to raise the profile of the school and UTS in the general and business communities, as well as within the university community.

These stages have been characterized by short, intense periods of major curriculum development followed by longer periods of consolidation and refinement. New programs are introduced, followed by a period of adjustment and fine tuning based upon the experiences gained. The next stage (expansion) is not pursued until the current programs are deemed to be successful. Another feature is that the pace of change has quickened due to the learning experience, greater resources, and changing environment. The strategy has been one of expansion followed by concentration and integration.

The evolution of the process of internationalization of the marketing program at UTS has been largely situation specific—internal change agent, university in the growth phase, separate international marketing programs versus integration within existing offerings (infusion). However, as the organizational environment changes and the issue of "internationalization" becomes more institutionalized and is accorded a higher priority within the faculty's strategic plan, then the nature of the existing program may change—perhaps greater infusion, or greater integration? This contingency approach is also consistent with current theories of the internationalization of business organizations.

OUTCOMES

An important part of the evolutionary process is the impact of the outcomes of internationalization on subsequent internationalization behavior. The knowledge, experience, and skills gained by participants in the various international programs and activities manifest themselves, behaviorally and attitudinally, in a number of ways. For example, graduates will influence the internationalization behavior of the organizations in which they work. Over time, these alumni become leaders in their organizations and can be potential resources for the educational institution for sponsorships, scholarships, and training programs, and they can function in advisory capacities. These important links should be fostered and maintained by the institution in order to realize the potential benefits. In addition, the enhanced international orientation of staff/faculty involved in internationalization activities (teaching, research, exchanges) will be a valuable input into future activities.

The most conspicuously successful activity in terms of "value added" experience has been the overseas program. As well as providing a unique opportunity for applying the marketing knowledge and skills taught in the classroom, a student's cross-cultural understanding, empathy, and sensitivity are greatly enhanced. This results in a demonstrably more mature and internationally oriented individual. Indeed, students generally rate this subject as the "best" subject studied in their entire undergraduate degree. It is also rated very highly in terms of "learning experience," "usefulness," "effectiveness," "practicality," "career relevance," and "excitement generation."

These overseas activities have also resulted in tremendously strengthened and expanded external business and institutional links and, more importantly, raised the profile of the international marketing program throughout the university, the business community, and the markets/countries visited. For example, such links led to the employment of a new faculty member with extensive international business and government experience. Inquiries concerning enrollment in the program have also been received from universities in both Australia and New Zealand.

PERFORMANCE AND LEGITIMACY

Successful performance of internationalization activities reinforces the process by creating a favorable environment for expansion. Performance may be measured in terms of student demand, revenue generation, value-adding outcomes such as international experiences, and changed attitudes and behavior.

It is important that internationalization activities be successful, and be viewed as successful, not merely by supporters but also by disinterested parties and skeptics who may have some influence in resource allocation affecting these activities. This includes not only faculty and staff members of the university but also those with whom external relationships are sought and established (e.g., sponsoring organizations). Attitudes and behavior—as reflected in an enhanced international orientation, sponsorship commitments, resource allocation—are more likely to be influenced in a positive way by a successful program.

In the overseas program, a great deal of enthusiasm and excitement is generated among participating students and faculty. Many faculty have consequently expressed an interest in participating in the overseas program. Success of the undergraduate specialization has helped to lend legitimacy and credibility to internationalization efforts, and thus, has facilitated the introduction and adoption of similar activities at the postgraduate level—the Master of Business (International Marketing).

COMMITMENT

ROLE OF SENIOR ADMINISTRATION

Consistent with the business literature on internationalization, the support, encouragement, international orientation, and commitment of senior administrators is seen as critical to achieving internationalization objectives. At UTS, the vice-chancellor is very supportive of the principle and practice of internationalization. He has willingly accepted invitations to participate in the school's international activities in his role as chief executive (chairman of Scholarship Selection Committee), and speaks at major public events such as the launch of the Centre for International Business and the annual overseas program presentations. A supportive dean and head of school have also facilitated innovation and change.

It is interesting to note some personal characteristics of such key influencers. They are relatively young, born overseas and/or lived and worked overseas for many years, and obtained tertiary qualifications overseas. Again, this is consistent with the business literature which suggests that similar characteristics exist in the top management of firms that exhibit higher degrees of internationalization.

ROLE OF CHANGE AGENTS

A major influence has been the emergence of a faculty member to "champion" the cause of internationalization—to innovate and lead the way in instituting the changes necessary for increased international involvement. Underlying this leadership is a strong commitment and dedication to "make the future happen."

This faculty member has a business background (both in Australia and overseas), and joined UTS in the mid-1970s. In 1979, a firm commitment was made to pursue an academic career in international marketing at UTS. This decision acted as the catalyst for the internationalization activities undertaken over the next eleven years.

The important role of change agents can also be traced to the early international activities of the faculty and school (mid-to-late 1970s) when "international" subjects were introduced in the undergraduate marketing program and the MBA. In each case one or two committed individuals pushed strongly for their introduction and adoption. The fact that these change agents were foreign nationals probably reflected a strong international orientation. Indeed, the senior administrators of the Faculty of Business during the 1970s was composed mainly foreign nationals.

STAFF AND STUDENT COMMITMENT

The time commitment involved in the planning and administration of the overseas program, together with the establishment of the necessary external links with government agencies and business organizations, should not be underestimated. It requires substantial commitment by staff and students; nonetheless, the potential payoff makes it worthwhile. The program is extremely challenging, exciting, and rewarding, and these characteristics operate synergistically as an incentive to additional commitment and dedication to internationalization activities, thus making it an extremely profound learning experience. Such experiences tend to be infectious and spread the spirit of international orientation and involvement among staff.

STRATEGIC PLANNING

Prior to 1990, internationalization of marketing education at UTS did not evolve within the context of a formal strategic plan, either within the school or faculty. In this sense, it has occurred in a relatively isolated manner. However, what is perhaps significant is that it is the favorable institutional environment that has greatly facilitated change.

It is surprising to note that the Faculty of Business, and by implication the School of Marketing, has only just reached this stage in its evolution of formalizing and implementing a strategic planning process. As part of this planning process, the dean has been an important change agent in developing and implementing the major strategic thrust towards the internationalization of business education at UTS. This has started to lead to greater coordination and integration of the several international activities of the Faculty of Business. Indeed, if the degree of internationalization is to increase—particularly in relation to the international orientation of faculty/staff—then a more formal planning-oriented approach must be embraced.

In the case of the School of Marketing, it should be noted that the change agent responsible for these internationalization activities has had specific objectives in terms of the broad activities that needed to be undertaken as, for example, with curriculum and research. The timing and implementation phases were not so clear. Indeed, this has been part of the gradual learning process especially as there were very few models of internationalization available in the tertiary education sector (none in Australia). Part of this learning process has been the purposeful "immersion" of the change agent in those activities that will add value, and significantly enhance this international orientation. This has had the effect of increasing the rate of change, and of adjusting the nature of the internationalization change process in the school.

APPROACH TO CURRICULUM DEVELOPMENT

The "ideal" strategy to adopt in internationalizing business education might be to make all subjects "international," and to have these subjects taught by truly "internationalized" faculty. Reality suggests, at least in the case of most Australian tertiary institutions offering marketing/business education (and perhaps also in the case of many institutions in other countries), that such a strategy would probably be impractical at this time. Unfortunately, there exist few academics with the necessary knowledge, skills, orientation, interest, and motivation to truly internationalize their individual subject areas beyond a cursory treatment of international issues.

Another approach to the internationalization of the marketing/business curriculum is to focus on the development of specializations (majors and minors) in international marketing. At the School of Marketing, UTS, this was seen as the most viable option given the prevailing environment—relative lack of an international orientation among marketing faculty and programs, a generally favorable institutional/managerial environment that encouraged innovation and change in curriculum, limited resources, and the need to institute change in the short-term to achieve a demonstrable result (value added). Simply, the barriers to change were fewer and not so well entrenched, and the potential impact was perceived to be much greater. In this case the context clearly dictated the strategic approach to be adopted.

SUPPORT STRUCTURES

INTERNAL SUPPORT STRUCTURE

Staff/Faculty

The human resources available to service the various international programs and activities have been limited. However, with increasing internationalization, access to funds (internal and external) have similarly increased. Extensive use of part-time lecturing staff with tremendous international business experience has been made to teach the various subjects; a part-time research/administrative position has been supported by externally generated funds since 1988; and a new full-time faculty member joined the school in 1989.

In addition to the servicing of existing programs, the issue of increasing the international orientation of faculty must be addressed. Fundamental changes in orientation and behavior cannot be effected easily in the short term. They need to be undertaken gradually over the longer term (depending of course on the degree of internationalization to start with). This involves activities such as professional experience programs—teaching, research, consultancy and travel in foreign countries; incentive schemes; and revision of criteria for reward/promotion and recruitment/selection of faculty.

Administration

In relation to administrative support designed to manage internationalization activities, these are few and tend to be task oriented (e.g., Centre for International Business, International Programs Department). Internationalization activities that do exist tend to receive administrative support from existing resources within the current school, faculty and university structures. Nonetheless, it is anticipated that new administrative structures will emerge over time as the internationalization imperative is reinforced and as these activities grow.

The importance of informal/personal networks of relationships among key influencers within the university should also be emphasized in relation to achieving change.

EXTERNAL SUPPORT STRUCTURE

Relationships/Linkages

The initiation, establishment, and cultivation of linkages and personal relationships in the external environment are seen as critical factors in facilitating change and achieving internationalization objectives. Experience has borne this out. For example, relationships established with world leaders in the field in the early 1980s have led to collaboration in research and teaching, and professional experience programs overseas. In addition to strengthening these relationships (both professionally and personally), such collaboration has expanded the network of relationships internationally. Similarly, links established with Australian colleagues in the 1970s have been strengthened and expanded through collaboration on international programs and research. This is expected to continue in new directions as their institutions engage in internationalization behavior.

In order to successfully run the faculty's international collaborative programs, the establishment and management of linkages in the task environment are critical to their success. For example, in the International Marketing Country Study Program, the network of relationships involves—participating universities (administration, staff and students); sponsoring organizations (business and government in Australia and overseas), consulates and trade offices of countries visited (in Australia and overseas), the Australian Trade Commission (in Australia and overseas); and market research agencies in the markets visited.

FUTURE ACTIVITIES

Important internationalization activities to be considered for the future include:
- development of industry/executive training programs in international business/marketing in Australia and overseas;
- development of new programs for full-fee paying overseas students;
- expanded research program, including strengthening of links with the international community of scholars in the area;
- effective management (including development and refinement) of new and existing programs and linkages (including opportunities for language study, new opportunities for student exchange, and establishment and nurturing of links with international marketing alumni, institutions, business, and government);
- generation of funds for maintenance and expansion of programs;
- internationalization of staff/faculty (increased involvement in teaching, research, and overseas programs, conferences, and exchanges);

- integration of internationalization activities with faculty and the university as the different organizational units become more internationalized.

CONCLUSION

This chapter has presented a framework for thinking about the issues involved in the internationalization of business education, and has outlined the evolution and dimensions of internationalization in the School of Marketing at UTS.

In summary, internationalization involves a multitude of factors:

- it is a gradual evolutionary process;
- it involves the incremental commitment of resources;
- it is, to a large extent, situation specific in which the institutional and external environments determine the appropriate approaches at particular points in time;
- it involves behavioral and attitudinal dimensions;
- the institutional environment should be one which facilitates and fosters change;
- it requires commitment from top management down;
- it requires key managers with sympathetic international attitudes;
- it requires dedicated change agents;
- it requires planning;
- it requires internal and external support structures;
- it requires the development and management of formal and informal networks of relationships; and
- the key players are students, academics, administrative staff, top management, bureaucrats and government officials, business organizations, and other educational institutions, not only from the home country but from many countries around the globe.

It is hoped that other institutions and individuals who have chosen to tread the internationalization path will find some useful guidance in the UTS experience thus far. It is a journey that we have only just begun. Sound planning, management, dedication and commitment are required to make it happen. It is an exciting and challenging endeavor and the rewards can be extremely satisfying. Bon voyage fellow travellers!

Strategic Alliances And Localization: The European Approach

TEVFIK DALGIC

INTRODUCTION

This chapter aims at explaining the European approach to the internationalization of business schools at the MBA level. Although originally a U.S. product, the MBA as an educational program has been imported into Europe, changed, repackaged and delivered in different forms at different locations. This chapter will attempt to identify the general trends shaping the West European MBA. The principal thesis is that the MBA is no longer an exclusive U.S. product but a European one as well, adapted to local needs on a country and industry-basis.

To understand the European MBA, it is a good idea to look back at the U.S. MBA, since that's where the European MBA originated. The idea of internationalizing business schools originated in the United States as a response to the poor performance of U.S. firms in international markets and foreign penetration into the U.S. economy. There were also other reasons like:

- Globalization trends,
- Increased trade and, as a consequence, more need for international contacts,
- Cross-cultural developments,
- Opening of financial markets to foreign investors,
- International acquisitions and strategic business alliances,
- Preparations for the Single European Market,
- Emerging newly industrialized countries and their growing role in the world trade.

U.S. business schools' reaction to these developments was to train managers who can cope with these changes and successfully conduct business with diverse cultures. Following the U.S. experiments, some European business schools also started to implement some changes toward internationalization. However, European schools have additional reasons to do so; these will be dealt with under the European approach later. U.S. business schools have developed long-term strategies and policies toward internationalizing themselves. Gradually, some forms of internationalizing emerged. These emerging forms may be grouped under the following headings:

1. Changes in Curricula,
2. Changes in faculty,
3. Changes toward more international cooperation,
4. International strategic alliances,
5. Foreign direct investments.

1. CHANGES IN CURRICULA

These changes have aimed to make the business curricula more adaptive and responsive to foreign cultures, political structures, and geographic conditions. They usually take place in the following forms:

- Adding foreign languages to the curricula; for example, teaching Japanese, Chinese, Spanish, Arabic, German, French, Russian, and other languages,
- Adding cross-cultural subjects and issues related to globalization and international management/marketing/business/finance/economics,
- Adding the study of international political relations/diplomacy/geography and legal issues.

2. CHANGES IN FACULTY

The emerging trends and forms may fall within the following groups:

- Recruiting foreign professors with international expertise and contacts,
- Faculty exchange programs with foreign business schools,
- Initiating programs for visiting professors as well as visiting researchers,.

- Supporting joint research projects with foreign business schools, as well as bidding jointly for international research projects and contracts for the World Bank, UN agencies, and multinational companies.

3. CHANGES TOWARD MORE INTERNATIONAL COOPERATION

These developments have been in the following forms:

- Visits to foreign countries, companies, and public organizations,
- Student placement in foreign companies,
- Student exchange programs with foreign business schools,
- Foreign student recruitment programs,
- Support for faculty members' international conferences,
- Other forms of international cooperation.

4. INTERNATIONAL STRATEGIC ALLIANCES

In this category, the following trends and forms have been observed:

- Joint teaching programs on modular or semester/term basis with foreign business schools. Students spend a limited period in a foreign school (London Business School; MIT Sloan School of Business; Erasmus University of Holland; and University of Michigan at Ann Arbor,
- Starting joint business education with local business schools or independent organizations in foreign countries (Huron University of the United States with a local teaching organization in London) Another example is the joint venture between University of Hartford and the American Business School (ABS) in Paris, France.

5. FOREIGN DIRECT INVESTMENT

This category in a way combines "internationalizing" with "internationalization" activities. In some instances they make available faculty members from the main campus in the United States and also recruit some members in the foreign country. They may also add new courses as electives to cater to the needs of local students. Webster university has been applying this system over the years in the Leiden campus in the Netherlands.

THE EUROPEAN APPROACH

European business education in general and MBA education in particular have a shorter history than the U.S. experience. Business subjects were treated as "business-economics" by many European universities. Even today management, marketing and other business subjects are taught under the category of business economics in many schools in Germany, Holland, and Belgium. One of the oldest private business schools of Europe, Henley Management College, has a history of less than fifty years. So when we talk about business education in Europe, in general we are talking about a comparatively recent history. The MBA education in Europe has an even shorter history. But after being imported from the United States, the MBA has been substantially transformed in the following ways:

1. Product Change: MBA general management programs courses have become functionally focused products; like an MBA with a finance orientation, industrial development orientation, or international marketing and information systems orientations. Stratclyde University of Scotland offers an MBA with an international marketing focus, Sheffield University's Management School offers one with an international business focus, and some British polytechnics offer MBA degrees with a European studies orientation.
2. Delivery Form Change: Some European business schools adapted the U.S. product to local conditions by developing in-company MBA degrees. Henley Management college runs company-based MBA courses along with a consortium MBA course for some selected company managers representing several UK firms. Cranfield School of Management (United Kingdom) provides a part-time MBA program in addition to its full-time MBA. Warwick University also offers a consortium MBA.
3. *Re-exporting the MBA*: Some European business schools, after developing their MBA programs have begun to re-export them. Bradford University of UK offers an MBA course in the Netherlands. Henley Management College of the UK has developed several international links to export its general management—focused MBA program to The Netherlands, Denmark, Singapore, Cyprus, Germany, and Hong Kong.
4. *Strategic Alliances*: Some European business schools have developed joint MBA courses by arranging study tours or

semesters to be taken in different locations in Europe provided by different schools. The Cranfield School of Management runs a full-time MBA program in collaboration with ESC Lyon in France. Students may study some courses in France. An example of a similar alliance by U.S. schools is the University of Texas at Austin: it runs similar semester exchange programs with several European business schools.

5. *English Language*: Another characteristic of the European MBA is language. The majority of MBA courses are taught in the English language. With the emerging internal market by the end of 1992, the English language is in a way asserting itself as the future business language in the united Europe of the 21st century. INSEAD in France and IMD in Switzerland run their MBA courses in English, as does Bocconi in Italy.

6. *Industry Influences*: Many European MBA courses have been influenced by the local/national industries in their course structure, syllabi materials and cases. There are many European cases developed over the years covering mainly European examples used by several business schools.

7. *International Faculty*: Many European business schools have established themselves as employers who recruit several faculty members from different countries. In addition to North American academics, other European, Middle Eastern, Far Eastern, and Japanese nationals are also employed by those schools.

European business schools did not react to the changes in the market place with the same urgency as did U.S. schools. They had their own additional factors for internationalizing and internationalization.

Some of these were:

1. Support of the EC for joint courses among member state universities and colleges, like the ERASMUS project aimed at creating an environment where credit transfers are possible for university level courses, and the Euroforum project which supports joint academic ventures in vocational training;

2. Reduction of state funding in the UK higher education sector has forced British universities to create extra funds, which has lead them to go nationwide and international;

3. Huge demand for a higher qualification in business management in Europe helped the European business schools to run profitable MBA courses;

4. Increasing demand in the Pacific Rim countries for business education, preferably in Europe, in anticipation of EC 1992, helped some European businesses schools to attract foreign students as well as establish themselves in the Far East—Henley Management College in Hong Kong;

5. Changes taking place in Eastern and Central European countries toward a market orientation and democratic political systems have also created additional demand for a business education, especially in English;

6. A support for joint business courses with East European schools for example, the TEMPUS project, prompted a network of strategic alliances among business schools throughout Europe;

7. There is no European parallel to the AACSB and hence no official recognition of the MBA as a degree. However, with the pressure exerted by business communities throughout Europe the trend is in the direction of a general acceptance. This lack of official accreditation in a way induced many individual investors to get involved in business education;

8. Formal links among European business schools for joint promotional campaigns, to reduce promotion costs as well as to establish a quality school image for themselves and to share each others expertise by an exchange of students and faculty. Members of this group of European business schools who have organized joint promotional programs in Europe and in the United States are Erasmus University of Rotterdam, Holland; IMD, Lausanne, Switzerland; ISA (Institute Superieur Des Affairs) Jouy-en-Josas, France; London Business School, England; Manchester Business School, England; Sda Bocconi, Bocconi, Italy; INSEAD, Fountaineblau, France; and IESE, Barcelona, Spain;

9. Increasing interest in private business schools with a reputation for excellence in teaching in Europe—IMD (Switzerland), INSEAD (France), Njonrade and ICBA of Zeist (Holland). The European Business School (EBS) is a private organization with centers in France, Germany, UK and Spain with offices in Brussels and Italy. This school offers a four-year diploma in European Business Administration; students graduate with a minimum of three European business languages (Coulson-Thomas 1989);

10. A greater role played by the chambers of commerce in business education and schools opened by them, e.g., ISA (France);

11. The growing British influence on business education in Europe at both the graduate and undergraduate level:
    - *Undergraduate level*: Wolverhampton Polytechnic and Netherlands Hooge School have established a modular BBA degree on European Business,
    - *MBA level*: The University of Bristol (United Kingdom) and Ecole Nationale des Ponts et Chausses' (Paris, France) have developed a joint MBA program in international business offering specializations in finance, strategic management, management of technology, and international marketing. This program will also be conducted in English.
12. Another observed trend is the development of a European Business degree. The current boom in the MBA market in Europe has also brought the accreditation issue into the picture. "In most of the European countries the MBA degree has no legal status, so anyone can offer a course of study—however inadequate. The situation reached such a pitch in Switzerland in 1988 that the Government decided to launch an inquiry. In the UK the award of the MBA is restricted to recognized universities and polytechnics" (*EFMD Guide* 1991).

Recommendations For U.S. Business Schools

U.S. business schools may find the developments taking place in Europe very useful for their future plans for internationalization as well as a resource for greater funds. The following strategies may be suggested to U.S. business schools for consideration in their efforts in this direction:

1. *Go European.* Opening a wholly-owned subsidiary in Europe as an extension of a U.S. school and positioning it as a unique blend of U.S. and European traditions, U.S. curriculum, and European business methods, politics, and culture. This option requires careful market research, funding may also pose a problem. Nevertheless, it is an option to be considered carefully.
2. *Joint Ventures with European Business Schools.* This option may be a better one, taking into account the risks involved in a foreign country without prior knowledge of the market place. The issue then becomes the choice of the European business school, its plans, its reputation and the feasibility of the new venture. This option may create an opportunity to

tap the European markets, expertise, and resources (in terms
of funds, faculty, courses, teaching material, and students).
Very recently, the University of St. Louis has started a joint
venture in Spain with a local Spanish college.

3. *Close Cooperation with a European, Far Eastern or Middle Eastern University.* This option may be the safest in terms of
financial risk. Joint courses and exchange of faculty and students may be started on a trial basis. Depending upon the
experience gained, further cooperation may be considered.
This may be a good option to recommend to U.S. business
schools considering internationalization of their programs.

According to the *Economist* (1988), the underlying features of
successful European business schools are their expensiveness, international character, and independence. These features may be taken
into account to create market niches in Europe. Expensiveness is a
matter of positioning and pricing. Many rich business people seem
to prefer expensive business schools in Europe. Independence and
international characteristics may also play important roles in establishing new business schools or joint ventures in Europe. A joint
venture with a distinctive name may be the solution, along with
high enrollment fee, very elegant environment, residential facilities, international faculty, a good library, audiovisual support, and
exclusivity.

The first action U.S. business schools should take is to recruit
non-U.S.-born academics. No matter how well a U.S.-born academic knows foreign cultures, he/she lacks the essential understanding of a foreign culture which can be gained only by growing up in
a foreign country. The recruitment policy should not necessarily
follow U.S. standards, but should take into account other considerations. For example, teaching excellence, international contacts,
and exposure to foreign business practices and managerial norms
should be top priority, rather than number of refereed publications
alone. University education is still considered primarily a teaching
activity, combining research and consultancy practices in Europe.
For this reason, the academics to be recruited should be good teachers and communicators in their fields first.

In the case of students, scholarships may be initiated for Euro-
pean/foreign students to attend U.S. schools. This may be further
taken up with the State Department for inclusion in the bilateral
trade/culture agreements with foreign countries. U.S. business
firms operating in foreign countries may be encouraged to finance
some scholarships and endow chairs in the business departments.

Reduced fees and sport-based zero-fee schemes and scholarships may be extended to foreigners in greater numbers to come and study in the United States.

More culture-based, geography-based courses and modules may be added to the curriculum. Entirely new courses may be designed combining foreign relations, cross-cultural matters, international marketing, and some regional subjects in detail. More cases can be developed based on experiences of foreign firms.

U.S. business schools may also look at the European MBA models and their applicability in the United States. Distant MBA, company-based MBA, and consortium MBA models may be further developed and refined to suit North American needs. If these activities can be combined with other measures of internationalizing, an entirely different type of business school may emerge in the United States. According to Muller, Porter and Rehder (1991), the U.S. business schools may "reinvent the MBA the European way." The *MBA Newsletter* (1991) states that "For those MBAs, national boundaries are becoming less important every year in defining the geographic areas for job searches. The leading business schools of the world recognize that they, too, compete globally—for students, faculty, jobs, and funding." Given the advanced level of technology in the United States for creation of educational tools and material, U.S. business schools may compete better in the international markets than their European counterparts. Perhaps, what is lacking is vision and determination.

CONCLUSION

Despite the current boom of MBA programs in Europe, the following facts should be kept in mind when a decision is to be made by U.S. business schools in the areas of internationalization. While there is a growing demand in Europe for MBA education, Europe has only around 100 business MBA programs while the United States has over 500. Strategic alliances with European business schools will be beneficial for both the U.S. and European schools, provided that localization issues are taken into account within the EC context and with an eye for East and Central European markets. If the Euromarket is taken into account within the context of Scandinavian nations like Sweden, Norway, and Finland, and East Mediterranean countries like Malta, Cyprus, and Turkey in addition to Israel and other Middle Eastern countries, as well as Balkan States and the former Soviet Republic, the size of the potential market for MBA education will be far more attractive. And that means there are plenty of opportunities for U.S. business schools to go global.

References

Coulson–Thomas, Colin. 1989. "The European Business Schools and Its Philosophy." *Journal of European Industrial Training* 13, no. 1: 30-34.

The Economist. 1990. "Which MBA?: A Critical Guide to Programs in Europe and the USA." London: The Economist Publications.

The Economist. 1988. "European Business Education: Who Needs MBAs?" 4 June, 62–63.

European Foundation for Management Development (EFMD). 1991. European Master's Degrees in Management, 1991–1992 Brussels: IMEC.

The MBA Newsletter. 1991. "The Global MBA." April.

Muller, J. Helen; James L. Porter, and Robert R. Rehder. 1991. "Reinventing the MBA the European Way." *Business Horizons*, 34, no. 3 (May/June): 83-91

Rogers, Jane. 1989. "European Business Schools Face the 1990s." *Multinational Business*, no. 3 (Autumn): 40-43.

Doctoral Studies and Research Activities in European Business Schools and Universities

DANIEL VAN DEN BULCKE

INTRODUCTION

Although the free movement of people is one of the basic tenets of European economic integration, it took about thirty years before the European Community (EC) moved into action with respect to its "institutions of higher learning." Firstly, there was the movement toward the integrated internal market which made universities and business schools realize that not only the enterprises, but they themselves would have to operate in a more competitive international environment. As the dynamics of international business (IB) development in Europe will to a large extent determine the European employment structure (Van Dijck 1990), education will be affected too. Secondly, a number of special programs launched by the EC in the field of education (Erasmus, Lingua, Comett, Tempus, Phare), were quite successful in awakening universities and business schools to the need for a more international approach.

This chapter does not intend to survey the educational initiatives taken by the European Commission. It will address issues of research and doctoral programs. Any serious evaluation of business schools has to be based on the quality of the research efforts of its faculty, as these provide the necessary insights for teaching and consulting. Additionally, the increasing internationalization of business operations inevitably pushes even the more local educational institutions to consider internationalization as a necessity.

A very basic strategy to achieve this is to develop a vital element of the future, i.e., the Ph.D. student. Such an intellectual investment is all the more prudent as many European universities are confronted with an aging academic staff. Professors are carrying heavier teaching loads; there is an increasing enrollment in business schools and the lack of financial resources prevents expanding the economics and business departments without infringing on the older and more traditional faculties where the student population has not increased to the same extent. It is estimated that France will need a net annual flow of 100 management professors in the next five years; meaning that thirty to forty doctoral theses would have to be presented (Labraty 1989, 105). The European system does not seem to be able to cater to this kind of demand.

The existing doctoral programs are few in number, of variable quality—especially with regard to methodology—and widely dispersed geographically. The "International Teachers Program" an intensive, six-week, residential development program for business educators, organized by a consortium of ten major business schools in Europe and the United States, although quite useful, is insufficient (Labraty 1989, 101). The higher remuneration in private business firms attracts many potential Ph.D. candidates. In addition private institutions such as banks and planning departments of large enterprise groups and international organizations also lure away fresh Ph.D.s., and sometimes even established professors, from the academic world (cfr. Rameau 1989, 101).

The second part of this chapter presents some evidence of the internationalization interests and efforts of European universities and business schools. The third part deals with doctoral studies in international business research. After placing the doctoral program in the overall picture, some examples of international and national initiatives to internationalize doctoral programs are discussed. These include not only pure international business initiatives, but also programs that expose doctoral candidates to international scientific and cultural diversity and increase their understanding of it.

Internationalizing the business curricula in a fundamental way cannot be limited to the introduction of special courses or programs in international business, but has to include the internationalization of faculty members who teach the core courses. The fourth part of the chapter presents international business research in Europe and illustrates the potential impact of the EC on the basis of the SPES programs.

International Business Education In Europe

According to the first systematic survey on international business education (IBE) in Europe (Luostarinen and Pulkkinen 1991),

197 out of 231 (i.e., 85 percent) of the responding institutions were engaged in some form of international business teaching. In fact practically all business schools (98 percent), polytechnic institutions (96 percent) and special MBA programs (100 percent) practiced international business in the broadest sense, i.e., at least as an extension of existing courses. The average proportion was brought down however, by the 135 responding *universities*, of which only 77 percent had some international business elements in their more general and economic oriented curricula.

The survey distinguished among four different categories of IBE. Fifteen percent of the European institutions are only at a *starting stage* where they offer IBE only as an extension of existing courses. Another 39 percent of the responding institutions are catalogued in the *development stage*, as they offer specific IB courses; and the balance (41 percent) in the *growth phase*, because they offer a distinct IB program; i.e., a program which is mainly composed of courses with an international business orientation. Only 5 percent are labeled 'international schools' as they have reached the *mature stage.*

Despite the claims of the glossy brochures, there are very few truly international business schools. Staubus (1988, 42), of *The Economist*, proffers three criteria for a school to qualify for the necessary international outlook to expose students to different cultures, business attitudes, labor relations, accounting rules, and so on. These criteria are: an international management board; an international faculty whose members still represent the countries from which they come, and an international student body, with no more than 10 to 15 percent of any one nationality, including the host country.

International business schools create an international microcosm (Naert 1990). This is achieved by bringing together students from a great number of countries, with no particular dominating country; by having a faculty of international composition, with extensive experience outside of the member's home country; by offering a curriculum that includes international subject matters and infuses international aspects even into their core courses; by hosting foreign guest professors, for short or long periods; by allowing its own faculty to regularly venture abroad for teaching, research, and consulting purposes; by establishing exchange programs with foreign universities for both students and faculty. Only IMD in Lausanne (Switzerland) and INSEAD in Fontainebleau (France) are therefore regarded as real "global business schools." INSEAD's MBA students come from forty different countries of which France and Great Britain each contribute 20 percent. Its seventy-five professors come from twenty different nations, with France and the U.S. each accounting for about 20 percent

Several institutions in the Scandinavian countries are clearly headed toward this global stage. Between 67 percent of Swedish and 83 percent of Danish schools already have well established IB programs (Finland and Norway are placed between these two percentages). In France, institutions with special IB programs represent 62 percent, as compared with only 14 percent in West Germany. In the latter country, 62 percent of the surveyed schools and universities only offered specific IB courses. In the UK, the IB orientation was more evenly divided, as 44 percent had created IB programs, 28 percent offered IB courses, 9 percent were considered international schools and 19 percent brought in IB only through an extension of existing courses. More than three out of four surveyed institutions provide only one IB program, while 15 percent offer two, and 7 percent have from three to five IB programs at the same school or university.

While IB programs are the most common approach to internationalization in Europe, there exists a wide variety in the IB program itself. Luostarinen and Pulkkinen (1991) distinguish different types of IB programs. First, about half (52 percent) of the responding institutions organize the so-called typical program, which is composed of special IB courses, language studies, and an international traineeship and/or foreign study period. Secondly, some IB programs concentrate on a special functional area such as international marketing, finance or management, while others are of a bilingual nature, courses being taught in two languages. Together both forms represent 37 percent. Thirdly, there are also joint programs in which students spend a long period at a foreign partner institution (11 percent).

Doctoral Studies

Overview

Doctoral studies form a very critical stage in the life cycle of academics. If, during that period in their career, students could be exposed to an international environment, the benefits that would accrue to the doctorandi themselves, and to institutions to which they belong, will be quite high. To integrate young doctoral fellows into an international interacting group of established researchers and supervisors should be a tremendously enriching experience.

An advantage of international doctoral research networks is that they not only involve the Ph.D. students themselves, but also their thesis supervisors and institutions. This is why they are likely to have a lasting effect on business education in general and international business education in particular. It can be extremely useful for Ph.D. students to become aware of the differences in traditions and orientations that exist among countries. This will allow them to participate in an active way in a more global network.

International business education in Europe is mainly geared toward graduate students (44 percent of the total number of schools and universities). One out of three (34 percent) surveyed schools and universities orients its IB toward undergraduate students, while one out of five (19 percent) aim at the so-called postgraduate MBA-level. Only three percent of the IBE initiatives are directed toward the doctoral level (Luostarinen and Pulkkinen 1991). This of course is commensurate with the limited number of candidates who actually take up doctoral studies.

However, the fact that doctoral IB students represent such a small part of the total IBE activities in Europe is, to some extent, indicative of the neglect of doctoral studies, both by the students and the universities. As doctoral IB studies could play a crucial role in the internationalization of business schools and universities, this is regrettable. The research efforts of Ph.D. students could contribute immensely to the research orientation of institutions, especially in the long run. Even if only a small proportion of Ph.D. candidates remain in academia, they are likely to have a more permanent impact on the internationalization of faculty than other types of initiatives in favor of existing faculty members.

In four business schools and universities (7 percent) in the Scandinavian countries—more particularly in Finland, Norway, and Sweden—there is a doctorate level IBE. The Scandinavian business schools are also setting up a common doctoral program. In France, doctoral studies in IBE are offered only in two institutions (6 percent of the total), while these percentages are even lower in Germany (2 percent) and Ireland and the United Kingdom (1 percent). In the Benelux countries there is no doctorate level IBE yet (Luostarinen and Pulkkinen, 1991).

In general, doctoral IBE programs are quite recent. At the Helsinki School of Economics, a doctorate program in international business was started in 1988, while INSEAD introduced a Ph.D. program in International Management in 1989.

THE EIBA-EIASM DOCTORAL TUTORIAL IN INTERNATIONAL BUSINESS

Inspired by its earlier initiatives, the European Institute of Advanced Studies in Management (EIASM) European International Business Association (EIBA) organized its first Doctoral Tutorial, on the occasion of its 13th annual conference in Antwerp, in December, 1987.

From 1973 to 1988, EIASM sponsored thirty-one tutorials in conjunction with the most dynamic management associations in Europe—the European Accounting Association (EAA), the European Association for Research in Industrial Economics (EARIE), the European Finance Association (EFA), the European Marketing Academy (EMA), the International Association for Research in Economic Psychology (IAREP), and the European International Business Association (EIBA). About 800 doctoral scholars participated in these programs. After a slowdown in these activities between 1982 and 1988, the launching of the new initiative EDEN (see further) was expected to inaugurate a new phase of growth (Bultez 1991a).

The first objective of the tutorial is to provide a forum for doctoral students in IBE to discuss their research plans and the progress of their work, both with a distinguished international faculty and their colleagues. Secondly, as the tutorials take place in concurrence with EIBA's annual conferences, the candidates also have the opportunity to meet other IB specialists and become acquainted with an international network working in IB in general and in their specific field of interest in particular. Since 1987, EIBA's doctoral tutorial has become a regular feature of the annual conferences.

The number of participants in EIBA's tutorial is strictly limited. The selection is based on an application form and a three-page abstract. Once they are selected, the students are requested to present a paper about their doctoral project. This paper and its oral presentation form the basis of the comments and suggestions from the international faculty. The most interesting thesis proposal or project is given an award of US$ 500, which is intended more as a distinction and a modest incentive rather than a real financial prize.

The faculty members at EIBA's doctoral tutorial number four to seven well-known professors from different countries (Exhibit 1). From the second tutorial onward, at least one American professor, who is familiar with European international business eduction, was a member of the doctoral faculty. Not only have American doctorandi participated in the doctoral tutorial, two out of the six award winning projects originated in the United States. For the 1990 tutorial only ten Ph.D. candidates out of thirty-six were selected to present their proposals.

EXHIBIT 1

EIBA'S Doctoral Tutorial (1987–1991)

Location	Year	Faculty			Participants			Award winner(s)
		Total number	Europe	US	Total number	Europe	US	(Nationality)
Antwerp	1987	4	4	–	6	6	–	Germany
Berlin	1988	4	3	1	10	8	2	Finland + US
Helsinki	1989	5	4	1	8	6	2	US
Madrid	1990	7	5	2	10	10	–	Netherlands + Sweden
Copenhagen	1991	6	5	1	8	6	2	US + Germany

EIASM's DOCTORAL EDUCATION NETWORK (EDEN).

Since its establishment in 1971, EIASM has tried to stimulate management education by developing a network of European (university based) faculty members, mainly based on their individual rather than institutional role. In 1987, EIASM reacted to the growing shortage of qualified management teachers, especially in view of the needs of the European single market of 1992, by proposing a special program for high-quality doctoral research in management and setting up a system of integrated seminars.

The EDEN (EIASM's Doctoral Education Network) program tried to attract to its doctoral seminars, top-level graduates from European business schools and universities, who are either enrolled in their first year of a doctoral program organized in Europe (which is focused on management-related disciplines), or are young research assistants with an equivalent profile and the necessary drive to conduct doctoral research. It is also expected that the thesis supervisors will be involved in the tutorship operations and benefit from being exposed to and collaborating in research projects originating from doctorandi of other countries and institutions. It is hoped that the interconnections and exchanges that will gradually evolve among European participating institutions will lead to effects of cross-fertilization and that synergies will be established.

According to one of the initiators of the program, it's no coincidence that the acronym is reflected in the Book of Genesis 2:8, as "EDEN evokes the attractive and creative surroundings required to motivate young promising scholars to undertake and complete (within a reasonably short period of time) the exciting doctoral adventure" (Bultez 1990b).

EXHIBIT 2

EIASM's European Doctoral Network (EDEN) Seminars
(1988 through mid-1991)

Year	Number of seminars	Number of participants	EDWN Fellowships	Faculty		
				Total	Europe	US
1988	2	51	20	7	5	2
1989	1	26	6	2	1	1
1990	4	112	68[a]	22	20	2[b]
1991	4	113	73[a]	23	20	3[c]
Total	11	302	167	52	46	8

(a) Not included are 17 FNEGE Fellowships from France
(b) Of the two, one faculty member was from Israel
(c) Two of which were from Canada

It might be useful to stress that EDEN is not an IB activity as such. Yet, its activities are highly relevant to a better mutual understanding of different academic and corporate cultures in Europe and therefore of indirect importance to future international business activities in European business schools and universities.

Exhibit 3 shows that since EDEN has become operational, forty faculty members have coached 240 Ph.D. candidates during nine doctoral seminars. Only one out of eight of these faculty members was a non-European. More than half of the doctorandi had obtained an EDEN fellowship. The proportion of participants who received a fellowship doubled from about 40 percent in 1988 to almost 80 percent in 1991.

Exhibit 4 lists the themes of the doctoral seminars of EIASM and the nationality of the participants. The high proportion of Finnish and Belgian Ph.D. participants—respectively 26 percent and 17 percent of the total—is due to the fact that most of the seminars were organized either in Belgium or in Finland. France, Germany and Sweden each represent each about 10 percent of the total number of participants, while the Netherlands take up 6 percent. In the case of France, two-thirds of the Ph.D. students enrolled for a seminar on "Interfaces: Research Ventures in Management," which was cosponsored by FNGE (Fondation Nationale pour l'Enseigne pour la Gestion des Enterprises). Almost nine out of ten Finnish doctoral participants followed a marketing seminar. Forty-three students, including fourteen Finns and twelve Belgians, took part in more than one of EDEN's doctoral seminars.

EXHIBIT 3

EIASM's Doctoral European Network:
Number of Participants According to Nationality and
Theme of Tutorial
(1988 through mid-1991)

Doctoral Seminar Theme and Location	Nationality of Participants [a]								
	Belgium	France	Germany	Netherlands	Other EC[b] Countries	Finland	Sweden	Other [c] Countries	Total
Theory of Organization (Brussels)	5	6	2	–	4	4	2	1	24
Research Ventures in Management (Louvain)	6	16	1	3	2	1	2	–	31
Discrete Time Theory in Finance (De Haan)	4	–	3	2	4	3	21	3	40
Continuous Time Theory in Finance (Louvain)	9	1	7	1	3	4	3	5	33
Theory of Corporate Finance (Konstanz)	3	1	1	3	11	2	–	4	25
Marketing Models and Modeling (Helsinki)	5	1	2	2	2	–	9	1	22
Marketing Theory (Helsinki)	4	–	1	–	2	1	18	4	30
Consumer Behavior (Helsinki)	3	–	1	–	–	2	16	3	25
Business Marketing (Helsinki)	2	–	4	3	4	2	12	3	30
Total number of participants	41	25	22	14	32	19	83	24	260
Total number of students	29	25	18	14	29	16	49	17	197

(a) Only those countries with at least 10 participants are listed separately.
(b) These other EC-countries with the respective number of students and participations were: Denmark (9/9), Ireland (4/2), Italy (9/8), Portugal (1/1), Spain (3/3), UK (6/6).
(c) In the other European countries are included: Austria(8/5), Norway(6/6), Poland(1/1), Turkey(1/1), Canada(2/2) and the United States(1/1).

The Belgian Inter-university College
of Management Sciences (ICM)

The Inter-university College for Management Sciences (ICM) was established in 1969 at the initiative of the Belgian Industry-University Foundation and the Institute of Public Administration-University, in order to train professors and researchers in the field of management. Although one of its original objectives was the organization of a doctoral program in management sciences, this was objected to by the participating universities. Because of this opposition from the universities that wanted to keep their own doctoral programs, ICM has concentrated on the allocation and management of Ph.D. fellowships in management. The financial contributions by ICM to Ph.D. candidates are conditional on the realization of stringent conditions regarding selection, orientation, and monitoring of their work in progress.

The prestige and high scientific quality of the ICM fellows abroad is the result of the following operating characteristics of the ICM program:

- The selection process is very severe. There is a written exam and oral presentation before an inter-university Belgian jury in order to be accepted in the program. Another test and oral presentation before an international jury measures progress in the first year;
- The obligation to study abroad during one year at a well-known foreign university on the basis of a program submitted to ICM;
- A permanent monitoring of the ICM fellows, during their three-year fellowship, by the scientific advisers of ICM;
- The obligation to complete their Ph.D. studies within a period of five years, of which period only three can be financed.

From 1970 to 1989, 133 candidates have been accepted in the ICM program. Twenty doctorandi failed, either because they were rejected after the first year or did not finish their Ph.D. studies within the accepted period. Twenty doctorandi are still in the system. This means that the remaining 93 out of 133 (70 percent) have completed their degree. This proportion is significantly higher than the more general system of doctoral fellowships allocated by the Belgian National Fund for Scientific Research.

The strong international element in the ICM program, especially the compulsory one year stay at a foreign university, leads to a very international outcome. Thirty six of the ICM fellows i.e., two out of five, have found employment at a foreign university (of which seventeen are in North America). Sixteen Ph.D. graduates are employed in the Belgian private sector, primarily in foreign or Belgian multinational enterprises. While only two out of five ICM fellows (i.e., thirty-nine) ended up at a Belgian university or business school, their impact with regard to the international orientation of their research activities and teaching initiatives is considered as quite important (*CIM* 1990, 6–7).

Following its prestigious doctoral fellowship, ICM launched postdoctoral programs for the training of professors and researchers in management. Although the objective of these postdoctoral activities was not internationalization as such, the fact that most of the sponsored initiatives are internationally oriented contributed a lot to the internationalization of Belgian universities and business schools. The opportunities created by this training program were:

- Fellowships for professors and researchers for study and travel abroad for four to six weeks on the basis of a proposed program for individual extra training;
- Support for new initiatives or restructuring of business schools, e.g., the induction of foreign scholars to start a new teaching program or research department;
- Financial intervention for sabbatical leave of Belgian professors to go abroad for a year, something which did not exist earlier in the Belgian academic system;
- Repayment of the participation fees for seminars and courses which are organized by EIASM in Brussels. This has allowed Belgian scholars to meet foreign colleagues on a regular basis on their home ground.

That the doctoral program is the central preoccupation of ICM is illustrated by their utilization of financial resources. During 1980-1986, 63 percent of their funds went into the Ph.D. program, as compared with 13 percent for postdoctoral activities and 24 percent for research programs. The funds for postdoctoral programs are released only after the necessary doctoral funds have been allocated. For its research programs, ICM had to rely on special subsidies from the Ministry of Economics. Totally, twenty-four research teams (thirty-six researchers) have been operational during a three-year period.

DANISH SUMMER RESEARCH INSTITUTE (DSRI)

An interesting new project was started in 1990 by the Institute of International Economics and Management of the Copenhagen

Business School. The objectives of the Danish Summer Research Institute of EEC Business and Economic Studies (DSRI) are to:

- Create an interest for research in problems relating to the EC internal market, particularly among junior scholars in Scandinavian countries, especially Denmark;
- Challenge Danish Ph.D. students to compare their research with ongoing Ph.D. research at some of the best universities and business schools in the world;
- Create new international research networks, each encompassing a number of doctoral programs and participation by senior scholars.

The executive steering committee composed of J. Dunning, N. Nielsen, L. Stetting, and A. Stonehill invited twenty senior scholars from European and non-European countries (mainly the United States) together with thirty-four junior scholars (of which fifteen were from the United States—eight of whom were Europeans pursuing doctoral studies in the United States and nine from Denmark, the sponsoring country) and brought them together for two weeks in a Summer Institute in Gilleleje.

Although it is still too early to evaluate the success of DSRI, it is promising that twenty-seven of the thirty-four Ph.D. students became active members in separate international research networks with their peers, and sometimes with senior scholars acting as network advisers (Nielsen, et al. 1990).

INTERNATIONAL BUSINESS RESEARCH IN EUROPE

OVERVIEW

The chapter on IBE research in "International Business Education in European Universities in 1990" (Luostarinen and Pulkkinen 1991, 107–14) is remarkably short and counts only four pages.

Two thirds (67 percent) of the 205 reporting institutions stated that they were engaged in IB research; 15 percent of the participating institutions were planning research activities; and 3 percent had previously completed IB research projects. Fifteen percent answered negatively as to their research activity in IB. No attempts were made to estimate the actual scope of the IB research undertaken. Moreover, the fact that the definition of the research activities was left to the respondents seriously limits the validity of the answers.

Country data show that the Scandinavian region scores highest on IB research programs. Information about the organizational arrangements supporting IB research was provided by 113 schools and universities. Almost one of five (18 percent) of the IB research was institutionalized in a separate IB research institute, unit or center. Two out of five institutions carry out their IB research on the basis of the individual efforts of their faculty members. It is hard to believe that a pure individual research approach would lead to long-term research programs. Yet 36 percent of the responding schools described their IB research as part of a long-standing program.

Luostarinen and Pulkkinen (1991, 114) conclude from their short survey: "Coordinated and permanent financed long-term international business research through a special IB research project, program, unit or center is not a common phenomenon yet." They assume that one of the reasons for the embryonic state of IB research could be the lack of qualified Ph.D. students. These hypotheses concur with their findings that the higher the internationalization degree of business education in European institutions, the higher the involvement in IB research will be. While 56 percent of the institutions that provide IBE only as an extension of existing courses engage in IB research, this proportion increases to 63 percent in the institutions with IB courses, 75 percent in those with IB programs, and 86 percent in the international schools. Surprisingly 57 percent of the universities and schools without IBE still mention IB research, which might mean that such research is being planned.

A relatively new feature is the increasing number of exchange agreements which have been concluded by European universities, not only because they have become fashionable, but also because they can be supported by the European Community. Of the 417 institutions with exchange agreements for students, faculty, and research, which were recorded in the EIBA survey, almost half dealt with student exchange while about one-third concerned faculty teaching. In 20 percent of the institutions with exchange programs, the objective was faculty research. Forty-four of the eighty-two institutions that reported an exchange of faculty research had concluded between one and five agreements. Thirty had signed between six and ten exchange programs and eight had more than ten partner institutions with which they conducted research (Luostarinen and Pulkkinen 1991).

THE EUROPEAN SPES PROGRAM

For 1989, the Council of the European Community adapted the proposal from the EC-Commission to allocate six million ECU from the EC budget for the period 1989-1992, to support economic research at the European level. The program was called SPES (Simulation Program for Economic Science), and aims to support cross-border economic research which is of relevance to European integration. SPES intends to upgrade the economic profession and to improve its international competitive position by providing financial support for cross-border research projects.

The international orientation and effects were already apparent from its first year of operation (March 1989—March 1990) as SPES received 180 proposals for EC research networks; and 100 personal applications for doctoral or postdoctoral research to be pursued away from the home country of the applicant (Emerson and Allgeier, 1990).

On the basis of the opinions of anonymous external referees and the deliberations of 'E-CODES' (Committee for the Development of Science and Technology, Economic Formation) thirty projects (ECU 12,037,00) and twelve scholars (ECU 572,000) were selected during the first year of operation. In recognition of the quality and abundance of the applications, the Commission decided to front-load to some degree the four-year budgetary allocation. In addition, the Commission proposed that the available funds should be increased from six to ten million ECU until 1992.

Although the name of the program suggests *economic* research, a wide variety of subjects were proposed. As a matter of fact, the three projects that deal with international trade (including the EC internal market) and the five concerning issues of industrial organization, are to some extent linked with IB. Topics such as 'Multinational Corporation Activity in Europe' clearly belong to the field of IB. However, while the majority (nineteen out of thirty) of the approved projects aim at establishing international research networks, support has also been given to:

- Workshops and summer schools (3);
- Programs for visiting researchers or seminars (4);
- Diffusion of research (2);
- Association for a branch of economics (1);
- Professional cooperation between a group of universities (1).

It would seem that the Commission does not want to create a "Research Fortress EC," as negotiations are taking place with the EFTA-countries (Austria, Finland, Norway, Sweden, and Switzerland) to join SPES by signing special protocols. After having paid their financial contribution in the proportion of their GNP in relation to that of the EC, these countries will become full members of

SPES. The applications from their universities and researchers will then be handled in the same way as those from the EC-countries.

Another extension which has already been carried out is the ACE program (Action for Cooperation in Economics) which was set up in 1989 especially for Poland and Hungary. The budgetary allocation of 1.5 million ECU comes from the PHARE program for broader economic assistance by the G-24 members and EC for these two countries.

It is planned to have an evaluation of the experience of SPES, before decisions are taken as to its continuation for a second period (1993–1997).

CONCLUSION

Cooperation among universities and business schools has been practiced for some time at the undergraduate level. The Erasmus program greatly broadened exchanges of students between European universities. The latest stage in the Erasmus program is its attempt to introduce ECTS, a European Community Credit Rating System (Braddick 1991), which would allow students to circulate more freely among the member states of the European Community.

Although Ph.D. students represent only a small segment of the student population, they should play a crucial role in the long-term internationalization of IBE education and research. Ten to twenty years ago, doctoral studies in many European countries were carried out mainly by isolated researchers who often had little or no support from their direct supervisors. In 1973, Wadell and Naslund (5) wrote: "By and large all doctoral candidates of a department get the same kind of training, an important part of which is to carry out one major piece of research, usually alone, and report it in the way which is prescribed by the academic community." After several universities have introduced doctoral programs based on the American model of Ph.D. studies, it is now perceived that the local and national institutions have their limitations. Their initiatives to internationalize doctoral programs are meritorious, but lack a more fundamental approach.

The internationalization of Ph.D. programs allows students to position their own research within the European research scene and compare it with the work of their peers from other countries. The participation of internationally known senior scholars and supervisors from foreign universities permits educational economies of scale. For many specialized topics the best professors are not necessarily available at the institute of the Ph.D. candidate. The contacts with foreign faculty are likely to make them aware of additional and new databases (which are useful for their research), and/or of the cultural differences relevant to a valid interpretation of the research results.

A more general advantage is that more harmonization would be created among the many Ph.D. degrees. Internationalization would provide more guarantees for comparable quality. The creation of a European and global network of faculty members, who are active at the doctoral level in management studies in general and international business education in particular, should be the avowed objective. The recent founding of the European Association of Doctoral Programs in Management and Business Administration (EDAMBA) is a step in this direction. It is the only approach that can simultaneously answer the dual challenges of more specialized studies on the one hand, and a more global attitude on the other.

REFERENCES

Braddick, B. 1991. "Postgraduate Management Education in Europe." *International Management Development*, no. 1: 15–16.

Bultez, A. 1990a. "Developper la recherche en gestion pour ameliorer l'enseignement." *Revue francaise de gestion*, no. 78 (March–April–May).

_____. 1990b. "Doctoral Research in Management: A New Eden?" *EIASM Newsletter* (Winter): 1–2.

College Interuniversitaire pour les Sciences due Management (CIM). 1990. *Rapport d'Activite*, 1989–1990: 23.

Emerson, M., and J. Allgeier. 1990. "Economic Research at the European Level: First Year's Progress Report for SPES." *European Economic Review*, no. 34: 1427–35.

Lebraty, J. 1989. "Vers un management a l'europeenne," *Revue francaise de gestion* (March–April–May): 104–10.

Luostarinen, R., and T. Pulkkinen. 1991. *International Business Education in European Universities in 1990*. EIBA, Helsinki, 300.

Naert, P. 1990. "Management en Managementvorming voor de jaren negentig." *Economisch en Sociaal Tijdschrift*, Key to Economic Science no. 2: 157–73.

Nielsen, N., L. Stetting, and A. Stonehill. 1990. *Summary Report of the Danish Summer Research Institute on EEC Business and Economic Studies*, (August–September) Internal Document.

Rameau, C. 1989. "Comment adapter l'enseignement de gestion aux besoins des entreprises en Europe." *Revue francaise de gestion* (March–April–May): 98–103.

Staubus, J. 1988. "MBA: The Best Business Tool? A Guide to British and European Business Schools." *The Economist*, Special Report, no. 1154, London.

Thepot, J. 1990. "Les etablissements de gestion face a l'ouverture europeen." *Revue francaise de gestion* (March–April–May): 92–97.

Van Duck, J. 1990. "Transnational Management in an Evolving European Context." *European Management Journal* 8(December): 474–79.

Wadell, B., and B. Näslund. 1973. "Doctoral Research and Practical Management." *European Training*, no. 2 (September).

Conclusion

S. TAMER CAVUSGIL

I am confident that this book will convey the seriousness of academia's response to the challenge posed by the internationalization of business today. I have never taken lightly the countless charges leveled by the business press against business schools—the arcane research done by business faculty, the scathing denunciation by corporate executives of their MBA employees, the missing contribution of American business education to the global competitiveness of U.S. businesses, and so on. And now we have the reality of unemployed MBAs and the threat of European business schools as serious competitors for our business students, right in our back yard! Are there any vestiges of self sufficiency and complacency (that over-enrollment success has bred) still lurking in our classrooms or deans' offices? Business schools that do not rise adequately to the challenge will produce products—students—who are rejected by the job market. As for those schools that are attempting change, they will have to be on their toes in this new and formidable competition for the enrollment and placement of students. The incipient ethnocentrism found in all of us, that students cannot receive a better business education than that found in the United States, has received a real shock. All is not lost, however! Students of overseas programs organized by American universities, still demand American instructors and American style of instruction!

Each of the chapters in this volume has lent very valuable insight into the task ahead by way of the author's particular experiences and knowledge. What I would like to do in the next few paragraphs is to place some of the major issues discussed in their proper perspective, and as the good old analogy goes, try not to lose the forest for the trees (and vice versa too).

323

Clearly a good starting point is faculty. Can you teach the old dog new tricks? And what about faculty of the future—the doctoral candidate of today? Nehrt places the figure of faculty who have participated in AACSB workshops/seminars as representing an average of two faculty members per school. He also states that the number of doctoral graduates who have taken courses in international business have fallen from 25 percent to 17 percent from 1976 to 1984. While all over the country graduate management schools have been updating MBA programs by adding pertinent new courses or integrating international business components into existing courses, little has changed in the training of those who teach the MBA. The trend is for Ph.D.s to specialize—at a time when they need to relate to the broader practices of management. Doctoral training has played down educational concerns in favor of research. An issue that may lend itself to an interesting research effort is how many of these Ph.D.s have had direct business experience. One of the more hard-hitting measures that could combat this perpetuation of "the old way" would be for some of the leading management schools, the AACSB, and other national professional associations, to establish strict requirements of international business expertise and experience for business faculty. For existing faculty, we could step up retooling workshops and put pressure on universities to evaluate their tenure, recruitment, sabbatical, grant giving, and other policies and procedures. so as to incorporate an international business bias. Would we be overextending ourselves if we advocated a recruitment policy or "job specification" type manual (as in industry) that included norms like teaching excellence, international projects, exposure to foreign business practices, and managerial norms, rather than number of refereed publications alone?

Several of the chapters in this book have chalked out detailed plans of curriculum reform. To them, I would like to add only this dimension of thought: when only 7 percent of a manager's learning takes place while he/she is at business school, the more appropriate approach would be that of "continuous learning" rather than the "in and out" concentrated orientation that exists now. I see the internationalization of business education as a lifetime learning process with the world as a stage. Wouldn't this new orientation translate itself smoothly into a series of shorter courses—in other words, executive education? Demographics also will support the above. The average age of the MBA applicant has now risen to 27 and, with industry increasingly voting for an MBA with a few years of work experience, the more receptive market for business schools will very soon be the executive in his/her mid-30s.

The profitability of these short executive programs could also be an incentive to administrators. Michael Czinkota relates that even though the preparatory effort for each of these (one-week programs in international business for corporations and government personnel) was high, annual contracts and frequent repetition of these courses made them easy to manage and also highly desirable for the teaching faculty. Also, over time alumni (students) from their courses become leaders in their organizations and can be potential resources for the educational institution in terms of sponsorships, internships, and scholarships. Great care must be taken to nurture these relationships and keep these individuals informed. This would demonstrate to them the fact that their money was well spent. And perhaps, too, encourage them to contribute more!

A large number of international business faculty members today have had their training in marketing. Popularly, international business is equated with international marketing. But the truth could not be further from this. International business education is a true integration of disciplines, of people and process, of theory and practice. It is an examination of business issues from the viewpoint of several disciplines. Knowledge of the culture and business practices of another country, and the cultural decentralization that this dictates will emphasize the skills that enable one to get different people to work together. Internationalism celebrates and appreciates the differences between people and why they act the way they do. This is the challenge for human resource management. No less a part of international business education is information technology and the ability to use it to gain the maximum advantage over one's competition. With the worldwide vision that globalization espouses and its underlying principle of "think globally but act as local conditions dictate," pricing, orders, payments, distribution, and scheduling, could be either the international executive's nightmare or strength. Foreign language fluency is no longer an exotic accomplishment—it is a working necessity. A word of caution, however. While international business education should teach one to be capable of managing a hotchpotch of products, consumers, and cultures, care should be exercised to ensure consistency in program components. Choices in area studies courses and language studies should complement (and not conflict with) each other so that we graduate students with a composite expertise.

Certainly the world is getting smaller with globalization; but that has made even more acute the need to promote "real-world problem solving." A task oriented, multi-disciplinary approach with a premium on communication, reasoning and problem solving skills, would go far to prepare managers for today's global corporation. We need to reinforce in our students an orientation toward action so that education and business may forge a powerful union to enhance U.S. competitiveness.

I have little to say in the area of curricular initiatives. Each school would undertake this after a careful appraisal of its particular set of goals and resources. Curriculum subjects for internationalization have a common core that includes dealing with cultural diversity, communication, the logistics of privatization, effective negotiation—all skills prized by the global economy. At this point, I would only urge that management schools see the necessity of including the study of specific industries and competitiveness in this curriculum and also direct a fair amount of attention to the study of third world countries and the development of case material on small- and medium-sized companies. The signs all point to the world's economic center of gravity moving, more certainly, from the United States to Asia. It would be appropriate for me to bring up at this point the "niche marketing" strategy that several business schools have chosen to adopt. Some have made the choice of specializing in an area that is the dominant local business interest (e.g., a Pacific Rim specialization by the University of Southern California, Latin American by the University of Miami). Others have chosen to teach capitalism to the economies of East Europe and the former Soviet Union. While these may certainly seem natural and open niches in the current perspective, let us not fall again into the "short-term specialization" trap.

Management schools are the viaduct (via media) between corporations and academe. In this position, they have a tremendous role to play in the process of internationalizing economic development and reform. The pace and direction of change in this new world order is so rapid and almost, one could say, so confusing that management schools face exciting possibilities of what they can do beyond the narrow confines of the classroom. We must express a genuine and great interest in new kinds of alliances with business. In working with federal and local government agencies and with corporate partners, we can develop exchanges and other specific programs to assist American executives and students in facilitating an understanding of what the issue/area involves. Through overseas linkages and involvement of foreign faculty, we could even introduce potential business partners to each other. We must not overlook our role in the public policy process through editorials, interviews with the media, and expert testimony. In this fervor to re-energize the U.S. economic engine, let us not also forget the loftier ideal of a civic education that the interdisciplinary component of internationalization affords.

Another few years will mark the end of the twentieth century. We have a sense of things ending and others beginning. We are witnessing the end of nationalism as we have known it. We are working on a program for the internationalization of business education that sees business education as a lifetime learning process taking place in a variety of stakeholder settings. We, business educators, see ourselves as part of an ongoing collaborative effort that emphasizes information sharing, team learning, and research that cuts across disciplines.

And, as gradually the winning verdict seems to be for free markets (versus controlled ones) the global demand for business education is poised for a big leap. We have much to teach others and a great deal to learn from others too. And if you choose to be part of this learning alliance, rest assured you have ahead of you an opportunity for tremendous excitement and growth.

About the Contributors

Jeffrey S. Arpan is the James F. Kane Professor of International Business and Director of International Business Programs at the University of South Carolina. One of the most outspoken proponents of internationalization, Professor Arpan has also served as Consulting Editor of the *Journal of International Business Studies* and as Vice-President of the Academy of International Business.

Nigel J. Barrett is Senior Lecturer at the University of Technology, Sydney, Australia, and holds a Ph.D. degree in international marketing from the University of New South Wales. His research interests focus on the export behavior of firms and company internationalization.

Paul W. Beamish is the Davis Professor of International Business at the Western Business School, the University of Western Ontario, in Canada. Director of the School's China Program, Professor Beamish was previously Director of the Center for International Business Studies and serves as Editor of the *Journal of International Business Studies*.

Claude B. Cellich is the Chief of Training at the International Trade Centre UNCTAD/GATT in Geneva, Switzerland. Over the past two decades, he has been involved in training trade promotion officials, business executives and trainers from developing countries. Mr. Cellich has published extensively on the subjects of training strategies, techniques, and issues in international business.

Michael R. Czinkota is Professor of Marketing and International Business at Georgetown University. Chairman of the National Center for Export-Import Studies from 1981-85, Dr. Czinkota then served as Deputy Assistant Secretary in the U.S. Department of Commerce during a leave from 1986-89. He is a member of the Board of Governors of the Academy of Marketing Science and is on the Editorial Board of several journals. He is the co-author of two books, *International Marketing* and *International Business*, both with the Dryden Press.

Tevfik Dalgic is Professor of Marketing and International Business and Director of Henley Research Centre at Henley, the Management College, Zeist, Netherlands. He has lectured extensively in Turkey, Ireland, and the United States. Professor Dalgic serves as the Editor of *Advances in Business Studies*. He is also on the Editorial Board of the *Journal of International Marketing*.

John D. Daniels is Professor of International Business at Indiana University. He also serves as the Director of the CIBER at Indiana. Co-author of a well-known international business textbook, Professor Daniels is also a past President of the Academy of International Business.

Susanna C. Easton is a Senior Program Specialist with the U.S. Department of Education, International Studies Branch, Washington, D.C.

Linda V. Gerber is Director for Academic Programs of the Center for International Business Education and Research, and a faculty member in the Department of Marketing and International Business, the University of Texas at Austin. She was previously Academic Coordinator of business programs with Boston University's Overseas Programs. In all these capacities, she has been directly involved in establishing and maintaining international academic partnerships.

Robert T. Green is the Harkins Professor of Business, and Director of the Center for International Business Education and Research at the University of Texas at Austin. In his capacity as CIBER Director and as Director of International Programs, Professor Green has been directly involved in the establishment of linkages with several business schools in other nations.

Robert Grosse is director of the Center for International Business and Education, and Professor of International Business, University of Miami, Coral Gables, Florida. His recent work focused on Latin American debt and its implications for U.S. firms. He recently edited a book, Private Sector Solutions to the Latin American Debt Problem.

Ben L. Kedia is the Robert Wang Professor of International Management at Memphis State University. He is also the Executive Director of the Center for International Business Education and Research (CIBER) at Memphis State University.

Duane Kujawa is Professor and Associate Dean for International Programs, University of Miami, Coral Gables, Florida; past President, Academy of International Business. Professor Kujawa was instrumental in the development of a new degree program, Master of International Business Studies, at the University of Miami.

Jack G. Lewis is Associate Director of IBEAR Programs, and Director, IBEAR Executive Programs at the University of Southern California. Lewis received his Ph.D. in comparative politics from Stanford University. His current interests include the social and political environment of business in Asia, and patterns of management training for international managers. He lived in Japan for six years and visits Asia often in connection with his IBEAR responsibilities.

Charles S. Mayer is the Nabisco Brands Professor of Marketing, and Associate Dean-External Relations at York University, Canada, where he was the founding director of the International MBA program. He has been a visiting professor in the U.S., Switzerland, France, England, New Zealand, PRC, Hong Kong, and Japan.

Lee C. Nehrt received his Ph.D. in International Business from Columbia University in 1962 and taught International Business at Indiana University from 1962-74. He has chaired professorships in International Business at Wichita State University and Ohio State University, and was Director of the World Trade Institute in NYC. He was President of the Academy of International Business (1972–74) and Dean of the Fellows of the Academy (1978–81).

Lee H. Radebaugh is the KPMG Peat Marwick Professor of Accounting and International Business at Brigham Young University and Co-Director of the BYU-University of Utah CIBER. Professor Radebaugh is the author of several books, including *International Business Environments and Operations* (6th Edition), *International Accounting and Multinational Enterprises* (3rd Edition), and *Introduction to Business: International Dimensions* (1992).

Ray Schaub is Director of the World College, and Professor of German, Eastern Michigan University, Ypsilanti, Michigan. Professor Schaub was instrumental in the establishment of the World College at Eastern Michigan University.

Michael G. Schechter has been a faculty member at James Madison College of Michigan State University since he completed his Ph.D. in Political Science at Columbia University in 1975. At

Michigan State, he has chaired Madison College's International Relations Program and served for four years as the Assistant Dean for International Studies and Programs. Professor Schechter has published numerous articles in his major area of research—intergovernmental organization decision making.

Robert E. Scott is Associate Director for the Center for International Business Education and Research at the University of Maryland at College Park, Maryland.

Brian Toyne is Professor of International Business and Director of the International Business Program at the University of South Carolina. His research and educational interests include the development of international business as a distinct field of theoretical and empirical inquiry.

Daniel Van Den Bulcke is Professor at the Center for International Management and Development, University of Antwerp, Antwerp, Belgium. Professor Van Den Bulcke has been active with both the Academy of International Business and the European International Business Association.

Gerard E. Watzke is Professor of Management at the A.B. Freeman School of Business, Tulane University, New Orleans, Louisiana, and past Executive Secretary, Academy of International Business

ABOUT THE EDITOR

S. Tamer Cavusgil is the Executive Director, Center for International Business Education and Research, and Professor of Marketing and International Business, The Eli Broad Graduate School of Management, Michigan State University. He is the author or co-author of several books in marketing and international business and over eighty articles that have been published in professional journals such as the *Journal of Marketing Research, Journal of the Market Research Society, Business Horizons, European Journal of Marketing, European Research, Journal of Business Research,* and *Journal of International Business Studies.* Currently Dr. Cavusgil is Editor of *Journal of International Marketing* and Editor of the JAI Press Annuals *Advances in International Marketing.*

Dr. Cavusgil's educational background includes MBA and Ph.D. degrees in Business from the University of Wisconsin. He has taught at Bradley University, the University of Wisconsin-

Whitewater and the Middle East Technical University in Turkey. Cavusgil's research on the export marketing behavior of firms is widely recognized and his microcomputer software, CORE (COmpany Readiness to Export) has been adopted by many firms in designing export strategies. He is an active member of the Academy of International Business, American Marketing Association, European International Business Association, and the Academy of Marketing Science. Dr. Cavusgil frequently advises businesses, public sector agencies, nonprofit organizations, and developing country governments.

GLOSSARY

AAA	The American Accounting Association
AAC	The Association of American Colleges
AACSB	The American Assembly of Collegiate Schools of Business
AASCU	The American Association of State Colleges and Universities
ACE	The American Council on Education
ACTFL	The American Council on the Teaching of Foreign Languages
AIB	The Academy of International Business
ALACCI	The Latin American Association for Training in Foreign Trade
AMA	The American Marketing Association
CIDA	The Canadian International Development Agency
CIEE	The Council on International Educational Exchange
CORE	COmpany Readiness to Export
DOE	U.S. Department of Education
EAA	European Accounting Association
EARIE	European Association for Research in Industrial Economics
EBS	European Business Schools
EFA	European Finance Association
EFMD	European Foundation for Management Development
EIASM	European Institute of Advanced Studies in Management
EIBA	European International Business Association
EMA	European Marketing Academy
ESADE	Graduate School of Business Administration and Management (Spain)

ESIC	Graduate School of Management and Marketing (Spain)
ESIDEC	Graduate School of International Trade (France)
FDIB	Faculty Development in International Business
GATT	General Agreement on Tariffs and Trade
GMAC	Graduate Management Admission Council
ICEE	International Cooperative Exchange Program
IMD	The International Institute for Management Development (Lausanne, Switzerland)
INSEAD	The European Institute of Business Administration (Fountainebleau, France)
ITAM	El Institut Technologico Autonomo de Mexico
ITC	International Trade Centre, UNCTAD/GATT
MCU	Ministry of Colleges and Universities (Canada)
MIBS	Master of International Business Studies
MITT	Ministry of Industry, Trade and Technology (Canada)
MNC	Multi National Corporation
MNE	Multi National Enterprise
NAFTA	North American Free Trade Agreement
NDEA	National Defense Education Act
OCGS	Ontario Council of Graduate Studies
OCIB	Ontario Center for International Business
OCUA	Ontario Council of University Affairs
OECD	Organization for Economic Cooperation and Development
PRODEC	Program for Development Cooperation at the Helsinki School of Economics
UNAM	Universidad Nacional Autonoma de Mexico
US AID	The U.S. Agency for International Development

Index

A

AACSB, 24, 31, 34-41, 43, 45, 49, 52, 66-67, 70, 109, 138, 194, 225, 229, 231, 300, 324

AIB, 32, 34, 35, 231, 232

Administration, 15-30, 33, 60-61, 147, 155, 187, 229-30, 233, 289, 292

Administrative: continuity, 148-49; position, 21, 26-27; support, 6, 24, 61, 73, 163, 187-88, 252, 289; unit, 11, 25, 142-43, 148-49, 195, 208, 258

B

Business community: linkages, 4, 6, 10-11, 95-96, 99-108, 179, 199, 249-62, 297; outreach. 10, 95-96, 113-14, 119, 125-26, 128, 130; relations between the Executive Board and business school: AIB Board, 35, IBBI Board, 100, 103-8; Business economics, 263-73, 298

C

CIBER, v, xi, xiv, 30, 52, 56, 65-81, 88-97, 119-28, 143, 237, 258; activities, 41, 67-77, 89-96; list of centers, 68-69; programs, 41, 67-81, 121-28; purpose, 11-12, 67-69, 88, 96-97, 119

Canadian perspective, 111, 144, 153-66, 197-208

Change agent, xi, 5, 9, 158, 196, 252, 284, 287, 289-91

Classroom internationalization, 119-28, 129-38, 141-51, 167-80

Collaboration, 6, 11-12, 36, 46, 57-58, 60, 68, 92-93, 96, 99-108, 112, 115, 119-28, 131, 190, 196, 252, 257, 258-59, 261, 271, 285-86, 292

Commitment, 6, 25, 32, 42, 62-63, 75, 81, 133, 136, 162-64, 187, 252, 278, 284, 289-90, 281-82

Company M.B.A. program, 62, 246

Concentration (major), 7, 18, 19, 20-21, 40, 49, 77, 89, 90, 132, 133, 134, 168-69, 173, 174, 286

Conferences, 24, 33, 34, 35, 92, 93, 111, 114, 127, 194, 221, 225, 284, *see also* Seminars; outlook conferences, 144-45

Continuing Education, 113, 324-25

Corporate hiring and development programs, 10, 12, 33-34, 192-93, 202

Curriculum, 2, 4, 6, 7, 12, 15-30, 31-44, 69, 74-77, 86-90, 122, 132-36, 167-83, 187, 209, 231-32, 252, 266-67, 283-87, 291, 296, 303, 310, 324, 326; CORE, 270; doctoral, 29, 40, 175-76, *see also*, Doctoral programs; M.B.A., 28,